The Confessional
Mosaic

THE PRESBYTERIAN PRESENCE:
THE TWENTIETH-CENTURY EXPERIENCE

Series Editors

Milton J Coalter

John M. Mulder

Louis B. Weeks

The Confessional Mosaic: Presbyterians and Twentieth-Century Theology

Edited by
Milton J Coalter
John M. Mulder
Louis B. Weeks

Essays by
Jack B. Rogers and Donald K. McKim,
James H. Moorhead, John McClure,
Beverly Ann Zink, Ronald P. Byars,
Morgan F. Simmons, Mark A. Noll and
Darryl G. Hart, Benton Johnson, and
Rick Nutt

Westminster/John Knox Press
Louisville, Kentucky

Book design by Gene Harris

First edition

Published by Westminster/John Knox Press
Louisville, Kentucky

PRINTED IN THE UNITED STATES OF AMERICA
9 8 7 6 5 4 3 2 1

Library of Congress Cataloging-in-Publication Data

The Confessional mosaic : Presbyterians and twentieth-century theology
/ edited by Milton J. Coalter, John M. Mulder, Louis B. Weeks ;
essays by Donald K. McKim . . . [et al.]. — 1st ed.
     p.   cm. — (The Presbyterian presence : the twentieth-century experience)
  Includes bibliographical references and index.
  ISBN 0-664-25151-X

  1. Presbyterian Church—United States—Doctrines—History—20th century. 2. Preaching—History—20th century. 3. Worship—History—20th century. I. Coalter, Milton J. II. Mulder, John M., 1946–   . III. Weeks, Louis, 1941–   . IV. McKim, Donald K.
V. Series: Presbyterian presence.
BX8937.C65 1990
285′.1—dc20   90-36838

Contents

Series Foreword

This series, "The Presbyterian Presence: The Twentieth-Century Experience," is the product of a significant research project analyzing American Presbyterianism in this century. Funded by the Lilly Endowment and based at Louisville Presbyterian Theological Seminary, the project is part of a broader research effort that analyzes the history of mainstream Protestantism. By analyzing American Presbyterianism as a case study, we hope not only to chronicle its fate in the twentieth century but also to illumine larger patterns of religious change in mainstream Protestantism and in American religious and cultural life.

This case study of American Presbyterianism and the broader research on mainstream Protestantism arise out of an epochal change in American religion that has occurred during the twentieth century. Mainstream American Protestantism refers to those churches that emerged from the American Revolution as the dominant Protestant bodies and were highly influential in shaping American religion and culture during the nineteenth century. It includes the Presbyterians, Episcopalians, Methodists, Congregationalists (now the United Church of Christ), Disciples, and American or northern Baptists.

In this century, these churches have been displaced—religiously and culturally—to a significant degree. All have suffered severe membership losses since the 1960s. All have experienced significant theological tensions and shifts in emphasis. All are characterized by problems in their organization as institutions. And yet they remain influential voices in the spectrum of American religion and retain an enduring vitality in the face of a massive reconfiguration of American religious life.

The result is a complex phenomenon that is not easily described. Some would say the term "mainstream" or "mainline" is itself suspect and embodies ethnocentric and elitist assumptions. What characterized American religious history, they argue, was its diversity and its pluralism. Some groups may have believed they were religiously or culturally dominant, but the historical reality is much more pluralistic. Others would maintain that if there was a "mainstream," it no longer exists. Still others would propose that the mainstream itself has changed. The denominations of the evangelical awakening of the nineteenth century have been replaced by the evangelical churches of the late twentieth century—Southern Baptist, charismatic, Pentecostal.

Some propose that the term "mainline" or "mainstream" should be dropped in favor of talking about "liberal" Protestantism, but such a change presents additional problems. Like "evangelical," the term "liberal" is an extremely vague word to describe a set of Christian beliefs, values, and behavior. Furthermore, virtually all the "mainstream" churches contain large numbers of people who would describe themselves as either evangelical or liberal, thus making it very difficult to generalize about them as a denomination.

Despite the debates about terminology and the categories for analyzing American Protestantism, there is general agreement that American culture and American Protestantism of the late twentieth century are very different from what they were in the late nineteenth century. What has changed is the religious and cultural impact of American Protestantism. A study of American Presbyterianism is a good lens for examining that change, for in spite of their relatively small numbers, Presbyterians are, or were, quintessential mainstreamers, exerting a great deal of influence because of their economic, social, educational, and cultural advantages.

When did the change occur? In a pioneering article written more than fifty years ago, Arthur M. Schlesinger, Sr., pointed to the period from 1875 to 1900 as "a critical period" in American religion. In particular, American Protestants confronted the external challenges of immigration, industrialization, and urbanization and the internal challenges posed by Darwinism, biblical criticism, history of religions, and the new social sciences.[1] Robert T. Handy has maintained that the 1920s witnessed a "religious depression." The result was a "second disestablishment" of American Protestantism. When the churches lost legal establishment in the U.S. Constitution, they attempted to "Christianize" American culture.[2] But by the 1920s, it was clear that both legal and cultural establishment had been rejected. Sydney Ahlstrom points to the 1960s as the time when American religion and culture took a "radical turn" and the "Puritan culture" of the United States was shattered.[3] Wade Clark Roof and William McKinney build on Ahlstrom's argument, proposing that the 1960s and 1970s represent a "third disestablishment" in which mainstream churches lost their religious dominance.[4]

These diverse interpretations underscore the fact that the crises of mainstream Protestantism did not appear suddenly and that the developments within one tradition—American Presbyterianism—are mirrored in other denominations as well. While some of our studies reach back into the late nineteenth century, most of our studies focus on the period after the fundamentalist controversy within Presbyterianism during the 1920s and 1930s. For a variety of reasons, that became a watershed for Presbyterians and ushered in the twentieth century.

The value of this substantial Presbyterian case study can be seen from at least two perspectives. First, this research is designed to write a chapter in the history of American religion and culture. It is the story of the attempt of one tradition—its people and its institutions—to respond to the crosscurrents of the twentieth century. Second, it is an attempt to illumine the problems and predicaments of American Presbyterianism so that its members and leaders might better understand the past as a resource for its future direction.

The series title was carefully chosen. Presence is more than passive existence, and it connotes the landmark that we hope these groups of studies provide for comparing the equally important pilgrimages of other mainline Protestant denominations through the past century. Missiologists have characterized the Christian responsibility as one of "profound presence" in the world, patterned on the presence of God in providence, in the incarnation, and in the work of the Holy Spirit. In the words of missionary and theologian John V. Taylor, Christians "stand" in the world in the name of Christ to be "really and totally present . . . in the present."[5]

Has the Presbyterian presence declined into mere existence? Have the commitments of Presbyterians degenerated into lifeless obligations? What forces have informed, transformed, or deformed our distinctive presence within the Christian community and the society? And can changes in Presbyterianism invigorate their continued yearnings to represent Christ in the world today? These are the questions posed in the series.

More than sixty researchers, plus students at Louisville Seminary and generous colleagues in seminaries, colleges, and universities throughout the United States, have cooperated in the research on American Presbyterianism. Many are historians, but others are sociologists, economists, musicians, theologians, pastors, and lay people. What has excited us as a research team was the opportunity of working on a fascinating historical problem with critical implications for the Presbyterian Church and mainstream Protestantism. Animating our work and conversations was the hope that this research might make a difference, that it might help one church and a broader Christian tradition understand the problems more clearly so that its witness might be more faithful. It is with this hope that we issue this series, "The Presbyterian Presence: The Twentieth-Century Experience."

Milton J Coalter
John M. Mulder
Louis B. Weeks

Acknowledgments

Every volume presenting the fruits of research reaches publication through the collaborative effort of a host of people whose contributions are largely hidden on the printed page.

One such group are the "widows and orphans" of this project, the editors' spouses and children. They have endured or perhaps sometimes enjoyed the negligence of scholar husbands and fathers. For their loving patience during our all too frequent absences, we say thanks to our families.

A second group of individuals deserves special credit: the students, staff, faculty, and administration at Louisville Seminary. Since each of us holds an administrative position in addition to teaching responsibilities, the patience of staff and administrative colleagues has allowed us the space to complete this project. Students and faculty have likewise contributed by broadening our perspective on the issues involved through generous offerings of their time for discussion. Their own examples of scholarship and the dedication of the entire seminary community to the church have inspired and enriched our labors.

Without the financial support and the intellectual challenge from the Lilly Endowment and its leadership, this project would not have been possible. We deeply appreciate the creativity and counsel of Robert Wood Lynn, Fred Hofheinz, and Craig Dykstra as well as the excellent support work their staff provided.

We also recognize the expert hand given to this volume by Davis Perkins, the Editorial Director of Westminster/John Knox Press. His incisive counsel enhanced the final form of the essays.

Finally, we acknowledge the burden that preparations for this volume placed on our secretaries. Elna Amaral, Beverly Hourigan, Kem Longino, Dana Rohde, and Ingrid Tanghe have skillfully managed a daunting paper trail of communications, revisions, and revisions of revisions. Without their singular goodwill and cooperation, this volume would not be offered at this time.

Milton J Coalter
John M. Mulder
Louis B. Weeks

Contributors

Ronald P. Byars is the pastor of the Second Presbyterian Church in Lexington, Kentucky. A graduate of Yale Divinity School and Michigan State University, where he completed a Ph.D. in history, he has served congregations in Fremont, Allen Park, and Okemos, Michigan.

Darryl G. Hart is the director of the Institute for the Study of American Evangelicals at Wheaton College, Wheaton, Illinois. His dissertation, completed in 1988 at Johns Hopkins University, is entitled " 'Doctor Fundamentalis': An Intellectual Biography of J. Gresham Machen." His essays on the history of Presbyterians have appeared in the *Journal of Ecclesiastical History,* the *Westminster Theological Journal,* and *Church History.*

Benton Johnson is Professor of Sociology at the University of Oregon. He has written extensively on mainline Protestantism, his most recent publications being "Is There Hope for Liberal Protestantism?" in *Mainline Protestantism in the Twentieth Century: Its Problems and Prospects* and "Winning Lost Sheep: A Recovery Course for Liberal Protestantism" in *Liberal Protestantism: Realities and Possibilities.*

John McClure is Assistant Professor of Preaching and

Worship in the Frank Caldwell Chair of Homiletics at Louisville Presbyterian Theological Seminary. He served previously in the parish ministry in Birmingham, Alabama, and has published several articles in such journals as the *Journal for Preachers, Liturgy,* and *Soviet Studies.*

Donald K. McKim has taught at Westminster College in Pennsylvania and the University of Dubuque Theological Seminary. He is the editor of a new *Encyclopedia of the Reformed Faith* to be published by Westminster/John Knox Press. Among his numerous publications are *What Christians Believe About the Bible, Theological Turning Points,* and *Puritan England: Essays in Religion and Society.*

James H. Moorhead is Professor of American Church History at Princeton Theological Seminary. Previously he taught at North Carolina State University and in 1976 received the Brewer Prize of the American Society of Church History for his work *American Apocalypse: Yankee Protestants and the Civil War.*

Mark A. Noll is Professor of History at Wheaton College in Wheaton, Illinois. He has written *Between Faith and Criticism: Evangelicals, Scholarship, and the Bible in America* and has edited *Charles Hodge: The Way of Life* (Sources of American Spirituality), and, with Roger Lundin, *Voices from the Heart: Four Centuries of American Piety.*

Rick Nutt is Associate Professor of Religion and Philosophy at Muskingum College in New Concord, Ohio. He is a Presbyterian minister and has served churches in Eldorado Springs, Missouri, and Tuskegee, Alabama. He has also taught at Auburn University. His most recent publications are "How the Religious Right Views History—and Why," in *Soundings,* 1989, and "Some Thoughts on Heritage USA and Modern Consumer Society" in the *Journal for Preachers,* 1989.

Jack B. Rogers is Associate for Theological Studies in the Theology and Worship Ministry Unit of the Presbyterian Church (U.S.A.). He is a graduate of Pittsburgh Theological Seminary and holds a Th.D. from the Free

University of Amsterdam. He taught theology at Fuller Theological Seminary for seventeen years and has written seven books, the most recent being *Presbyterian Creeds: A Guide to the Book of Confessions.*

Morgan F. Simmons has served as organist and choirmaster of the Fourth Presbyterian Church of Chicago since 1968. He received a master's and a doctoral degree from the School of Sacred Music of Union Theological Seminary in New York, and was Assistant Professor of Church Music at Garrett-Evangelical Seminary in Evanston from 1963 to 1977. He also studied at the Royal School of Church Music in Croydon, England, as a Fulbright scholar, and he served as reader-consultant for *The Hymnal 1982* of the Episcopal Church and for *The Presbyterian Hymnal* (1990). He has contributed articles to a number of professional journals, including *The Hymn, The American Organist,* and *Reformed Liturgy & Music.*

Beverly Ann Zink is a graduate of Dickinson College and Princeton Theological Seminary, where she received a fellowship in history. She is Associate Pastor of the Neshaminy-Warwick Presbyterian Church in Hartsville, Pennsylvania.

Introduction

This volume of essays explores the development of Presbyterian theology and worship during the twentieth century. Christian thought and liturgy have varied widely across cultures and history. All forms of Christian reflection and worship stem from the seedbed revelation in the Bible. Yet each represents a distinctive translation of that divine disclosure into a contemporary idiom. In this way, Christianity remains intelligible, persuasive, nourishing, and responsive to the questions of particular societies in time.

The theology of American Presbyterians has been seriously tested by the translation demands from several new developments in the twentieth century. The essays in this work focus on Presbyterians' struggle to respond to this wide array of challenges. However, their findings provide much more than the isolated story of a single denomination's reply to the modern world.

All the denominations known traditionally as mainstream American Protestantism have shared in the effort to provide alluring but faithful theological foundations and worship experiences in the contemporary setting.[1] All have likewise been involved in increasingly intimate ecumenical contacts with one another throughout the century. Because these common conversations nurtured a blending of perspectives, the story of one of these denominations is emblematic of the larger ferment in theology and worship throughout mainstream Protestantism as a whole in the twentieth century.

When one examines this emblem of twentieth-century confessional translation, the image of a mosaic comes to mind. The rudimentary lines of traditional Reformed thought and liturgy continue in present-day Presbyterian theology and worship, but the overall picture is now one of diverse forms and visions. This diversity has troubled some who equate confessions, creeds, and Reformed liturgical practice with static definitions requiring uniformity and consensus. Variety in Christian opinion and ritual has historic precedents, of course, reaching back to the Reformation and beyond.

The Protestant Reformers agreed on the preeminence of biblical authority, the priesthood of all believers, and the need to cleanse the sacramental system of unscriptural rites and ordinances. But they allowed latitude for diversity of interpretation and practice in numerous areas deemed to be "adiaphora." Adiaphora included those aspects of Christian faith and practice not clearly determined by scriptural example or instruction and, therefore, of secondary importance.

The Reformation debate over the boundaries of adiaphora continued in the English setting at the Westminster Assembly. The resulting confession and accompanying catechisms sustained the distinction between those aspects of Christian life and thought essential to the faith and those best left to conscience. Theology was defined more rigidly at the Westminster Assembly than were polity and liturgy, but the principle of conscientious objection remained in tact.

When the conflict moved to North America, a major controversy in the Presbyterian Church centered around the question of subscription to the Westminster Standards. Here again the prerogatives of conscience were ultimately upheld as subscription was required but the possibility of conscientious objection recognized.

During the nineteenth century, the limits of pluralism were further challenged. A stringent theology of biblical infallibility developed by Charles Hodge and others at Princeton Theological Seminary claimed the perfection of the original scriptural manuscripts. This doctrine found ready reception in a fundamentalist movement emerging throughout Protestantism. Instead of enlarging the margins of permissible variation, fundamentalists during the first two decades of the twentieth century insisted on more precise definitions of belief. These definitions were to be binding on all who wished to participate in their communions.

Several concurrent factors counteracted these constricting influences. Among Protestants, extensive historical research on the early church and Reformation raised new awareness of the church's diversity of thought and worship across time. Higher criticism of the Bible also brought greater consciousness of the potential, honest differences of interpretation among Christians trying to separate the kernel of scriptural revelation from its cultural trappings.

More recently, the ecumenical movement, among not only Protestants but also Roman Catholics and other Christian communions throughout the world, extended American mainstream Protestants' appreciation of alternative forms of witness to Christ. Similarly, sustained contact with non-Christian societies and with other living religions through the missionary movement, mass communications, and other avenues of interaction have heightened Christian sensibilities to the plurality of sincere convictions.

Some see blessings in the resulting expansion of Presbyterian toleration and individual freedom under God. These developments symbolize for them a hard-won spiritual insight into the multiform call for human reformation found in the Christian gospel itself. It is believed that this fuller understanding of gospel truth recognizes world

Christianity's various, yet genuine, perceptions of the biblical witness.

At the same time, voices of protest have been heard within the Presbyterian denominations. Individuals and groups regard the developing theological diversity with alarm. They claim that current Presbyterian theology and worship have strayed from the straightforward path they once trod.

These two quite different perceptions of the current Presbyterian situation epitomize the peculiar predicament and potential genius of the contemporary Presbyterian confessional mosaic. The church has been engaged in the creation of a flexible but consistent frame for its theology and worship that surrenders neither the need for communal identity nor the right of conscientious diversity.

The first two offerings in this volume consider how the sometimes conflicting tendencies of identity and diversity have stretched Presbyterians' perspectives of the Bible and the creeds. Jack Rogers and Donald McKim examine how the scriptures have been variously interpreted in the twentieth century. James Moorhead then considers the denomination's redefinition of what it means to be a confessional church.

The research by Rogers and McKim supports the well-known thesis propounded by Lefferts Loetscher in his work *The Broadening Church.* Loetscher proposed that a decision in 1927 by the Presbyterian Church U.S.A. General Assembly "opened the present era of theological pluralism."[2] At the time the church was in the throes of a fundamentalist challenge. The 1927 Assembly decided to reject the fundamentalist demand for theological precision by allowing a wider diversity of opinion. As a result, theological definition of orthodoxy was decentralized. Presbyteries and the judicial process of the church became the final arbiters of individual cases.

The implications of this move for biblical interpretation were not fully evident until the late 1960s because an informal theological consensus developed for a time within the church. Neo-orthodox theology crossed the Atlantic in the 1930s to capture the minds of Presbyterians north and south. The widespread acceptance of the neo-orthodox identification of the Word of God with its perfect content, Jesus Christ, rather than its imperfect text, the Bible, was confirmed in the United Presbyterian Church U.S.A.'s adoption of the Confession of 1967 and the Presbyterian Church U.S.'s educational use of the 1962 "Brief Statement of Faith."

The victory of the neo-orthodox biblical perspective proved short-lived. The official sanctioning of neo-orthodoxy marked the beginning of its demise. Theologians were already moving away from that position by the mid-1960s. Under assault for both its theological and philosophical affirmations, neo-orthodoxy rapidly fell from favor. It left in its wake a range of important but issue-oriented theologies. This latter development in theology coincides with what Robert Wuthnow has identified as a political transformation in American mainstream Protestant denominations. Namely, they lost their internal cohesion in the 1960s as their membership divided into a host of issue-oriented constituencies. Many people found a primary identity in special interest group allegiance rather than denominational affiliation.[3]

Rogers and McKim chronicle the growth of several influential issues around which theological positions have developed since the 1960s. They also discuss the particular methods of interpreting scriptures promoted within each system. Feminist, liberation, and process thought, as well as theologies arising during controversy over the ordination of homosexuals, were all important. In 1988 the Presbyterian Church (U.S.A.) officially blessed this plurality of biblical interpretation. But Rogers and McKim contend that the majority of Presbyterian members still maintain a "centrist" perspective. They accept biblical criticism's value but retain a sense of the scriptures as the "Word of God written."

James Moorhead paints a strikingly similar picture, but he focuses on how Presbyterians have redefined what it means to be a confessional church. He draws data largely from the denomination's creeds and confessions, as well as from cultural and theological trends that determined which biblical texts exercised authority and how. Moorhead pinpoints the Presbyterian Church U.S.A.'s 1927 General Assembly decision as a landmark on the road to greater theological pluralism. The Presbyterian Church U.S. lagged behind its northern counterpart, but it too eventually rejected the constraints of fundamentalist biblical literalism and theological rigidity.

Neo-orthodoxy provided the initial source of theological consensus following the fundamentalist challenges. Its emphasis on the centrality of the Bible, the fallibility of scriptural authors, the transcendence of God, human sinfulness, and the dynamism of theological reflection provided the necessary flexibility for diversity without abdicating theological clarity.

But neo-orthodoxy in America proved to be less a coherent theological program than a critique of earlier "liberal" theology. Its focus on the dynamic changes of theological understandings over time propelled the Presbyterian community to ever greater tolerance of plurality. It also shifted the church's view of its creeds and confessions. As Moorhead notes, this new definition of confessionalism "has emphasized dynamic conceptions of truth, has eschewed narrowly propositional understandings of theology, and has increasingly identified the secular world as the arena in which it must define its faith."

The latter move has proved particularly troubling for Presbyterian theology. The "moral consensus" that prevailed outside the church in American culture prior to 1960 was disintegrating into a pluralistic collage of varying personal opinions just as the church turned its attention to the "world" for signs of divine activity. Moorhead suggests that the church remains unable to find "a theological perspective powerful enough to encompass diversity." It, therefore, turns to polity to provide unity and clarification in theological matters.

The recent draft of the proposed Brief Statement of the Reformed Faith indicates that Presbyterians can still articulate where they share common ground theologically. The ability of that base to sustain the spirit and bind their fellowship remains to be tested.

Just as the Bible and creeds have been the traditional authorities for Presbyterian theology so also liturgy, hymns, and preaching have been major avenues for the transmission and expression of that theology. John H. Leith has recently observed that "the Protestant Reformation was born in the conviction that the church could be revived and reformed by preaching 'the most holy gospel of the glory and grace of God.' "[4] If this assertion is true, then no Protestant tradition has put more stock in preaching than the Calvinist community. John McClure and Beverly Ann Zink chronicle how even this basic staple of Reformed worship has been affected by dramatic changes during the twentieth century. Ronald Byars and Morgan Simmons then follow with illustrations of how the tradition's emphasis on preaching stunted the development of other liturgical aspects of Presbyterian worship.

John McClure investigates the fluctuating authority, methods, and messages of preachers in the Presbyterian Church U.S.A., the United Presbyterian Church of North America, and the United Presbyterian Church in the U.S.A. As early as the 1920s, McClure sees signs that ministers sensed a loss of authority. They responded by trying to earn the laity's respect through sermons that were "interesting, relevant, simple, and clear." The liturgical movement of this era moved preaching away from an "oratorical, persuasive, and expository" style. Truth was now discussed from the human standpoint rather than from that of the divine sovereign. Human depravity gave place to an assumed continuity between humanity and the divine, and social gospel notions of human potential and self-esteem were stressed. Harry Emerson Fosdick's "project method" undergirded a focus on ethics and life situations. The preacher began sermon preparation not with the Bible but with a problem or question to be solved.

The 1950s witnessed a revival of preaching authority. Church membership peaked during this decade, and neo-orthodoxy exalted the preaching event as the objective Word of God for today. Neo-orthodoxy also altered the theological content of sermons by insisting on continued social involvement, but tempering the social optimism of former "liberal" theology with a self-critical realism. Human and ecclesiastical "prejudice, parochialism, and complicity in a host of social sins" were linked with an emphasis on human reliance on God's grace.

Despite this revival, the institutional authority of the preacher continued to decline. Sermon content focused increasingly on the psychological needs of the congregation. At the same time, biblical studies and homiletics training were separated in the seminaries. English Bible classes linked to preaching instruction, which had once been the norm, now disappeared. The historical-critical method became dominant in biblical studies. Homiletics students found it increasingly difficult to use the results of their biblical exegesis for theological exposition in preaching. They resorted to preaching on unified scriptural themes rather than on specific theological points drawn from particular texts.

By the mid-1960s the preaching task generated little enthusiasm in seminaries amid a broader cultural attack on "authoritarian" communication. A new dialogical method checked the declining interest in preaching. It inaugurated a new age of proclamation in a "conversational-interactive" mode with the congregation. Ministers spoke much of the personal dynamics of faith through a new set of theological terms borrowed from Paul Tillich and Søren Kierkegaard. In place of classic theological dualities like sin/grace, they employed existential and/or psychological concepts of alienation/reconciliation and fragmentation/wholeness.

These developments allowed preachers to relocate the authority of the sermon in what McClure calls the "performative power" of its language rather than in the person occupying the pulpit. In the 1970s and 1980s, American culture became especially sensitive to the power of words in shaping worldviews. The church also accented the central place of the powerless in Christ's ministry. Consequently, the preacher became the "storyteller of a congregation's 'lived world' " through an inductive, narrative style of presenting gospel liberation. The former neoorthodox emphasis on social advocacy sounded new themes with the introduction of feminist and third world theologies in which liberation was the dominant motif.

The challenge of science, McClure argues, is the single thread that links all these shifts in twentieth-century Presbyterian preaching. Modern science has redefined truth as "subjective, situational, and verifiable only through the five human senses." Although this scientific perspective was widely disseminated in popular culture, Presbyterians also absorbed it where it was most dominant, that is, in the colleges and universities.

Presbyterian preaching was already dealing with the challenge of modern science in the 1920s by what McClure calls its "philosophy of religion" messages. Later, Presbyterian proclamation followed neo-orthodoxy's lead by evading or ignoring conflicts with the scientific viewpoint in its sermon content. But after the 1950s, the Presbyterian pulpit began to employ psychological and sociological themes to provide at least the appearance of a "common currency" with science. The end result has often been less than satisfactory as theological substance has frequently been omitted from Presbyterian sermons in the interest of scientific respectability.[5]

Beverly Ann Zink's analysis of southern Presbyterian preaching follows McClure's in scrutinizing homiletical themes. Rather than emphasizing change, though, Zink sees a remarkable continuity in southern Presbyterian sermons. The one persistent theme of the southern Presbyterian pulpit in the twentieth century has been personal spiritual regeneration. Despite radical transformations in southern culture during the century, "southern evangelicalism" continued to exercise a powerful influence on pulpit proclamation.

Within this basic framework, Zink does perceive more subtle but significant shifts in emphasis. The denomination's preachers generally maintained a hostile attitude toward the social gospel until World War II. The doctrine of the "spirituality of the church," which James Henley Thornwell propounded in the southern church during the nineteenth century, circumscribed involvement in political affairs. Similarly, the commonly held belief that personal regeneration was the precondition for and best approach to social transformation fostered further antagonism toward any "social" gospel.

World War II dissipated the South's cultural isolation, and the spirituality of the church disappeared with it. After a flurry of evangelism sermons in the heyday of membership growth during the 1950s, concerns over the emerging secularization, materialism, and racial tensions in southern society began to emerge from the pulpit. More prominent than any of these themes was the collapse of theological vocabulary into psychological language.

Despite the dominance of preaching in Reformed worship, sermons alone do not exhaust the experience of worship. Indeed, sermons may not even be the most powerful liturgical element shaping Presbyterian piety and practice. Morgan Simmons and Ronald Byars confirm this possibility by providing accounts of the significant transformation in Presbyterian hymnology and liturgy.

Byars's study of directories for worship and books of common worship suggests that pre-Puritan Reformed practice recognized the importance of liturgy. However, English Puritans' interest in free, spirit-led worship inadvertently conspired to reduce the richness of Presbyterian worship until the twentieth century.

Byars admits that periodic surges of liturgical reform during the last eighty years were not always theologically sound. They were, however, motivated by several understandable factors. First, while the Protestant Reformers cleansed their churches of religious symbols in the interest of freeing the laity from superstitions, their English Puritan offspring purged their liturgies of all but their barest outlines in the interest of freeing worship for the direction of the Holy Spirit. An unintended consequence was the surrender of the laity to the "varying talent and sensitivity" of the clergy who led worship. This error led some twentieth-century Presbyterians to create liturgical directories and handbooks that officially structured congregational worship. The biblical theology movement and historical studies of ancient Christian and Reformation ritual further loosened the grip of those claiming free worship alone represented scriptural and early church practice. Finally, ecumenical interaction with other Protestants and Roman Catholics awakened Presbyterians to the significance of liturgy in the worship experience.

Byars insists that the Presbyterian denominations' appropriation of ritual practices from other communions was consistent with the best pre-Puritan Reformed practice and with the Reformed tradition's persistent rejection of narrow sectarian practices. He acknowledges that this "remarkable ecumenical convergence" has led Presbyterians and other mainstream Protestant churches to lose "a sense of denominational distinctiveness, with a corresponding decrease in denominational loyalty." He is convinced, however, that the gains outweigh the losses for Presbyterian spirituality.

Morgan Simmons chronicles a similar pattern of ecumenical impact on the church's hymnology. Simmons observes that at the turn of the century only the United Presbyterian Church of North America retained the Reformed psalm-singing tradition. Other Presbyterian denominations used hymnals with eclectic selections. In fact, a double standard prevailed in many Presbyterian congregations, where two different hymnals were frequently used. One was employed for formal worship and the other for informal occasions like Sunday school and evening services. The contents of the latter hymnals exhibited the strength of the gospel hymns of the late nineteenth and early twentieth century. Despite the powerful appeal, Simmons contends they taxed neither the laity's intellect nor musicians' skills.

Simmons closely surveys the unique strengths and weaknesses of the various editions and revisions of Presbyterian

hymnals in the twentieth century. Often a particular
hymnbook reflected the peculiar cultural and denominational conditions in which it was created. The 1972 *Worshipbook,* for instance, illustrated the "uncertainty" of the
church in the face of the social unrest spawned by the civil
rights movement and the Vietnam war. Archaic pronouns
and verbs were quickly altered without regard to musical
consequences while issues of inclusive language, which
were just beginning to arise in the church, were not addressed. Simmons also argues that the *Worshipbook*'s alphabetical arrangement of hymns illustrated "the sense of
drift that was prevalent" throughout American mainstream Protestantism during the period.

The most recent hymnal published by the Presbyterian
Church (U.S.A.) in 1990 follows closely the pattern Byars
describes for current liturgical resources. Its selections dis-
play the contemporary pluralism of the denomination but
also recall the musical heritage of Presbyterians.
Psalmnody, even from the *Genevan Psalter,* is included
alongside ethnic and indigenous hymns and texts in non-
English languages. This diversity of content has enriched
Presbyterian worship, according to Simmons, but it also
marks the end of the distinctively "denominational"
hymnal.

While Simmons and Byars provide insights into the evolution of Presbyterian corporate worship, Mark Noll and
Darryl Hart consider materials produced for Presbyterian
devotions by Westminster Press and John Knox Press.
Their "preliminary probe" into this literature again finds a
growing pluralism.

During the early part of the century, scriptural witness
to God's transcendence and exemplars of piety from
church history provided the major sources for Presbyterian devotional materials. Indeed, Noll and Hart are
struck by the uniformity in the devotional literature.

By the late 1950s and certainly in the turbulent 1960s, a
dramatic shift occurred. A "new language of spiritual life"
did not replace "traditional concepts of evangelical piety."
Rather it grew "alongside of, and sometimes [was] inter-

woven" with the older vocabulary. What Noll and Hart call the "modern devotion" emphasized the development of greater self-understanding over an individual's life span. Self-realization became a major concern. The division between the sacred and the profane became blurred as the holiness of all life gained prominence. Scriptures continued in use, but the references concerned self-fulfillment and divine immanence. The spiritual was expected in the world rather than in retreat from it. Church history was seldom mentioned.

Noll and Hart see much in these developments that is endemic to Christianity. For example, they regard the recent turn inward into the self to be part of a continuing post-Reformation debate as to whether spiritual growth comes primarily from external revelation or from resources within the individual. However, they do see other cause for serious concern. Specifically, they ask whether the range of theological questions addressed by the "new language of Zion" in Presbyterian devotions is broad enough to nurture either a distinctive or a healthy Reformed spirituality.

Benton Johnson's article on Presbyterians' move from an old social agenda to a new one shifts attention from devotional life to the practice of piety, a movement that the Reformed tradition has consistently stressed as the natural goal of theological reflection and worship. Johnson's particular interest is the claim made by many that American political liberalism has co-opted the social consciousness of mainstream Protestantism.

Johnson tests this thesis by comparing General Assembly pronouncements with the editorials and articles in *The Nation,* a forum for Democratic liberalism. He wishes to see if Presbyterians followed or preceded the latter over time in order to trace the influence of liberal opinion on the church.

Johnson finds that General Assembly statements on social issues "vastly" increased over the century. Particularly after 1965, General Assemblies expended much greater amounts of time and energy on social issues. The type of social issues addressed also changed significantly. In the late 1920s and early 1930s, temperance, Sabbath observance, and world peace dominated Presbyterians' attention. By the 1980s only peace remained in the forefront of the denominations' concerns. Moreover, even in its peace advocacy, earlier General Assembly statements exhibited little understanding of the connection between peacemaking and social justice that was emphasized in later pronouncements.

According to Johnson, the "new agenda" to which Presbyterians eventually turned did closely resemble the political stance of American political liberalism. The shift to this new agenda was persistent and without retreat but also gradual and relatively free of conflict until the late 1960s. Johnson accounts for the early, moderate speed of this development by postulating generational differences in Presbyterian advocates for the social gospel. Early proponents of the new agenda avoided pushing their positions too hard or on too many fronts until the 1960s. After that date, a more militant generation of politically active clergy were encouraged to advocate more aggressively for their positions by contemporary civil rights agitation, liberation movements elsewhere in the world, and the prospect of nuclear holocaust.

The Presbyterian Church U.S. exhibited a slightly different pattern from that of the PCUSA, UPCNA, and UPCUSA, though again the process moved inextricably to the same ends. During the twentieth century, PCUS General Assembly pronouncements assumed similar stances to those of other Presbyterian denominations, but they avoided specific recommendations or references to politicians or laws. Leaders of the new agenda in the PCUS were hampered in their promotion of new issues by their denomination's unique doctrine of the spirituality of the church. In the 1970s, this barrier was surmounted, but not without significant conflict.

Johnson finds the range of issues addressed in the Presbyterian Church's new agenda impressive. Nevertheless, he cautions that its proponents may have "neglected to refuel the engines that produced" enthusiasm in the first place. Rising disaffiliation from the denomination is evidence of that fact. Johnson further suggests that a third agenda may now be needed. This new agenda would revitalize the spiritual and theological base of the church, while simultaneously avoiding the creation of any "latter-day version of the spirituality doctrine."

Rick Nutt's examination of the creation of the Presbyterian Church in America provides an interesting counterpoint to Johnson's work. The PCA's birth was a specific, direct result of the new agenda's triumph that Johnson describes. Nutt illustrates that the final schism of the PCA from the PCUS had been developing for some years. Conservative groups within the PCUS had spawned various organizations and even a seminary to combat the growing influence of the new agenda that was, in their view, corrupting their church.

The PCA schism also exemplifies a Presbyterian version of what Robert Wuthnow has called "the Great Divide" of recent American religious realignment. Wuthnow insists that the main demarcation lines between American Protestants are no longer denominational boundaries. Instead, even within denominations, mainstream Protestantism is divided between religious "conservatives" and "liberals."[6] The PCA follows the patterns of religious conservatives generally in its biblical stance. Its founders maintained a fundamentalist view of scriptures born from the Princeton theology of the previous century. That theology had become the common property of many non-Presbyterian fundamentalists by the twentieth century. But the PCA diverges from other conservative patterns on one significant point. Its leaders believed that the Westminster Confession was as perfectly inspired as the scriptures. Where Moorhead has noted that the larger Presbyterian churches came to emphasize the historical relativity of all humanly constructed creeds and confessions, those who formed the PCA were convinced that confessions were not period pieces growing out of the human conviction of a particular time and place. Instead, the Westminster Confession was the absolutely firm and true system of doctrine found in scripture.

The departure of PCUS members to the PCA says as much about the PCUS as it does about the church that separated from it. Nutt acknowledges that the PCUS leadership wanted rapid change and, in service to that end, "may have appeared insensitive or unresponsive to the grass roots." The liberal hierarchy also promoted a more politically and socially active Christianity but was less exacting toward theology and Bible. At the same time, Nutt observes that the very cultural captivity that the PCA abhorred in their liberal brothers and sisters proved to be the PCA's greatest temptation. In their advocacy of their own conservative agenda, its members became heavily involved politically. Thus, their efforts in behalf of a pure gospel did as much, if not more, to preserve southern culture's status quo as it did to free the gospel from the secularizing influences of American society generally. Ironically, Nutt points out, such flying too close to the cultural flame may ultimately prove to be the primary characteristic shared by the PCA and the PCUS.

Expanding pluralism is without a doubt the central theme of Presbyterian theological and liturgical development in the twentieth century. For some like the members of the PCA, its emergence has been a curse. For others, it has been a blessing. But for many more, the challenge of a pluralistic church is both a boon and a bother.

As a boon, the expanding vision of twentieth-century mainstream Protestantism represents a religious awakening of sorts. The church has become acutely aware of the rich variety of sincere religious expression both within the church and beyond the Christian community in other living faiths. This new consciousness of religious diversity has opened Christians' eyes to significant but formerly ignored aspects of the gospel. The equality of all under God, the priesthood of lay as well as clerical believers, the life-giving balance of multiple forms of witness and worship, and the necessity of verbal proclamation with active demonstration of divine grace have all acquired a deeper meaning in this situation. Mainstream Protestantism now exhibits a new appreciation for the persistent but formerly overlooked contributions of women and ethnic minorities to Christian witness.

With this refreshing recognition of the many who comprise the community of faith, how can the church be said to live as one? With this growing consciousness of its various constituencies' differing needs, how can the body of Christ serve all? If all are equal, who shall lead? If representative organization be the answer, how shall that representation be measured? And if historical and cultural forces do, indeed, influence all theology and worship, what can the church proclaim and practice as true to the gospel, trustworthy across time, and necessary to all for salvation? These and many other unexpected and perplexing questions now trouble the soul of mainstream Protestantism as never before.

The image of a mosaic mentioned earlier as a paradigm for contemporary Presbyterian theology and worship is, in one sense, misleading in the face of these questions. A mosaic requires a mixture of variety and structure. The miscellaneous pieces that fill a mosaic pattern provide detail, color, and energy to what is oftentimes a commonplace design, but the design itself supplies the framework or outline for coordinating what seems otherwise a mere hodgepodge of random fragments.

Certainly, the abiding contribution of Presbyterian theological and liturgical development, as well as that of other mainstream Protestant communions in this century, has been the unprecedented recognition of the multiplicity of gifts brought to Christ's body by its many parts. This new vision has expanded the acceptable scope of theological and liturgical expression within the denomination. Consequently, the Presbyterian Church can now draw on a rich array of theological perspectives and worship styles. But the church still lacks a commonly accepted, overarching design to harmonize the parts into a whole.

The Presbyterian mosaic then remains inchoate, at best,

and fragmented, at worst. Indeed, the very plurality that promises remarkable depth and breadth of vision in Presbyterian thought and worship threatens to become a network of fault lines for future division. For this reason, a central question for the church in the 1990s is, How can it achieve an intimate community, a corporate solidarity, and a clear witness even as it embraces the plurality that arises from the profundity of the gospel itself?

Milton J Coalter
John M. Mulder
Louis B. Weeks

1

Pluralism and Policy in Presbyterian Views of Scripture

Jack B. Rogers and Donald K. McKim

Presbyterians in America have experienced diverse and often disputed approaches to the authority and interpretation of the Bible. For the first century of its American existence, views of the Bible and its function did not seem to occasion much comment or controversy in the Presbyterian Church. But in the nineteenth century and the first third of the twentieth century, a scholastic doctrine of scripture similar to that of seventeenth-century Post-Reformation orthodoxy in Europe prevailed. Its literalistic interpretation of scripture was treated as confessional for several decades. This approach became the subject of intense dispute during the fundamentalist-modernist controversy of the 1920s. The scholastic approach was officially abandoned in 1927 when the General Assembly declared that no judicatory could state in categorical terms which doctrines in the church's confessions were "essential and necessary." This constituted a functional rejection of the Assembly's deliverances in 1910, 1916, and 1923 of five articles to which all candidates for ordination had to adhere. From the 1930s until the mid-1960s an alternative neo-orthodox view gained wide acceptance and application. It was taught in seminaries, used in denominational curriculum, and guided preaching in mainstream churches. This neo-orthodox consensus collapsed under the pressures of intellectual and cultural changes shortly after it was made the official denominational position in the Confession of 1967. After much confusion in the 1970s, a third, mediating model was described and commended in official studies by the two larger Presbyterian bodies just prior to their merger in 1983. Controversy over moral and social issues during a period of restructuring following the reunion of the northern and southern Presbyterian churches, however, evidenced a wide variety of understandings of both the nature and the function of scripture, yet, with no new models receiving explicit sanction in the late 1980s.

Scripture in Neo-Orthodox Theology (1936–1967)

The story of the scholastic period and its controversies from 1869 to 1936 has been ably documented in Lefferts Loetscher's classic study *The Broadening Church.*[1] It concluded with the 1927 decision that no one, not even the General Assembly, had the constitutional power to define what were "essential and necessary doctrines."[2] That decision decentralized theological decision making to the presbyteries and the judicial process. It opened the present era of theological pluralism. Loetscher noted in 1954 that the principle established in 1927 "has much broader implications than the Church has yet had occasion to draw from it."[3]

The full impact of the 1927 decision was delayed in part because by the mid-1930s, American Presbyterianism was being influenced by a movement newly arrived from Europe, neo-orthodoxy. Karl Barth (1886–1968) was the major figure, but in America the works of Emil Brunner (1889–1966) were also influential. Neo-orthodoxy attempted to rediscover the central themes of the Protestant Reformation and restate them in contemporary fashion. Barth reacted strongly against liberal theology and its view of scripture as the record of religious experiences of ancient people which could be repeated anew in each generation.

For Barth, scripture as the written Word of God bears witness to God's decisive revelation in the living Word, Jesus Christ. As a "witness," the Bible always points beyond itself to Christ. The Bible is written in human words and needs the work of the Spirit to "become" the Word of God in a personal sense. It should not be expected to be technically perfect (in the Old Princeton sense of "inerrant") since scripture writers have the "capacity for errors." "The Bible is God's Word," said Barth, "to the extent that God causes it" to be God's Word, to the extent that God "speaks through it."[4] Barth was the primary author of the Theological Declaration of Barmen in which the Confessing Church in Germany declared its resistance to Nazi encroachment. The substance and style of this document proved formative for the later Confession of 1967 of the United Presbyterian Church in the U.S.A.

Scripture in the Southern Presbyterian Church

Change in the Presbyterian Church in the U.S. came gradually. In 1930, Kenneth Foreman in a *Union Seminary Review* article openly questioned the notion of a plenary, verbal inspiration of scripture and urged the acceptance of some of the conclusions of biblical criticism.[5] In the 1930s and 1940s, R. L. Dabney's *Theology* was removed as the basis for theological instruction in southern seminaries, and students began to read Calvin as well as more contemporary exponents of Reformed theology such as Barth and Brunner.[6] In the 1940s, the biblical departments of the southern seminaries gradually added professors who did not believe that a conservative view of the Bible as the Word of God was necessarily bound to a belief in inerrancy. These same professors felt free to incorporate many of the conclusions of higher criticism in their teaching even though it mitigated against the widely held literalistic interpretation of scripture.[7]

By the late 1950s both northern and southern branches

of Presbyterianism had a relatively well established theological consensus at least among the leadership in the denominations and in the seminaries. It seemed appropriate to make room for a moderate neo-orthodoxy in the confessional understanding of the churches. The year 1958 was pivotal. The General Assembly of the Presbyterian Church in the U.S. acted to establish a committee to prepare a statement in the "language of our day" to replace a similar Brief Statement adopted in 1913 to clarify certain passages in the Westminster Confession of Faith.[8] In 1962, the PCUS Assembly adopted "A Brief Statement of Belief." It both presented the theology of the Westminster Confession in contemporary language and seemed to open the door to some of the emphases of neo-orthodoxy and its companion in America, the "biblical theology movement."[9] A statement that "the Bible becomes a means of grace through preaching, teaching, and private study, as the Holy Spirit speaks to human needs and reveals the living Word of God who is Jesus Christ" could be heard as reflective of the cadences of Barth and Barmen.[10] The 1962 Brief Statement was not submitted to the presbyteries for approval as a confessional document. It was adopted by the General Assembly as an educational tool and was printed in the back of editions of the Westminster Confession.

Scripture in the United Presbyterian Church of North America

Also in 1958 the Presbyterian Church in the U.S.A. and the smaller United Presbyterian Church of North America united to form the United Presbyterian Church in the U.S.A. The confessional basis of the merger was the Westminster Standards. This was done despite the fact that the UPCNA had a confessional standard adopted in 1925 and amended in 1945 which had superseded the Westminster Confession of Faith and Catechisms.[11] The UPCNA statement, "Of Holy Scripture" declared:

> We believe that the Scriptures of the Old and New Testaments are the Word of God and are inspired throughout in

language as well as thought; that their writers, though moved by the Holy Spirit, wrought in accordance with the laws of the human mind.[12]

This article evidenced the moderate conservatism which had characterized the denomination. Drafted at a time when the larger Presbyterian Church U.S.A. was sharply polarized over inerrancy, it declined to use the word and yet appeared to allow both inerrantists and noninerrantists to subscribe in good conscience.[13]

Scripture in the Confession of 1967

At the merging General Assembly of the UPCNA and the PCUSA to form the United Presbyterian Church in the U.S.A. in 1958, the Committee on a Brief Contemporary Statement of Faith was named. Edward A. Dowey, Jr., of Princeton Theological Seminary was appointed chair.[14]

The members of the committee and a majority of the ministers, and through them, the elders, of the denomination had been shaped by what they experienced as the "thrilling revival of theology," occasioned by neo-orthodoxy in the 1940s and 1950s.[15] They understood this approach not just as one model among others but as the normative way of doing theology. They intended, therefore, to give a neo-orthodox approach to scripture's confessional status in the Confession of 1967.[16] Edward Dowey was convinced the neo-orthodox approach alone could save scripture from the ravages of higher criticism.[17]

The neo-orthodox consensus shared by the committee defined the Word of God, not as the written text of scripture, but as the content of scripture, Jesus Christ. The explanatory discussion of "the Place of the Bible" in the "Introductory Comment and Analysis" made the reasons for this choice clear.

> This section is an intended revision of the Westminster doctrine, which rested primarily on a view of inspiration and equated the biblical canon directly with the Word of God. By contrast, the preeminent and primary meaning of the Word

of God in the Confession of 1967 is the Word of God incarnate.[18]

Revelation in Jesus Christ replaced the inspiration of the book in order to avoid the limitations of the older doctrine of inerrancy.

Following presentation of the proposed confessional changes in 1965, a Special Committee of Fifteen was established by the General Assembly to receive responses and consider amendments. At the end of this process, a compromise was reached between those who wanted to speak only of Jesus Christ as the Word of God and those who believed it was proper to speak of scripture as the Word of God. The final draft stated:

> The one sufficient revelation of God is Jesus Christ, the Word of God incarnate, to whom the Holy Spirit bears unique and authoritative witness through the Holy Scriptures, which are received and obeyed as the word of God written.[19]

Dowey, in a subsequently published commentary, made clear the committee's intention to maintain a distinction between Jesus Christ as *the* Word of God and the Bible as a witness to Christ. A capital *W* was used to designate Christ as the Word, while a lowercase *w* was used for word of God in reference to scripture.[20]

On biblical interpretation the confession said that while the scriptures are "'given under the guidance of the Holy Spirit," they are also human words, "conditioned by the language, thought forms, and literary fashions of the places and times at which they were written." They reflect the "views of life, history, and the cosmos which were then current." Thus, the church must "approach the Scriptures with literary and historical understanding" (9.29).

The approach to biblical interpretation in the Confession of 1967 was one of two reasons cited by a newly formed special purpose group, the Presbyterian Lay Committee, Inc., in urging Presbyterians to vote against the proposed confession. The continued resistance by some conservatives to biblical criticism was evidenced in full-page advertisements in leading daily newspapers purchased by the Lay Committee. They alleged the confession represented a "humanizing" of the Bible.[21] Despite this outcry, the confession was approved by the presbyteries.

The theological consensus of the 1940s and 1950s in the Presbyterian Church was given confessional status just as the general culture and academic theology were abandoning the assumptions on which it was built. As the 1960s unfolded a new cultural climate, and new issues arose, neo-orthodoxy waned.[22] It had always been less of a coherently constructed school of thought than a movement in reaction to liberalism. It offered an alternative to both liberal and fundamentalist approaches to scripture. It did not, however, provide solid answers to the questions in dispute. Is the Bible objectively or only existentially true? Will higher criticism support a biblical theology that assumes a consistent and coherent biblical message? Changes in cultural context after the formative leaders of neo-orthodoxy were no longer active also contributed to the lessening of its influence. Neo-orthodoxy had been formulated in a Euro-American setting but presented itself as universal in import. That assumption was challenged in the 1960s by the contextualized theologies of the third world and racial ethnic theologies in the United States. With a reawakened interest in science in American culture, the antiempirical orientation of Barth and others seemed unhelpful. Philosophy had passed from an interest in existentialism in the 1940s and 1950s to analysis of language in the 1960s. In this context, Barth's claim to have removed philosophical elements from his theology seemed naive. In a period when the cultural emphasis was on wholeness, Barth's thundered insistence on a dualistic separation of God and humanity was unacceptable. American theology in the 1960s became issue-oriented and "secularity" became popular. Black theology, theology of revolution, ecological theology, and other issue-oriented theologies developed. For a few years around 1965, "God is dead," with its roots in a critique of theological language, became a theological slogan.[23] The Confession of 1967 thus marked the end of an era of relative homogeneity in the understanding and use of scripture.

Pluralism and Schism in the 1970s

While the Confession of 1967 was being prepared and debated in the northern Presbyterian church, some southern Presbyterians began actions designed to resist a similar eventuality in their denomination. In 1964, a group of conservatives in the PCUS formed Reformed Presbyterian Seminary in Jackson, Mississippi. Central among the distinctives of the new school was a commitment to "plenary, verbal inspiration" of the Bible and "its absolute inerrancy as the divinely revealed and authoritative Word of God."[24] A signal was thus given that some intended to hold to the theology of Charles Hodge and Benjamin B. Warfield, of James Henley Thornwell and R. L. Dabney, as the normative understanding of the nature of scripture. Some of these people, led by Professor Morton H. Smith of Reformed Seminary, participated in a schism in the PCUS, which occurred in 1973 with the formation of the Presbyterian Church in America (PCA) with 250 former PCUS churches.[25]

Scripture in "A Declaration of Faith" (1976)

In 1976 the PCUS General Assembly approved and sent to the presbyteries for their vote a *Proposed Book of Confessions.* It was similar in format to the *Book of Confessions* adopted by the UPCUSA in 1967. In place of the Confession of 1967, the PCUS was presented with its own contemporary statement entitled "A Declaration of Faith." The style of the PCUS Declaration was poetic and liturgical. The material on the Bible, contained in chapter VI, generally paralleled its counterpart in the Confession of 1967. The issue of the relationship between Christ as the living Word and scripture as the written Word which proved so controversial in the Confession of 1967 was, however, handled in a more nuanced manner. It both identified Christ and the Bible as the Word of God and yet sought to differentiate the way in which that was true. A study guide accompanying the confession explained,

The Declaration places the "written" Word after the "living" Word for a reason. We must say of Christ that he is God himself with us, but we cannot say that of Scripture. We can worship Christ but we cannot worship the Bible. Jesus Christ is the Word of God in a more direct way than the Bible. Nevertheless, once we are clear about this, we must say that the Bible too is the Word of God.[26]

Despite extensive preparation and enthusiastic presentation; the proposal failed to receive an affirmative vote in three fourths of the presbyteries as required for adoption. Press comments at the time attributed the defeat to moderate conservatives who had remained loyal during the PCA schism but who were not ready for union with the UPCUSA and its theological perspectives.[27]

Ordination of Women

In the northern Presbyterian stream two social issues, the ordination of women and the ordination of homosexuals, provoked further discussion of scripture in the 1970s.

Northern Presbyterians had ordained women as deacons as early as 1906, as elders in 1930, and as ministers of Word and sacrament in 1956.[28] The matter became controversial when a 1974 graduate of Pittsburgh Seminary, Walter Wynn Kenyon, applied to the Presbytery of Pittsburgh to be ordained and installed as Stated Supply in a small congregation in western Pennsylvania. Kenyon made clear that he believed the Bible forbade the ordination of women as office bearers in the church. The presbytery voted to ordain him nonetheless, but its action was interrupted by a formal complaint. This led to a judicial case that finally reached the Permanent Judicial Commission of the General Assembly, the highest court of the denomination.[29]

The decision of the Permanent Judicial Commission of the General Assembly contradicted Kenyon's assessment of the ordination of women as a nonessential of Presbyterianism. It made clear that the status of women in the church was an essential tenet which Presbyterians had to hold in order to be ordained. The Judicial Commission's decision was rendered on the grounds of scripture and confessions stating,

> The question of the importance of our belief in the equality of all people before God is thus essential to the disposition in this case. . . . The UPCUSA, in obedience to Jesus Christ, under the authority of Scripture (and guided by its confessions) has now developed its understanding of the equality of all people (both male and female) before God. It has expressed this understanding in the Book of Order with such clarity as to make the candidate's stated position a rejection of its government and discipline.[30]

Some ministers sharing Kenyon's views left the church following the Judicial Commission's ruling. A number of congregations split, with the dissidents who rejected the ordination of women reconstituting themselves as congregations of the formerly southern PCA.[31]

Ordination of Homosexuals

The matter of the ordination of homosexuals released both more heat and more light regarding the way in which northern Presbyterians viewed scripture in the 1970s. In response to several overtures, the General Assembly in 1976 established a Task Force to Study Homosexuality related to the Advisory Council on Church and Society. The task force reported to the 1978 General Assembly with a 201-page study including both majority and minority recommendations.[32] The study contained data from psychotherapy and empirical sciences, and also a 70-page section entitled "Homosexuality and the Bible: A Reexamination." A subsection on "How to Read the Bible?: Problems and Models of Biblical Authority and Interpretation" drew much attention. For the first time in decades, Presbyterians were presented with four alternative approaches to biblical interpretation with both their presuppositions and suggested applications to the issue at hand carefully laid out. The report labeled them Models A, B, C, and D.[33] When these models were assessed in rough relation to identifiable theological movements the following correspondences could be discerned: Model A was the view of the scholastic theology of the Old Princeton School of the Hodges and Warfield which dominated in the northern Presbyterian Church from 1812 to 1927; Model B could be identified with the neo-orthodoxy of the 1930s through the 1960s, citing as its referents John Calvin, Martin Luther, Karl Barth, Emil Brunner, Dietrich Bonhoeffer, and the Confession of 1967; Model C moved in the direction of liberation theology citing for reference Gordon Kaufman, Dorothee Soelle, Paul Lehmann, and Rosemary Radford Ruether among others; Model D combined the liberation motif with the emphases of process theology represented by Norman Pittenger, John Cobb, David Ray Griffin, and Daniel Day Williams.[34]

Liberation theology and process theology were new theological models that came into significant use in the general culture and the Presbyterian Church in the 1970s. Liberation theology's basic concern was for justice. It had been developed in various ways by Black and feminist theologians and especially in the struggle for justice in Latin America, where it emphasized God's preference for the poor and dispossessed. Scripture functioned as a foundation for freedom providing paradigms and goals for human liberation and presenting humanity's ultimate human liberator, Jesus Christ. A UPCUSA committee studied the theology of liberation and recommended in 1976 that ways be found of "introducing programs on liberation theology in each of the United Presbyterian seminaries."[35] Process theology became an option especially for those seeking a theological framework coherent with contemporary science. It posited a dipolar nature in God, with one part of God, the primordial nature, being absolute and changeless while the other part of God, the consequent nature, was constantly engaged in the change and relativity of the universe of time and space.[36] The Bible in process thought described God as lovingly luring humans and all other entities in the world to be what they most fulfillingly could become. When scripture concurs with one's own experience it can become a source of seeing the unfolding action of God in the world as God evolves along with creation into future possibilities.[37]

Requests for New Definitions of Scripture at the End of the 1970s

Also before the UPCUSA General Assembly in 1978 was the report of the Committee on Pluralism in the Church. This group had been created by the 1976 General Assembly on the recommendation of the General Assembly Mission Council as part of its review of the spiritual welfare of the whole church. The task of the committee was to study sources of conflict in the church. The decisive area of conflict was biblical authority and interpretation. The committee's conclusion was:

> Of all the factors that contribute to divisiveness in our denomination, the Committee found none is more pervasive or fundamental than the question of how the Scriptures are to be interpreted. In other words, the widely differing views on the ways the Old and New Testaments are accepted, interpreted, and applied were repeatedly cited to us by lay people, clergy, and theologians as the most prevalent cause of conflict in our denomination today. . . . It is our opinion that until our church examines this problem, our denomination will continue to be impeded in its mission and ministry or we will spiral into a destructive schism.[38]

The conclusion of this report seemed amply illustrated by the conflict over homosexuality and the two together no doubt encouraged the 1978 General Assembly to set up a Task Force on Biblical Authority and Interpretation under its Advisory Council on Discipleship and Worship.

In October, 1978, the PCUS Council on Theology and Culture authorized a study entitled "The Understanding and Use of the Bible in the Presbyterian Church in the United States." The task given the PCUS study group was more general.

Since the Bible is so vital to us, its use in the church needs to be the subject of study and discussion from time to time to provide opportunity for gaining perspective, raising the level of mutual understanding, and, one would hope, reaching fresh agreements about the nature of its authority and the ways in which it may be faithfully interpreted.[39]

Thus both denominations looked toward the 1980s and toward their potential reunion by preparing definitive statements on the authority and interpretation of the Bible. They apparently hoped thereby to find ways of reducing conflict and finding agreements on the many issues that lay before them.

An unsettling event, outside the official structures of the larger Presbyterian denominations but affecting them, was the formation in 1978 of a group named The International Council on Biblical Inerrancy. This group initiated a ten-year drive in which it would "attempt to win back that portion of the church which has drifted away from this historic position" of inerrancy.[40] The chairperson of the group was James M. Boice, pastor of the Tenth Presbyterian Church in Philadelphia, a congregation of the UPCUSA. The first publication of the group was a book, *The Foundation of Biblical Authority,* edited by Boice with a chapter by former Pittsburgh Seminary church historian John H. Gerstner. The book and the papers given at a "summit" meeting in Chicago in October 1978 made clear that this group would continue to insist on the Hodge-Warfield theory of inerrancy as the only theologically sound and historically valid approach to biblical authority and interpretation.[41]

Presbyterian Statements
on Scripture in the Early 1980s

UPCUSA Report (1982)

The UPCUSA report was received for study and its guidelines and recommendations adopted in 1982. As part of its response to the first mandate to understand the di-

verse ways of understanding biblical authority then prevalent in the denomination, the task force conducted an
opinion poll by a sampling of Presbyterians through the
Presbyterian Panel. At one point, panelists were asked to
choose from five positions the one they preferred regarding
the inspiration of the Bible.[42] The report indicated that
"the five positions were seen as describing a range from a
maximum recognition of divine inspiration and control in
position 1 to a minimum of no divine inspiration in position 5, with a corresponding scale for the human element."[43] A most instructive finding was that Presbyterians,
far from being polarized between the far right and the far
left theologically, represented an almost bell-shaped curve,
weighted somewhat more heavily in a conservative direction regarding the inspiration of the Bible.[44]

Two overall conclusions were drawn. An overwhelming
82 percent of Presbyterians chose one of the center three
positions. UPCUSA representatives in 1979 were centrists
regarding the Bible. Another way of reading the data noted
that 85 percent of the panelists favored one of the first
three, more conservative, positions. The report concluded:
"It is clear that the *Panel,* speaking for the church constituency, affirmed that the Bible is indeed the word of God
written."[45] This did not negate, for most Presbyterians,
that the Bible is also a human document requiring continued critical examination and investigation as a literary-
historical work. The final conclusion from the Panel data
was that: "since the Bible is considered uniquely authoritative for the church, proposals, arguments, and conclusions—drawn from or based upon the Bible—have an
important place in the life and work of the church."[46]

The second mandate to the task force was to explore
the Reformed tradition and the denomination's confessional standards regarding their views of the Bible. Noting that "in many cases, the way people understand the
history of the Reformed tradition is inextricably bound
up with their theological position," the task force described three models which represented major attitudes
that had prevailed at points in American Presbyterian

history.[47] The first of these, "Model A: The Bible as a Book of Inerrant Facts" was the Old Princeton position which prevailed from 1812 until the 1930s. The second position, "Model B: The Bible as a Witness to Christ, the Word of God," was the neo-orthodox position which prevailed in the 1930s through the 1960s culminating in the Confession of 1967. "Model C: The Divine Message in Human Forms of Thought" was offered as a third model operative in the 1980s. Its distinctive characteristics included openness to the insights of the social sciences, a functional understanding of the way in which the message of scripture communicates in all cultures, and the acceptance of human, relational metaphors, rather than scientific or propositional statements as the best descriptors of the way in which God has communicated with people through scripture. The task force thus described a moderate, centrist, confessional approach that treated the Bible as both divine and human. They believed that such an approach was being used and was of service to the church at the time the report was written.[48]

Results of the task force's analysis of the confessional standards were incorporated into the final section of the report, "recommended guidelines for a positive and not a restrictive use of Scripture in theological controversies." The task force offered six Reformed confessional guidelines with a seventh added by the standing committee of the General Assembly in 1982 which accepted the report. In summary form the guidelines were:

1. Recognize that Jesus Christ, the Redeemer, is the center of Scripture.

2. Let the focus be on the plain text of Scripture, to the grammatical and historical context, rather than to allegory or subjective fantasy.

3. Depend upon the guidance of the Holy Spirit in interpreting and applying God's message.

4. Be guided by the doctrinal consensus of the church, which is the "rule of faith."

5. Let all interpretations be in accord with the "rule of

love," the twofold commandment to love God and to love our neighbor.

6. Remember that interpretation of the Bible requires earnest study in order to establish the best text and to interpret the influence of the historical and cultural context in which the divine message has come.

7. Seek to interpret a particular passage of the Bible in light of all the Bible.

These theological guidelines were followed by some recommended epistemological guidelines on how people know and learn and by some ecclesiastical guidelines on how to deal fairly with controversy in the church.[49]

PCUS Report (1983)

The report entitled "Presbyterian Understanding and Use of Holy Scripture" was adopted by the PCUS General Assembly in 1983 just prior to the act of uniting with the UPCUSA.[50] This report appears to be a careful elaboration of the Reformed confessional guidelines adopted by the UPCUSA in 1982. While the UPCUSA report merely asserted that its seven principles were derived from the Reformed confessions, the PCUS study carefully added a section on "Confessional Background Material" with citations after each of its nine guidelines. The editor of *Presbyterian Outlook* commented, "The two papers came out at the same place and differ chiefly in approach."[51]

Use of Scripture in General Assembly Reports Since 1983

The two Presbyterian streams entered reunion in 1983 with a clear consensus on the authority and interpretation of the Bible. This consensus was evidenced in the two freshly minted documents which had been adopted in the two years immediately prior to reunion.[52] Both documents took a centrist position rooted in the Reformed confessions and avoiding the distinctives of either the scholastic or neo-orthodox models which had previously dominated American Presbyterian thinking. Interestingly, although liberation, process, and various kinds of feminist and other theologies were in use in the early 1980s, the documents produced at the time of the reuniting of the church did not give sanction to these models of biblical interpretation. The behavior of the church constituency, reflected in actions of the General Assembly, seemed to expect something like the consensus of 1982–1983 to prevail in official church pronouncements when the issue of the nature and function of scripture was explicitly invoked.

In General Assembly reports after 1983, the Bible was used in a multiplicity of ways which evidenced that persons and committees preparing such reports were either unaware of the 1982 and 1983 guidelines or felt no obligation to follow their guidance as to scripture's authority and its interpretation. Several examples illustrate the diversity of uses of scripture since 1983.

Two reports reflected the view of scripture found in Latin American liberation theology. In 1983, the PC(USA) General Assembly adopted a paper, "Adventure and Hope: Christians and the Crisis in Central America," which came from the task forces of both the UPCUSA and the PCUS that had been studying Central America for two years.[53] The 1984 General Assembly approved "Christian Faith and Economic Justice" originating from the Council on Theology and Culture of the PCUS on authorization from its 1978 General Assembly. Part of the study was "a theology of economic justice from a specifically biblical perspective."[54]

Other reports presented in 1986 and 1987 appeared to reflect a moderate neo-orthodox approach to scripture with the door left ajar in each case to possible new approaches. "The Confessional Nature of the Church" was adopted by the 1986 General Assembly.[55] A more detailed treatment of scripture was presented in "The Nature of Revelation in the Christian Tradition from a Reformed Perspective" (1987). The study had been called for by some who were not satisfied with the 1982 UPCUSA report on "Biblical Authority and Interpretation." They were unable to defeat the report or significantly modify its conclusions so they persuaded the standing committee of the 1982 General Assembly to append to the report a call for a new study of "Revelation."[56]

Revelation in the paper was defined as "the self-disclosure of God," "received by faith," and "received in experience" with Jesus Christ as "the central revelation of God" by whom "all other apparent revelation must be tested."[57] By the Spirit, "the Scriptures are recognized as the word of God"; "in and through the Scriptures the Holy Spirit speaks to us primarily, not about the Scriptures themselves, but about Christ" (28.193). But "to affirm that the Bible is the word of God is not to commit oneself" to any one theory about it. In particular, "it is not necessary to commit oneself to the view that the sacred text is 'inerrant,' that what the biblical authors intended to say is identical with what God is saying to us, or that we must not disagree, for example, with Paul about anything" (28.212). "The most important interpretive question about the Bible . . . is what God is saying to us now in it" (28.226). While Jesus Christ remained "the supreme criterion . . . interpretation of Christ's significance must draw on the whole range of human experience, so far as it is accessible to us" (28.236).

"Theologies Written from Feminist Perspectives" (1987) asserted more emphatically the importance of human experience in interpreting scripture and formulating theology.[58] The presenting problem was that "the Bible has been used for centuries to justify the view that women are necessarily, by the plan of God and order of creation, subordinate to men."[59] The experience of women contradicted that interpretation of scripture.[60]

Recent Perspectives on Scripture in the Late 1980s

Pluralism gained official stature as a positive factor in the Presbyterian Church (U.S.A.) with the reception by the 200th General Assembly (1988) of a report later published as *Is Christ Divided? Report of the Task Force on Theological Pluralism Within the Presbyterian Community of*

Faith.[61] In the reorganized structure of the denomination, a Theology and Worship Ministry Unit was created. One of its departments was an office of Pluralism, staffed by Joseph D. Small III, former chair of the task force and writer of the report.

The report treated the Bible positively, but noted its pluraformity.

> Presbyterians confess that the Bible is "the unique and authoritative witness to Jesus Christ" and "the only infallible guide to faith and practice." Yet the reality of the Bible is plural rather than singular. The Bible is a collection of witnesses and guides.[62]

It went on to affirm that "what unifies the various writings of Scripture and joins them together as canon is their consistent testimony to God's story with humankind, culminating in the story of Jesus Christ."[63] The paper affirmed the unity in diversity of the Bible as a preface to affirming the value of a theological unity amid enriching diversity in the church. Its concluding plea was that "open theological discourse in the church is a realistic and creative possibility."[64]

Finally, the Presbyterian Church (U.S.A.) in 1989 was in the process of a potential confessional revision. It was part of the Articles of Agreement of the reunion between the Presbyterian Church in the United States and the United Presbyterian Church in the United States of America to form the Presbyterian Church (U.S.A.) that

> the General Assembly of the reunited Presbyterian Church shall at an early meeting appoint a committee representing diversities of points of view and of groups within the reunited church to prepare a Brief Statement of the Reformed Faith for possible inclusion in the *Book of Confessions* as provided in G-18.0201.[65]

The first Moderator of the reunited church, J. Randolph Taylor, in May 1984 appointed a Special Committee of twenty-one persons to prepare a new confessional statement.

In February 1988 the Special Committee published a proposed statement and asked for response from the church at large. The statement on scripture came in the section on the Holy Spirit and read: "The same Spirit who inspired prophets and apostles still speaks through Scripture read and proclaimed."[66] The Special Committee received over fifteen thousand responses and revised the document to clarify its intentions where there seemed to be misunderstandings. In early 1989 a revised draft of the proposed new Brief Statement of Faith was submitted to the 201st General Assembly (1989) for its consideration. The revised section on scripture declared: "The same Spirit who inspired the prophets and apostles rules our faith and life in Christ through Scripture."[67] A constitutionally mandated Committee of Fifteen was appointed by the Moderator of the 1989 General Assembly to consider amendments to the Brief Statement. The draft on scripture approved for submission to the 1990 General Assembly by both the revision committee and the original drafting committee added to the 1989 text a further line: "engages us through the Word proclaimed."[68]

Presbyterians as Mainline Protestants

This analysis of the road Presbyterians have traveled regarding scripture in the past fifty years provides interesting confirmations and contrasts with recent studies on mainline Protestantism. The Presbyterian Church is always listed in the category of a "liberal" mainline church. The decision of 1927 not to identify "essential and necessary articles," among them the "inerrancy" of scripture, represented a turning away from conservative leadership in the denomination. Denominational leaders in the late 1980s remained nervous about and resistant to initiatives based on a conservative view of scripture.

Robert Wuthnow has asserted that American religion in the mid-1980s was deeply and almost equally divided between conservatives and liberals and that this antagonism was as divisive within denominations as between denominations.[69] That Presbyterianism is almost equally divided between conservatives and liberals would not be confirmed by a review of attitudes toward scripture in the Presbyterian Church.[70] The national opinion surveys appeared to underestimate the numbers and the importance of the "moderate middle" within mainline denominations like Presbyterianism.[71] One reason the data in mid-1980s opinion polls may have distorted the picture is that conservatives were identified as those who interpreted the Bible "literally." Few conservative Presbyterians, or other mainline Protestants, would feel comfortable selecting that designation but might do so if that was the only choice on a questionnaire for a basically conservative orientation.[72]

A further evidence of fragmentation within mainline denominations was the formation of special purpose groups which focused people's energies on a single issue or task.[73] In the 1960s both the Presbyterian Lay Committee and Presbyterians United for Biblical Concerns evidenced a conservative attitude toward scripture as among their distinguishing marks. In the 1980s, special purpose groups tended to fall into either "evangelical" or "humanistic" categories.[74] Of the former, home Bible study groups were the most common with one in five persons surveyed having participated in such a group.[75] Presbyterians undoubtedly comprise part of the reported participants. Yet, despite nineteen Chapter 9 special purpose groups recognized by the denomination, none were dedicated to promoting home Bible study. Nor were there national staff or programs dedicated to that purpose.

What became apparent in the late 1980s was that moral issues, especially those related to family and gender, proved the most divisive. Women's roles, abortion, and homosexuality aroused the greatest passion and provided the occasion for special purpose groups.[76] Scripture was cited within Presbyterianism and outside it by those on opposite sides of these issues. Ironically, what seemed to make these issues the most divisive was that there was no agreed-upon understanding of either the authority of the Bible or the appropriate means of its interpretation on

these matters. Despite the centrist positions approved by
the General Assemblies in 1982 and 1983, Presbyterians,
like other mainstream Protestants, were unable to use
scripture to come to common understandings of these controversial issues.

Conclusion

As Presbyterians celebrated two hundred years as a fully
organized denomination in America, their official views of
scripture seemed to reflect the language and ethos of the
dominant traditions that had prevailed historically, now
recast in a mediating, centrist form. The continuing aller-
gic reaction to the excesses of the fundamentalist inerrantist approach dominant prior to 1927, and the subsequent
affirmation of a variety of confessions in 1967, however,
seemed together to prejudice Presbyterians toward pluralism. The appropriate limits of that pluralism tended still,
in accordance with the 1927 decision, to be tested only in
judicial cases. When pressed, in representative bodies, to
articulate a position regarding scripture, Presbyterians
came down near the center of their confessional tradition.
Rather than justifying unlimited pluralism, these reports
seemed to indicate acceptable Presbyterian parameters for
the use of scripture. When functioning in day-to-day policy
making on matters where scripture might be invoked,
Presbyterians behaved pragmatically and appealed to
pluralism.

2

Redefining Confessionalism: American Presbyterians in the Twentieth Century

James H. Moorhead

In the late 1920s, the General Assembly of the Presbyterian Church in the U.S.A. reversed a policy of more than thirty years' standing by opting for what Lefferts Loetscher has called "theological decentralization." Although the church prior to the 1890s had often tolerated a measure of ambiguity about its theological boundaries, a number of Assemblies, beginning in 1892, sought a more restrictive interpretation of the denomination's confessional base. Fearing that liberalism and the destructive effects of modern biblical criticism might seep into the church, these Assemblies enumerated allegedly essential tenets of the Westminster Confession, for example, the inerrancy of scripture, and thus in theory made assent to these doctrines mandatory for every minister in the PCUSA. During the early 1920s in the midst of the fundamentalist controversy, a party of conservatives sought to enforce this restrictive view of Presbyterian identity by purging theological liberals from the church. Faced with the prospect of protracted conflict and possibly schism within the denomination, the Assembly chose a more moderate stance designed to allay controversy. In 1926 and 1927, it adopted a report which denied that any General Assembly possessed the power to define categorically the essential articles of the Westminster Confession. In effect, this action declared unconstitutional previous Assembly attempts to dictate such essentials and thus safeguarded a degree of theological pluralism within the denomination. A few years later the Presbyterian Church in the U.S. took a more guarded step toward inclusivity. Dr. Hay Watson Smith had openly avowed moderately liberal sentiments when he assumed a pastorate in Little Rock, Arkansas, in 1924. Doubters of his orthodoxy demanded action against Smith, but presbytery ruled that his views did not disqualify him as a minister. Subsequently, the case went back and forth from presbytery, to synod, and General Assembly. The Assembly finally resolved the issue in 1934 by allowing the presbytery's initial ruling to stand. Although the decision to tolerate Smith's views did not indicate a formal shift in the church's doctrinal stance, it did signal a tentative broadening of theological identity.[1]

Viewed in the retrospect of more than a half century, these events marked the beginning of a major theological change. Presbyterians had self-consciously permitted diversity, and in subsequent years an even greater pluralism would flourish in their midst. Presbyterians were also on the verge of redefining the nature of what it meant to be a confessional church. To confess, according to the view soon to emerge, was not so much to affirm a set of truths as it was to witness to God's saving activity. Moreover, Presbyterians would increasingly locate that saving activity in the secular world itself. Thus in the last half century, formal theological pronouncements have functioned as general guidelines for religious discourse rather than as specific prescriptions for belief; and theology has assumed an increasingly ad hoc character as Presbyterians have sought to discern God's presence in the diverse issues posed by the world.

Both of the major branches of American Presbyterianism experienced this change. The so-called northern church, the Presbyterian Church in the U.S.A.—after 1958 it became the United Presbyterian Church in the U.S.A. as a result of a merger with the United Presbyterian Church of North America—officially achieved a new confessional identity in 1967. Although the Presbyterian Church in the U.S. (popularly termed the southern church) never formally altered its confessional basis, it also moved in the same direction as its northern counterpart. When the two denominations reunited in 1983 as the Presbyterian Church (U.S.A.), they left to their successor a new understanding of Presbyterian theological identity. Tracing the rise and the central features of that identity is the goal of this essay.[2]

Northern Presbyterianism: From the 1920s to the Confession of 1967

When the General Assemblies of 1926 and 1927 turned away from controversy, they did so largely because they were unwilling to pay the price of continued conflict; but soon a new theological perspective rendered the old battle cries obsolete. That theology, usually called neo-orthodoxy (but sometimes termed dialectical theology, the theology of crisis, neo-Reformation theology, or Christian realism) exerted a powerful influence upon American seminaries in the 1930s. Associated with such figures as Karl Barth, Friedrich Gogarten, Eduard Thurneysen, and Emil Brunner in Europe and Reinhold Niebuhr, H. Richard Niebuhr, and Edwin Lewis in America, neo-orthodoxy was not a single intellectual system but rather a common mood shaped by a common perception of crisis. The movement took shape as some liberals grew disenchanted with their theological tradition and attempted a course correction. The slaughter of World War I, the Great Depression, and the rise of Fascist dictators made former confidence in Western superiority and faith in progress appear to have been naive. Since Protestant modernism had often underwritten that optimism by stressing an immanent God manifest in the spirit of the age, many found liberalism woefully inadequate to the current crisis. With renewed appreciation of Christian themes neglected by their recent predecessors, the neo-orthodox returned to older sources of wisdom—preeminently to the Bible and the Protestant Reformers—in order to frame a more sturdy theology.

Although neo-orthodoxy cannot be reduced to one set of ideas shared by all, several salient emphases of the movement may be noted. First, it affirmed the centrality of the Bible as the instrument of God's revelation. Unlike modernism which tended to portray the scriptures as a record of humanity's evolving religious consciousness, neo-orthodoxy viewed the Bible as the medium through which *God* spoke, often in accents alien to those people expected. Yet for all of its respect for the biblical witness, the movement did not relapse into a fundamentalist doctrine of inerrancy. The Bible told of God's encounter with humanity, but it was also written by fallible people; and the neo-orthodox did not repudiate the results of critical scholarship. Second, the transcendence of God moved to the fore of theological discussion. Third, the neo-orthodox took seriously the biblical account of the Fall and the classic Christian idea of original sin, for they found in these symbols an accurate portrayal of the human predicament. Fourth, they conceived theology in dynamic terms. One did not approach the truth of faith through precise, changeless propositions. Faith was primarily a response of trust to the encounter with the living God in Jesus Christ.[3]

The changed face of Princeton Seminary, once the stronghold of conservative Presbyterianism, provided a dramatic example of the new theological mood. The reorganization of the institution in 1929 had augured a more inclusive stance, and that promise was fulfilled in 1936 when John Mackay assumed the presidency. A native Scot who had been trained at the seminary and had served as a missionary in Latin America, Mackay reshaped Princeton in accordance with his own ecumenical vision and desire to transcend the sterile categories of fundamentalism and modernism. He assembled a faculty sympathetic to the neo-orthodox impulse. Elmer G. Homrighausen, professor of Christian education and one of Mackay's appointees, exemplified the altered temper of the seminary in a 1939 article in the *Christian Century* series "How My Mind Has Changed in This Decade." Homrighausen averred that his intellectual encounter with the dialectical theology had convinced him that liberalism was inadequate and that "classic Christian theology is still the truest interpretation of Christianity," but at the same time he had learned that one could not simply repristinate orthodoxy. The faith needed "translation into the thought-forms and mentality of our day, without compromising the content."[4]

At the heart of this effort to recover orthodox themes without succumbing to fundamentalism was the so-called biblical theology that flourished among Presbyterian scholars in the 1940s and 1950s. Whether biblical theology ever constituted anything as unified as a movement is a subject of scholarly debate; but many Presbyterians—among them G. Ernest Wright, Floyd V. Filson, Otto Piper, and James D. Smart—approached the scriptures in a way transcending the polarity between modernists and fundamentalists. They believed, in the words of W. Eugene March, that it was "possible to draw together the results of critical scholarship in such a way that fully honored scientific objectivity while at the same time presenting the Bible in a manner appropriate to its status as Canon." They readily acknowledged that criticism had demolished many traditional views of the Bible, but they also believed that scholarship had shown a thematic unity within the scriptures. That unity was dynamic, based upon the action of a God revealing himself to men and women in particular historical events as God worked out a saving purpose culminating in Jesus Christ.[5]

By the late 1940s, biblical theology along with its neo-orthodox ally had established a broad (if ultimately fragile) consensus within Presbyterianism. That consensus shaped a significant revision of the Sunday school curriculum: *Christian Faith and Life, A Program for Church and Home,* formally launched in 1948. *Christian Faith and Life* provided a decidedly content-oriented curriculum focused on several major themes, one for each year of a three-year cycle: Jesus Christ, the Bible, and the church. These emphases reflected the neo-orthodox commitment to the centrality of revelation through Jesus Christ and to the importance of the church and its traditions. Although *Christian Faith and Life* stressed classical content, it sought to avoid any suggestion that Christian education was merely the imparting of concepts and facts. As James Smart, who played a major role in preparing the new curriculum, declared: "The content of a Christian curriculum ought never to be regarded as static, external or impersonal. A truly content-centered curriculum is simply one which is Christ-centered, that is, in which it is recognized that all else is of no avail unless somehow through the Church's teaching Christ is increasingly becoming known to the learners as a present living Lord and Saviour." Once again one hears the characteristic accents of neo-orthodoxy. The new curriculum handled problems posed by the higher criticism in the manner of advocates of biblical theology. Authors freely acknowledged these difficulties, then sought to transcend (if not resolve) them by reaffirming the basic message of the Bible. In part because of its success in giving serious acknowledgment to contemporary scholarship while simultaneously reaffirming traditional Protestant themes, the curriculum proved acceptable to a wide constituency. Its success was perhaps the high-water mark of neo-orthodoxy's influence in the Presbyterian Church in the U.S.A.[6]

By the 1950s, neo-orthodoxy had apparently triumphed, in the words of William Robert Miller, as "the normative religious outlook of the educated Protestant." Certainly the success of the *Christian Faith and Life* curriculum would appear to justify that claim, at least with respect to the Presbyterian Church in the U.S.A. Yet the neo-orthodox consensus, while real, was never as firm or as powerful as it seemed. It acquired an appearance of exaggerated strength because observers did not always distinguish it carefully from other forms of the postwar revival. This revival—sometimes dubbed the Eisenhower Revival—is usually dated from about 1945 to 1960; and it consisted of several components: increased religious affiliation, a building boom in church construction, a resurgence of conservative Protestantism in a form less strident than the fundamentalism of the 1920s, and the increased popularity of inspirational books, many of them best-sellers. These trends drew strength from the widespread conviction that religion, in whatever guise, was vital to the American way of life. Long a major theme in American thought, the idea acquired new timeliness with the United States now engaged in a cold war with the avowedly atheistic Soviet Union. These various streams of piety eddied in and out of one another, giving the postwar revival a diffuse or amorphous character. Critics—some neo-orthodox prominent among them—derided the blander aspects of the revival, its lack of theological content, and its inability to utter a prophetic word against American culture. And yet neo-orthodoxy itself benefited from the success of the revival, especially among men and women in the pew who were uninterested in making precise theological distinctions. In part, neo-orthodoxy lent itself to this confusion because it invoked classic Christian themes and therefore often received a sympathetic hearing from traditionalists who had little appreciation for its subtleties or the new meaning it had given ancient symbols.

Moreover, some of the leading theologians of the movement had shifted since the 1930s to positions that made it harder for them to be distinguished from the general surge of piety and its patriotic overtones. Reinhold Niebuhr, for example, had largely abandoned the stinging critique of American capitalism which informed his *Moral Man and Immoral Society* (1932) and now defended the government's policy of containing communism and of relying on nuclear deterrence. When a 1948 article in *Presbyterian Life,* the newly created magazine of the Presbyterian Church U.S.A., introduced readers to Niebuhr, it compounded the possibilities of confusion. While the article noted that he had once been a socialist and had spoken on behalf of industrial workers, the major thrust was to portray Niebuhr as a man made "unforgettable by his thundering insistence that the Bible was right: Sin was important, we all had it, and trying to blame it on society was the worst thing we could do." The "only answer . . . is recognizing our dependence upon God, and the regaining of the humility of obedience." Although one can scarcely fault the author for presenting a popularized account to a lay audience, one must wonder whether readers gained a very clear picture of his neo-orthodoxy, which they probably perceived as mere variation on the general themes of the postwar revival.[7]

The deeper problem of neo-orthodoxy, however, was that it had never constituted a fully unified movement; and it had left many theological questions unanswered. From the beginning it was united chiefly by an awareness of crisis in Western culture, a sense of the inadequacy of liberalism, and a willingness to look seriously at classic Christian doctrines. Once the immediate sense of crisis faded and liberalism (at least in its more exuberant nineteenth-century forms) had passed from the scene, much of the common focus of the movement had also disappeared. In their desire to go beyond the old fundamentalist-modernist debates, the neo-orthodox ignored or touched only lightly on several major issues: For example, does critical study actually yield a single overarching biblical theology as many of the neo-orthodox suggested? In what sense is scripture normative and how does it become so for the community of faith? While Sydney Ahlstrom was perhaps too harsh in suggesting that the neo-orthodox attempted to solve the problems created by modern critical thought by "putting down only a very thin sheet of dogmatic asphalt" over them, it is clear that many issues still cried out for attention. Moreover, the fact that it conceived theology in dynamic rather than static terms created within neo-orthodoxy a principle of self-criticism and volatility conducive to further change.[8]

By the 1960s neo-orthodoxy was disappearing but it left an enduring mark on Presbyterian theology. In 1967, the church—now broadened as a result of a merger—achieved a significant constitutional revision which embodied many of the insights of the theological ferment of the previous thirty years. That revision was at once the fruition of neo-orthodoxy, broadly defined, and a sign of the new theological climate to follow it.

Creedal change in the united church took a form more thorough than originally envisioned. When the Presbyterian Church in the U.S.A. and the United Presbyterian Church of North America merged in 1958, the first General Assembly of the new denomination charged a committee with the task of preparing a "brief contemporary statement of faith"; but a year later the committee, chaired by Edward A. Dowey, requested and received a mandate to make a broader review of the Reformed confessional heritage. In 1965 the group proposed a Book of Confessions; and two years later, after some changes, it was officially adopted by the denomination. The book included not only a contemporary statement (the Confession of 1967) but also documents from various periods of church history. Although most discussion during the revision process focused upon C-67, one must underscore the significance of the entire book. The fact that the denomination now had a multiple confessional base, composed of documents with somewhat different emphases and reflecting diverse historical settings, stood as an implicit reminder that no one creed could capture the fullness of the faith and that every creed was at least in part a creature of its own time and place.[9]

The Confession of 1967 summarized its message with admirable brevity: "In Jesus Christ God was reconciling the world to himself." Explicating that motif, the confession echoed many of the themes of the theological renaissance of the previous thirty years: the priority of God's activity in redemption, the radical sinfulness of humankind, the Christocentric nature of revelation, and the role of the Holy Spirit in bringing God's work in Christ to fulfillment. The last two themes shaped the confession's much discussed treatment of scripture. To avoid any hint of bibliolatry, C-67 subordinated the Bible to Christ: "The one sufficient revelation of God is Jesus Christ, the Word of God incarnate." The central theme of scripture was its witness to that living Word—a witness that could only be made efficacious by "the illumination of the Holy Spirit." Although the Bible remained the indispensable "witness without parallel" and although the church received it "as the word of God written," the confession deliberately rendered the *w* in word in the lowercase to avoid any suggestion of inerrancy and to prevent the notion that one could somehow establish the authority of scripture without reference to its Christocentric focus or independent of the work of the Holy Spirit. This emphasis freed the confession to acknowledge the fully human character of the scriptures; and for the first time in a creedal statement, American Presbyterians endorsed modern biblical scholarship: "The Scriptures, given under the guidance of the Holy Spirit, are nevertheless the words of men, conditioned by the language, thought forms, and literary fashions of the places and times at which they were written. . . . The church, therefore, has an obligation to approach the Scriptures with literary and historical understanding."[10]

While affirming the necessity of theological language, C-67 also recognized its limitations. Formulations about God's reconciling work were "expressions of a truth which remains beyond the reach of all theory." Denying that it offered a "system of doctrine," the document exhibited a decided antipathy toward any notion that confessions are primarily compendia of propositions. Indeed C-67 moved toward a functional or mission-oriented understanding of confessionalism. To confess was not primarily to affirm certain beliefs (though the act entailed these), but rather, to bear "a present witness to God's grace in Jesus Christ."[11]

That witness was decisively oriented toward the world. As God was in Christ reconciling the world to himself, Christians were summoned to a ministry of reconciliation. All of the church's words and actions were to be evaluated in the light of this mission; and all of its ordinances and polity were to be instruments to that end. Or as C-67 succinctly summarized, "To be reconciled to God is to be sent into the world as his reconciling community."[12]

The responsibility of the church to be a reconciling agent

was not left in the abstract. The Confession of 1967 listed four examples of concerns to which the church should address itself: (1) racial and ethnic discrimination, (2) the dangers of nationalism in the achievement of peace, justice, and freedom, (3) the prevalence of "enslaving poverty" throughout the world, and (4) "anarchy in sexual relationships." To a degree unprecedented in a confessional document, political, social, and economic issues emerged as matters of theological import. Equally important was the tone of the statements which implied a new commitment to prophetic judgment of existing inequities within society and which appeared to cast the church in the role of social critic. That prophetic stance was epitomized in a much-debated passage in which the confession asserted that the search for peace, justice, and freedom would require "fresh and responsible relations across every line of conflict, even at risk to national security." Moreover, the confession warned that "the church which identifies the sovereignty of any one nation or any one way of life with the cause of God denies the Lordship of Christ and betrays its calling."[13]

The adoption of C-67 as well as the other documents in the *Book of Confessions* represented a theological milestone. On the one hand, these actions deepened the church's historic confessional identity. Presbyterians now possessed a creedal foundation more nearly representative of the breadth of the Reformed tradition. Arnold Come and others have argued that the confession also "recaptured and intensified" the dynamic Christocentric understanding of faith held by Luther and Calvin—an understanding subsequently overlaid with emphasis on biblical inerrancy and on rational assent to intricate systems of doctrine. Viewed in this light, C-67 marked a return to Protestant roots. Moreover, the church's new confessional basis, though broader and theoretically less restrictive than the Westminster Confession of Faith, may in some instances have worked against doctrinal laxity. During the time that the denomination retained Westminster as its sole standard, many ignored it as a virtual dead letter; but the intense discussion of theological issues prompted by C-67 helped to clarify viable modern boundaries for Presbyterianism. Yet in another sense, C-67 clearly presaged a looser style of confessional identity. The drafters of that document had reminded the church that all creedal formulations were provisional and time bound, and they had, to a significant degree, made the "particular problems and crises" of the secular world the occasions of confession. Despite the intentions of its authors, C-67 gave a potential charter to redefine Presbyterian theological identity by retail—that is, on a case by case basis in response to "particular problems and crises."[14]

Southern Presbyterianism: From the 1920s to "A Declaration of Faith"

By contrast to its northern counterpart, the Presbyterian Church in the United States maintained for much of its life a more nearly monolithic theological identity. When, for example, the Presbyterian Church split into separate Old School and New School denominations in 1837–38, southern Presbyterians adhered in overwhelming numbers to the more conservative Old School. The southern portion of the Old School then withdrew in 1861 to form the Presbyterian Church in the Confederate States of America. Although several years later it incorporated a much smaller contingent of New Schoolers, the southern church remained decidedly Old School in thought; but to that conservative faith it added its own distinctive stamp. In the words of the 1861 Assembly, "the power of the church is exclusively spiritual." No ecclesiastical body possessed the right to address matters pertaining to the secular sphere, for the church and the civil order were "as planets moving in different orbits." This radical sundering of faith from the world of politics, economics, and culture represented in part the southern church's response to abolitionist critiques of slavery; but long after the "peculiar institution" had died, Presbyterian commitment to the spirituality of the church would continue to inhibit serious engagement with "profane" issues. Similarly, Southerners emphasized a *jure divino* Presbyterianism which asserted that the church could not go beyond the express commands of scripture in shaping its theology, worship, polity, and mission. Until the early twentieth century, scarcely any voices challenged these distinctives; and the church gloried in its rigid confessionalism, its freedom from contamination by the secular world, and the clear biblical sanction of the Presbyterian way of life.[15]

But a new theological identity was finding its voices in the church's seminaries and colleges during the 1920s and 1930s. Ernest Trice Thompson, beginning a long career at Union Theological Seminary in Virginia in 1922, wrote gentle but firm challenges to denominational shibboleths such as the precritical use of scripture, the spirituality of the church, unquestioning allegiance to the Westminster Confession, and *jure divino* Presbyterianism. Kenneth J. Foreman, professor at Davidson College from 1922 to 1947 and subsequently a teacher at Louisville Seminary, also reflected the spirit of openness and questioning. Expressing his rejection of inerrancy and the spirituality of the church—the latter he believed should fall "into the everlasting discard"—Foreman flatly stated that the Westminster Standards would no longer suffice for the modern age and called upon the church "to do for our own day what the seventeenth century thinkers did so ably for theirs": namely, to confess the faith in the idioms of modern thought. Joined by Aubrey Brown, Thompson and Foreman made the popular weekly *The Presbyterian in the South* (later renamed *The Presbyterian Outlook)* an effective instrument of the dissemination of more liberal views. In 1938 and 1945, Samuel Cartledge of Columbia Theological Seminary published two widely read introductions to the Bible in which he contended that conservative Christians need not espouse inerrancy and that they could readily accept such critical views as the composite nature of the Pentateuch and the nonhistorical nature of Jonah. In the 1940s, Union's Bible Department gained a powerful triumvirate of scholars—John Bright, Balmer Kelly, and

Donald G. Miller—who played a major role in fostering the new biblical theology which went beyond static conceptions of revelation to emphasize the scriptures as a dynamic record of the "mighty acts of God." In 1947, their approach won a significant medium of expression when Union Seminary's quarterly was transformed into *Interpretation.* In 1963, the denomination gave the fruits of this theological revolution to its lay people in the Covenant Life Curriculum, which in many respects was analogous to the northern church's *Christian Faith and Life* curriculum.[16]

In 1962, the General Assembly gave formal expression to southern Presbyterianism's changing theological outlook by adopting "A Brief Statement of Belief." Although the statement neither substituted for nor amended the official standards, the Assembly directed that it be used for educational purposes and that it be appended to future editions of the *Book of Confessions.* The statement treated six major topics: God and Revelation, Man [*sic*] and Sin, Christ and Salvation, The Church and the Means of Grace, Christian Life and Work, and Judgment and the Life to Come. Although much of the Brief Statement presented traditional views to which conservatives would not object, the document did accent many of the theological insights generally associated with neo-orthodoxy. While allowing that the Bible was the "written Word of God," the statement ignored the question of the mode of inspiration. It emphasized instead the role of the Holy Spirit through which the "Bible becomes a means of grace," and the preaching of the Word was the telling of the "mighty acts of God in history" more than it was a setting forth of doctrinal propositions. The statement depicted total depravity in terms redolent of Reinhold Niebuhr: "Sin operates not only within individuals but also within society as a deceptive and oppressive power, so that even men of good will are unconsciously and unwillingly involved in the sins of society." In a related passage, the statement decisively rejected without naming the shibboleth of southern Presbyterianism—the spirituality of the church. "The range of

Christian responsibility is as wide as human life. . . . Christians as individuals and as groups have the right and the duty to examine in the light of the Word of God the effects on human personality of social institutions and practices." The task of shaping and influencing social policies was deemed integral to the church's "basic responsibility both for evangelism and for Christian nurture." Moreover, the doctrine of election, treated in Westminster as part of the eternal plan of God whereby some were predestined to eternal life and others to everlasting death, received a very different interpretation in the 1962 statement. Following Calvin and the more recent neo-orthodox theologians, the Brief Statement placed election exclusively in the context of faith in Christ. There it provided no hint of the double decrees but served to testify to God's "eternal inclusive" purpose of redemption. Finally the statement banished any suggestion of *jure divino* Presbyterianism. The most the General Assembly claimed for denominational polity was that it "followed scriptural precedent"; but, the document quickly added, "The form of government of a church, however, is not essential to its validity." In sum, the Brief Statement embodied many of the features of the previous thirty years' theological renaissance and without explicitly acknowledging the fact signaled a major retreat from tenets once deemed the distinctive marks of the Presbyterian Church U.S.[17]

The following decade the church attempted a major revision of the standards themselves. The General Assembly in 1976 sent to the presbyteries a proposed *Book of Confessions,* including a contemporary statement called "A Declaration of Faith." Although the proposal failed to win the three-fourths vote necessary for enactment, the majority of presbyteries did support it; and the General Assembly subsequently commended the declaration to the church for use in worship and study.[18]

The Declaration was structured in narrative form. It told the story of God's activity, beginning with creation, moving through the history of Israel, Jesus, and the church, and culminating in eschatological hope. Even the printed form of the confession conveyed the sense of motion. The authors chose to render the document in a short-line, broken sentence format, in part because they believed that this style suggested "the active, moving, dynamic character of the story the Declaration tells." In employing the narrative form, the drafters neither neglected traditional theological loci nor denied that confession entailed the affirmation of specific propositions, but these achieved their meaning only in the context of the story of God's "mighty acts in history." Like C-67 and to a much lesser extent the Brief Statement of 1962, the Declaration accented the functional nature of theological language: God is what God does, and to confess faith in that God is to respond in trust to God's redemptive activity, not to possess a thoroughly elaborated set of ideas about God.[19]

The Bible, said the Declaration, plays an indispensable role in mediating the story of God's saving activity. It is "the written word of God . . . , [the] authoritative standard of faith and life . . . [to which] we subject . . . all our understanding of doctrine and practice." Yet the Declaration fully affirmed the historically conditioned character of the Bible. Written under diverse circumstances, its traditions had been "shaped and reshaped." To understand the Bible, one must use the best available historical and literary tools, remember that God's action in Christ is the final key to the meaning of scripture, and rely on the guidance of the Holy Spirit. Read as a whole, the Declaration's statements about scripture subordinated it to the living Word, Jesus Christ, and were consistent with the general view of theology in the document: it was the use, more than the nature, of the Bible which concerned the drafters. The Bible was given that humans might be incorporated into the story of God's saving acts.[20]

The same practical note resonated in a statement on the church's mission. "We serve humankind by discerning what God is doing in the world and joining him in His work." That task entailed, of course, the calling of men and women "to repent and believe the gospel"; but the church could not fulfill that mission by words unrelated to the specific social and political contexts of those to whom the message was addressed. True proclamation of the gospel required confrontation of the idolatry of nationalism, advocacy of peace, support of efforts "to correct the growing disparity between rich and poor nations," and a willingness "to stand with women and men of all ages, races, and classes as they struggle for dignity and respect and the chance to exercise power for the common good." Although the Declaration claimed for the church "no expert knowledge" about the policies needed to realize these objectives and although it affirmed that the gospel did not ignore individuals in its quest "for justice in the social order," it was equally clear that the spirituality of the church had, as Kenneth Foreman had long wished, been cast "into the everlasting discard." In its place was the ideal of joining God in God's work in the world.[21]

The Problems of "Discerning What God Is Doing in the World"

In one sense the idea of joining God in God's work in the world was scarcely new, for Presbyterians had long believed that faith should shape this world as well as the next. The style of engagement with social and political questions, however, shifted in the mid-twentieth century. The older stance assumed the priority of what Robert Wuthnow has called a "culture of values." If individuals were made to feel accountable to certain shared principles, American culture would then exhibit a moral consensus conducive to a just social order. By inculcating those values, the churches could thus exercise responsible influence on the public domain without becoming embroiled in specific issues of policy or program. "A Letter to Presbyterians," written to the denomination by the General Council of the Presbyterian Church in the U.S.A. on the occasion of the McCarthy hysteria in 1953, illustrated this approach. Denying that the church should "present blueprints for the organization of society and the conduct of government," the General Council added that the church should "proclaim those principles, and . . . instill that spirit, which are essential for social health, and which form the indispensable foundation of sound and stable policies in the affairs of state." Ten years later on Independence Day, Eugene Carson Blake, the United Presbyterian Stated Clerk, provided a powerful symbol of a new style of social witness. After joining Black and white leaders attempting to integrate an amusement park in Baltimore, Blake was arrested; and newspapers around the nation carried photos of him entering a police van. Blake's action, one of many instances of Presbyterian involvement in public protest during the turbulent 1960s manifested a style of direct advocacy in the public realm. Various Assemblies of both denominations displayed this style when they expressed grave reservations about the war in Vietnam, opposed particular weapons systems, approved economic boycotts, supported women's right to terminate pregnancy, and argued that the private sexual behavior of consenting adults should not be regulated by the state. The list of similar actions could be extended considerably, but all (at least by implication) rested upon the theological principle enunciated in the Confession of 1967: "In each time and place there are particular problems and crises through which God calls the church to act. The church, guided by the Spirit, humbled by its own complicity and instructed by all attainable knowledge, seeks to discern the will of God and learn how to obey in these concrete situations." In a word, the church's social witness was contextual, always conditioned by and addressed to particular settings. Hence faithful witness was not a matter of enunciating general values—as an older style of social engagement was wont to do—and then trusting that these values would work themselves out in effective action. Direct engagement with particular issues was required.[22]

Considerable irony attended this trend. At the moment when Presbyterians moved toward more immediate engagement with social questions, the larger culture was losing the moral consensus that could sustain such a venture. Sydney Ahlstrom has written of the disintegration of "national confidence, patriotic idealism, [and] moral traditionalism" during the 1960s. Robert Wuthnow has traced the emergence in the post-World War II period of two distinct civil religions, holding divergent views of the basic values which should undergird American life. Wade Clark Roof and William McKinney have contended that since the 1960s a new moral pluralism has emerged in American life with the result that recent efforts to articulate a common purpose and common values for the culture "reflect a fractured interpretation, more a legitimation of interest-group politics than an overarching canopy of national meaning."[23]

This loss of an "overarching canopy" was evident among Presbyterians when they debated the Confession of 1967 and the Declaration. In 1965, two groups in the northern church—the Presbyterian Lay Committee and Presbyterians United for Biblical Concerns—formed to fight the proposed Confession of 1967. After revisions in the document, PUBC eventually endorsed it; but the Lay Committee continued its opposition, even to the extent of taking out ads in newspapers to arouse public opinion against the confession. While most opposition centered on alleged doctrinal deficiencies—for example, insufficient emphasis on the Bible as the inspired Word of God—it was difficult in practice to separate resistance motivated by purely theological questions from hostility animated by the prophetic style of social advocacy that C-67 represented. J. Howard Pew, one of the founders of the Presbyterian Lay Committee, epitomized the linkage by his consistent attacks on church leaders who "meddled" in political matters. In the southern church, the Declaration also generated considerable debate. Critics faulted it for supposed overtones of universalism, neglect of the bodily resurrection of Christ, a weak view of scripture, inadequate formulation of the imperative for missions, and unclear guidance about sexual morality. Frequently lurking behind doubts about particular statements—or the lack thereof—in the Declaration was an objection to the form of the document itself. Some feared that the use of the story or narrative form lent itself to theological imprecision. It encouraged, said one group of protesters, "romantic, mystical" conceptions; and another critic called for a confession of "straightforward propositional statements." As in the case of C-67, opponents of the Declaration sometimes suspected that the call for engagement with the world served as a cover for dubious political and social advocacy by the church. In short, the dynamic conception of confessionalism and the attendant ramifications of "discerning what God is doing in the world and joining him in his work" had become sources of dissent and controversy for Presbyterians.[24]

As Presbyterians tried to sort out their differences in the years after these confessional controversies, they found themselves without a theological perspective powerful enough to encompass diversity. A resurgent conservative evangelicalism, representing emphases which some thought had died with the fundamentalist controversy, exhibited new strength; but its voice scarcely dominated church councils. Nor was there any longer a powerful middle group of neo-orthodox thinkers to serve as a bridge between liberal and conservative concerns. Neo-orthodoxy had been replaced by various theologies, emphasizing liberation, Black consciousness, and feminism among other issues. In this confused setting, the hermeneutical question, to which neo-orthodoxy had generally given insufficient attention, assumed new urgency as Presbyterians sought—but generally failed—to find a commonly accepted principle for the appropriation of the Bible's message. Faced with major divisions about fundamental issues, Presbyterians have turned increasingly to polity and process as a way of handling issues about which theological consensus is lacking. A report to the 1988 General Assembly of the Presbyterian Church (U.S.A.) lamented this fact. Using the debate over homosexuality as an instance of many similar controverted points within the church, the report commented: "Simple conversation between groupings with differing views on the issue is resisted lest such dialogue be perceived as shifting the balance of power or granting legitimacy. Groupings on both sides of the issue are content to engage in polity struggles while failing to address vital theological concerns."[25]

The case of Walter Kenyon, a theological candidate under the care of Pittsburgh Presbytery in the former United Presbyterian Church in the U.S.A., is illustrative. In his examination by presbytery, Kenyon avowed that on biblical grounds he could not support the ordination of women elders, would so inform any congregation he served, and would refuse to participate in the ordination service if women were elected. Although presbytery voted to ordain Kenyon, an appeal to synod reversed that decision—a reversal that was sustained by the Permanent Judicial Commission of the General Assembly in 1975. The commission based its decision in part upon the fifth question which ordinands were required to answer affirmatively: "Do you endorse our Church's government, and will you honor its discipline?" Since the denomination's *Book of Order* had expressed its commitment to women's ordination "with such clarity as to make the candidate's stated position a rejection of its government and discipline," his view "by itself would constitute a negative answer to Question 5." While major theological issues, for example, the equality of all believers in Christ and the proper mode of interpreting scripture, were vitally involved in the Kenyon case, it is significant that the commission chose to decide the matter primarily on grounds of polity.[26]

Another sign of the reliance on polity to contain differences was the effort to institutionalize diversity. Both churches made greater effort to be sure that committees have proper representation of women and minorities as well as of persons of diverse theological persuasions. The UPCUSA recognized a variety of extraecclesiastical groups seeking to promote particular goals and made constitutional arrangement for them to report annually to the General Assembly—a procedure carried over into the reunited church in 1983 when the southern and northern churches finally ended their 122-year split. By 1988, these groups numbered twenty. Their purposes ranged across a wide spectrum: among others, antiabortion lobbying, support for the concerns of gays and lesbians, the eradication of oppression in all human institutions and systems, and support of democracy and the free enterprise system. The sheer diversity of these aims would seem to lend credence to Robert Wuthnow's theory that modern denominations are becoming holding companies for special purpose groups.[27]

Recognizing the magnitude of the problem, the United Presbyterian Church in 1976 created a Committee on Pluralism. Growing out of a General Assembly mandate that there be an annual review of conflicts within the church and of instances "where diversity is dealt with creatively," the committee issued reports identifying divisive issues within the denomination, assessing the adequacy of Presbyterian polity to address these, and suggesting procedural and organizational strategies for handling conflict.[28]

Early in its deliberations, the committee identified diverse approaches to the Bible as a major source of conflict in the church and recommended the formation of a special task force to investigate the issue of biblical authority and interpretation. The latter group presented its report to the General Assembly in 1982. The task force did not endorse one view of scripture in preference to another. Rather the group saw itself as an adjudicator among contending parties and sought to offer principles whereby these groups might communicate with one another. Or in the language of the task force, it offered "guidelines and recommendations to the General Assembly for a positive and nonrestrictive use of Scripture in matters of controversy." Drawing upon and enlarging themes from the *Book of Confessions,* it suggested a number of rules for interpretation: among others, recognition of the centrality of Christ to the canon, focus upon the plain text of scripture, dependence upon the Holy Spirit, and willingness to be guided by the doctrinal consensus of the church. The task force anticipated that Presbyterians would not always agree about the meaning of the Bible for specific questions. "In fact," said the report, "a more faithful and constant reading of Scripture might provoke more and not less controversy. Nor should this be something to be afraid of. Controversy is a part of life and growth; it may give us the experience of struggling together with Scripture in an authentic and helpful way." In order to promote such life and growth, the report suggested specific procedures for the study of the Bible in reference to controverted issues. Like the Committee on Pluralism whose work had spawned it, the task force did not attempt to impose or articulate a fully formed theological consensus. Instead it suggested "the dynamic process" by which differences could be constructively addressed.[29]

The theological diversity within contemporary Presbyterianism has not, of course, been unlimited. The initial draft of a recent proposed Brief Statement of Reformed Faith, unanimously approved by a General Assembly committee representing most shades of theological opinion and submitted to the church for possible adoption, testified that Presbyterians could still find common ground. In sixty-five short lines written in broken sentence format, the statement used a trinitarian structure to affirm the centrality of Christ, the unfailing love of God despite human sin, the reality of new life in the Spirit, and the hope of eschatological fulfillment. While the document contained strands of varied theological concerns—among others, feminism, liberation theology, evangelicalism, and environmentalism—it wove these together in an artful tapestry.[30]

Yet because of its brevity and the fact that its authors designed it for liturgical use, the statement necessarily omitted many issues and left others imprecise. For example, on the matter of scriptural authority, the initial draft offered only fifteen words: "The same Spirit who inspired prophets and apostles still speaks through Scripture read and proclaimed." As a commentator observed, the document contained generalities in which everyone could feel at home. Although a subsequent revision has amplified the statement, it still remains a remarkably short document characterized by fairly general affirmations. This agreement is not to be minimized—it is solid and real—but its depth is uncertain. It is unclear whether at present there exists a denominational consensus which could go much beyond short generalities.[31]

Conclusion

Why has Presbyterianism changed in this fashion? One might argue that American Presbyterianism in the twentieth century recovered the moderate confessional stance which had characterized much of its life prior to the late nineteenth century. When, for example, the clergy were first required in 1729 to subscribe to the Westminster Confession, they were permitted a measure of latitude in the interpretation of the document, even the freedom to reject some of its teachings if these were not among the conveniently unspecified "necessary and essential articles of faith." After bitter struggles in the mid-1700s and again in the mid-1800s—struggles in part over the extent to which Presbyterianism should be theologically monolithic—the church composed differences by allowing confessional boundaries to remain somewhat imprecise. Viewed from this larger historical perspective, the effort of Assemblies in the generation after 1892 to define essential doctrines was an aberration from the central direction of American Presbyterianism; and the movement in the 1920s toward a more inclusive confessionalism marked a return to that path.[32]

Yet Presbyterianism in the last sixty years has done more than resume and deepen its tolerance for diversity. Redefining the nature of confessionalism, it has emphasized dynamic conceptions of truth, has eschewed narrowly propositional understandings of theology, and has increasingly identified the secular world as the arena in which it must define its faith. Neo-orthodoxy provided a major impetus for this change, and for a time that movement appeared to provide a canopy under which discordant theological elements could coexist with a degree of consensus. Neo-orthodoxy, however, left as many potentially disruptive questions as it supplied unifying answers.

For example, it begged the question as to whether the Bible contained a unified message; and aside from assertions about the role of the Holy Spirit, it seldom systematically explored the ways in which contemporary persons could appropriate the Bible. When biblical scholars and theologians subsequently turned to these issues, they discovered nearly as many biblical messages and hermeneutical strategies as there were scholars. Moreover, Presbyterians set loose a potentially disintegrative principle when they acknowledged that true theological confession occurs in response to the "need of the time" (C-67). This assumption prepared the way for a host of radically contextual theologies, taking their cues from gender, race, economic class, or culture. Or to state the matter in a slightly different fashion, this assumption cleared the ground for various efforts to "do theology"—the verb is significant—in an ad hoc fashion, responding to particular issues raised by contemporary culture.[33]

To the extent that this theological situation was exacerbated by the crumbling of moral consensus in the larger culture, Presbyterianism possessed little to insulate itself from the disintegration. Unlike many sectarian groups that have self-consciously withdrawn into countercultural enclaves, Presbyterians have always been actively engaged in the main currents of American life. Sometimes glorifying it, sometimes trying to change or criticize it, they have nevertheless always seen themselves as close to the center of their culture. But what does a church with this vision do when, in the words of William Butler Yeats, "the center cannot hold"? The story of Presbyterianism in the last half century suggests that such a church is destined to recapitulate within its own life the divisions of the culture and that its theology will enjoy no sanctuary from the painful process.

3

Changes in the Authority, Method, and Message of Presbyterian (UPCUSA) Preaching in the Twentieth Century

John McClure

There have been three significant areas of change in mainstream Protestant and Presbyterian preaching in the twentieth century. First, the authority of preaching has changed. Notable shifts have taken place in the influence of preaching and its importance and acceptance as a valid source of information in the eyes of parishioners, the general public, and preachers themselves. Second, there have been important changes in the methods of preaching. The way preachers conceive of preaching and go about the task of preaching is reflected best in fundamental shifts in homiletical theory and seminary education. Third, the theological message of preaching has changed.

It is impossible to separate Presbyterian preaching from preaching in other mainstream Protestant denominations in the twentieth century. By "mainstream" is meant those "establishment" churches defined by Dorothy C. Bass as including the "Presbyterian, Congregational, Episcopal, Methodist, and Northern Baptist churches together with the Disciples of Christ and some Lutheran bodies."[1] The societal and ecclesiastical forces that influenced one mainstream denomination during this period of time influenced all other denominations. Most of these denominations went through similar changes in both preaching and the training of preachers. For this reason, Presbyterian preaching can be seen against the background of what was happening more generally in mainstream Protestant churches in America.

This essay will focus primarily on preaching in the former northern Presbyterian church, the United Presbyterian Church in the United States of America (UPCUSA). Analysis of the distinctive qualities of preaching in the southern Presbyterian denomination, the Presbyterian Church in the United States (PCUS), is outside the scope of this study. However, there are many similarities between the preaching and homiletical education in these two denominations. Therefore, where applicable, examples have been taken from the southern church which coincide with developments in the northern church.

Changes in Cultural and Ecclesiastical Authority

In the early years of this century, preaching had substantial power in the formation of public opinion. Until 1930, mainstream Protestant pulpits were major platforms for entire social and ecclesiastical programs. Although many Presbyterian preachers were preoccupied with internal debates within the denomination,[2] preachers such as Henry van Dyke, Henry Sloane Coffin, George Buttrick, Charles Stelzle, Norman Thomas, Edmund Chaffee, and Alexander McKelway were demanding social and economic justice in the major cities of the nation.[3] From influential pulpits and at civic and national forums they demanded living wages, better working conditions, the abolition of slums, better housing, and the regulation of child labor.[4]

Several of the principal battles of the fundamentalist-modernist controversy were fought from Presbyterian pulpits in the early decades of this century. The best known of these was the debate in the 1920s between fundamentalist Clarence Macartney of Arch Street Presbyterian Church, Philadelphia, and liberal Harry Emerson Fosdick of First Presbyterian Church, New York City. This controversy received national publicity following Fosdick's famous sermon in 1922 entitled "Shall the Fundamentalists Win?"[5]

Presbyterian evangelist J. Wilbur Chapman was a leader in urban evangelism until his death in 1918. The preaching and leadership of Chapman were vital to the New Era Movement in the Presbyterian Church.[6] Evangelist William E. Biederwolf was a world-renowned leader in missionary evangelism. Biederwolf trained pastors of the rapidly growing Korean church in methods of revivalism and mass evangelism. The use of advertising by Presbyterian evangelists kept the opinions of a large, theologically conservative segment of the denomination at the center of the public eye. With self-confidence these preachers promulgated the optimistic belief that Christian civilization would soon prevail in the cities of the land and throughout the whole world.[7]

During prohibition years, the evils of alcohol were preached from both liberal and conservative Presbyterian pulpits. Between 1901 and 1909, conservative Presbyterian clergyman Francis Scott McBride campaigned for prohibition and led Armstrong County, Pennsylvania, to enact prohibition laws. During the same decade in New York City, social gospel advocate Charles Stelzle was underscoring the connection between the liquor problem and the social and economic problems of the city.[8]

No matter what the theological issue, social problem, or historical movement, the Presbyterian pulpit was widely perceived as an authoritative platform for processing information, debating perspectives, and generating interest and involvement in the first three decades of this century. It was important what mainstream and Presbyterian preachers thought on public issues, and these preachers believed that their perspectives were crucial and integral to the formation of public opinion and the witness of the church in society and history.

This authority was traditional for Presbyterian preachers. It was assumed largely as part of the preacher's institutional and social role. Preachers "filled pulpits." Their identity was linked closely to the institution of the pulpit which was an established "office" or official function of the church.

One parishioner, recalling a new pastor's first sermon at Second Presbyterian Church in Richmond, Virginia, in 1926 spoke of the pulpit in dramatic language which showed clearly the parishioner's view of the institution of the Presbyterian pulpit.

> On Sunday, January 17, 1926, a new minister was to mount the pulpit of the Second Church, a pulpit that had felt the stamp and tread and heard the wonderful voice of Moses D. Hoge for fifty-four years. . . . On this winter Sabbath morning an expectant congregation was waiting for their first glimpse of the new pastor. The door to the right of the pulpit opened. A man of medium stature entered, clad in a nicely fitting scholar's gown. He was a man of arresting dignity . . . a man of intense seriousness. . . . The Rev. William Edwin Hill, D.D., was at that time forty-six years old.[9]

This institutional authority was often accorded to rank-and-file Presbyterian preachers as well as those more famous preachers whose names covered the pages of newspapers, evangelistic tracts, and weekly religious periodicals. Presbyterian ministers in smaller churches argued that there were no distinctions between large and small churches when it came to the preaching of the gospel. Rev. Roswell C. Long, writing the history of First Presbyterian Church of Greenwell, South Carolina, in 1932 noted that

> By reason of her heritage, standards, and traditions the Presbyterian Church has a right to great preaching. . . . By reason of his training and personal equipment every preacher in our Church—from the smallest mission church to the largest city church—is prepared to do great preaching. It is not the size of the field—(is there any difference in the size of fields?)—but the size of the man that makes great preaching.[10]

Parishioners of small churches made little distinction between the authority of their preacher and that of well-known preaching personalities. *Presbyterian Survey* carried occasional articles written by lay people about their preachers. In a typical one of these articles the preacher was extolled as "a saint" whose "one desire was to preach His unsearchable riches" and who had "thoughts that an angel might share."[11]

By 1920, there were signs that the nature of the authority of the preacher was changing—a barely perceived shift in the role and identity of the preacher. Arthur S. Hoyt, then professor of homiletics and sociology at Auburn Theological Seminary, noted in 1921 that preachers believed that they had to earn authority through personal conduct and pastoral involvement. According to Hoyt, the "authority of mere position is felt to be less" so that the preacher "strives to be more."[12] The "more" which the preacher strived to become was interpreted by Hoyt as "human." Preachers were becoming more concerned to be interesting, relevant, simple, and clear in their preaching. Weekly sermons were abandoning the promulgation of theological and social programs and focusing on "practical living" and the "lofty ideal of living."[13] According to Hoyt, preachers began to "discuss truth from the standpoint of man, from his nature and need and actual experience."[14] There was a change from reliance upon the external authority of position and office to a more internal authority based upon the quality of the pastoral relationship between the preacher and the congregation.

One reason for this change was that congregations were looking for less in the way of knowledge and information from their preacher. The level of education and the quality of information available to the parishioner increased rapidly in the latter part of the nineteenth and early twentieth centuries, due partly to improvements in Christian education and public education and partly to wider exposure to religious issues in the mass media. The pulpit no longer served as "the chief agent of culture"[15] as it had for many people in the nineteenth century.

Even more significant during these early decades was what Robert Handy called the Protestant "religious depression" of the 1920s. The disillusionment of the postwar decade brought with it a suspicion of religion, a decline in Protestant missionary activity, and a sense within Protestantism that it no longer prevailed as the national religion.[16]

All of this meant that by 1930, the Presbyterian preacher could no longer assume that those in the pews on Sunday morning saw themselves as part of a Christian society or culture in which he had a central authoritative role. The Presbyterian preacher could not "presuppose the general recognition of his authority as a clergyman, or the authority of his institution, or the authority of Scripture."[17]

The ideas of the social gospel movement also affected the status and authority of preaching in Presbyterian churches, though that impact did not occur until the social gospel movement had nearly run its course. The Old School Presbyterian disengagement from culture was no longer possible by 1910 when the General Assembly of the northern church issued its historic declarations on social problems.[18] Northern and southern Presbyterians such as Henry Sloane Coffin, D. Clay Lilly, Charles Stelzle, and Alexander McKelway were preaching a socially engaged message which began to receive a wider audience in the midst of cities beleaguered by problems of rapid industrial expansion. The influence of these preachers was due partly to their ability to rely upon an institutional authority still accorded the pulpit by parishioners and society in the early years of the twentieth century.

As time passed, however, the primary impact of the engagement of Presbyterian preaching with social issues, particularly in the North, was that it instilled in parishioners and in preachers a keen sense that it was ultimately "actions, not words," which counted in the church. New specialized ministries were developed to meet the urban social situation and the needs of the large suburban churches. The idea that "great preaching" was the central feature of the ministry began to change. New forms of ministry developed in health care, home visitation, relief, athletics and youth activities, and other areas.[19] In the parish, authority was vested in those who could start soup kitchens, organize parishioners into involvement in various social projects, and administer a vibrant church program.

As early as 1930, Presbyterian preachers, homileticians, and theologians were feeling this change in the status of preaching acutely. In 1932 Elmer G. Homrighausen, professor of practical theology at Princeton Seminary, wrote an influential article entitled "Can the Protestant Sermon Survive?" In this article he noted that on Sunday mornings "folks expect nothing higher than they get in the Sunday paper, the lecture room, the club, [and] the lodge."[20] He was concerned that preaching had become relativized in its importance. Methodist preacher Gerald Kennedy observed of mainstream Protestant preaching that in the 1930s there began to be a "lack of confidence in the pulpit" which "affected many of the preachers themselves."[21]

Rather than analyzing the changing social and cultural conditions that were causing this change in the status of their preaching, preachers tended to blame themselves. This self-attack was almost overwhelming in the homiletical literature between 1920 and 1950. Preachers repeatedly attacked themselves and other preachers for lack of belief in the "plain word of God"[22] or for preaching only "ethics and the philosophy of religion"[23] or for preaching with a "sole emphasis" on "personal salvation"[24] or for preaching "morality sermons" which "rise no higher than the psychological makeup of the preacher."[25] Throughout the literature there is a sense that if preachers could only get the pieces of their craft in order and renew their personal commitment, the traditional authority of the pulpit would return.

In the 1950s there was a brief recovery of confidence in the significance of preaching by Presbyterian preachers. Several things contributed to this recovery. In Presbyterian seminaries, students had been exposed for several years to Karl Barth's emphasis on the objective authority of preaching as a form of the Word of God. The rapid growth and spread of suburban churches, and the renewal of parish and worship life encouraged the sense that preachers were preaching to congregations who valued worship as a "central fact of the church's presence in the world."[26] As these churches grew, especially in the South and West,[27] Presbyterian preaching seemed to enjoy a brief vote of confidence.[28]

This approbation appeared to be a revival of a more traditional, institutional authority for preaching. The perception was facilitated by an identification of preaching with images from a reconstructed past. Preachers appealed to images of congregations and preaching from eras of Presbyterian history before war and depression had clouded their vision. They spoke of "hardy preachers taking the gospel westward against great odds,"[29] or of great models of faith from the distant past.[30] They placed these images in opposition to the decay which would ensue if parishioners lost sight of these historical exemplars as models for their own self-understanding.[31] Some churches hired preachers from Scotland to fill vacant pulpits. Preachers such as Peter Marshall and Ernest Somerville restored models of preaching that linked American Presbyterian congregations to positive images of the past.

Beneath this recovery, however, the trend away from institutional authority continued. Preachers and psychologists investigated the psychological needs of the congregation, the psychological dynamics of the preaching event itself, and the psychological profile of the preacher. During the late 1950s and 1960s the journals *Pastoral Psychology* and the *Journal of Pastoral Care* were filled with articles examining these concerns. These studies illuminated the unconscious role of preaching as symbolic of the "cultural conscience,"[32] preaching's hypnotic transmission of "nervous tension by suggestion,"[33] misuses of the preaching "role,"[34] the psychology of the location for preaching (pulpit versus openness, elevation versus "coming down," etc.),[35] the psychological diversity within the congregation, and the depth of needs present there.[36] The urge toward humanness and shared humanity challenged dramatically the conception of the preacher's authority as potentially authoritarian: authority rooted in position of leadership, symbolic role, or personal dynamism.

The desire to purge the preaching office of authoritarianism hardened into distrust in many cases. The question by the mid-1960s was whether preaching should have any special authority in the life of the church and community at all. Although most Presbyterian preachers continued to preach using traditional methods, there was a general suspicion and apathy about preaching as a whole in mainstream denominations.[37] A few Presbyterian preachers experimented with nonauthoritarian dialogical methods of preaching. Most ministers placed the accent of their ministry on other things, especially counseling and social issues.

In the 1970s and 1980s, Presbyterian homileticians and preachers began to search for monological forms of preaching that would be dialogical and nonauthoritarian in style and approach. Preachers today are interested in maintaining the role of the preacher as one who speaks alone, interpreting a biblical text, while using language and forms of logic that invite cognitive and emotional participation by the congregation. Many preachers are exploring narrative, inductive, and phenomenological models that relocate the authority of preaching in the power of language to form human consciousness and communal identity.[38] Others, with roots in the pastoral care movement, seek to locate this authority in the professional competence of the preacher as therapist, counselor, community person, or liturgist. Such roles are interactive, yet maintain the role differences between clergy and laity.[39] There has been an attempt to retain kinds of authority which come from earned trust and relationship while restoring an objective authority to preaching which is not identified with office, institution, or tradition.

There are more traditional and conservative options. Some Presbyterian preachers and homileticians refuse to allow that the authority of preaching should be rooted in what is attributed to it by either congregation or culture. There is a continuing concern to rejuvenate the office and institution of preaching after the pattern of the nineteenth century or after the pattern of the 1950s.[40]

Given the enormous crosscurrent of interests scrambling for authority in shaping the life of each individual daily, what kind of authority can preaching have in shaping the final mix of messages that actually forms the values, life-styles, and beliefs of this generation of Presbyterians? Questions regarding the nature and future of the authority of preaching in the church and in the wider community have become fundamental issues confronting preachers and homileticians in the Presbyterian Church.

Changing Methods for Presbyterian Preaching

At the turn of the century, the typical homiletics curriculum in Presbyterian seminaries was an extensive, three-year process that involved the learning of "Sacred Rhetoric" or "theory of preaching," the studying and outlining of the English Bible, the learning of principles of elocution, and the practice of public speaking. For instance, in 1900 at Union Seminary in Richmond, Virginia, a student could expect to begin immediately in the junior year reading *On the Preparation and Delivery of Sermons* by Southern Baptist homiletician John Broadus. At the same time, students would learn homiletical theory in class. Then, during the second semester, the English Bible was studied and exercises in outlining would be practiced. At the same time the student would be required to take a course in "Training the Speaking Voice." For the next two years, each student would be required to take a semester of English Bible, studying and outlining the Old Testament during the middler year and the New Testament during the senior year. Students were also required to take a course in the "Oral Interpretation of the Bible" during their middler year and a course in "Sermon Delivery" during their senior year. At each stage of the process, opportunities to preach were provided to every student either in nearby churches or in the seminary chapel, often with several faculty members present to critique. Similar patterns and emphases could be found in other Presbyterian seminaries during this period, and only small revisions in curriculum were made until the mid-1930s.

Presbyterian preachers during this period conceived of their task as largely oratorical, persuasive, and expository.

They were trained to believe that preaching was the primary function of the minister. Their method of sermon preparation was an ordering of a biblical text into a preachable outline: the development of points which could then be preached. The sermon was the result of a critical and devotional interaction between the individual minister and the biblical text. The preacher was trained to become a master of the pulpit or a pulpiteer.

As the liturgical movement began to influence mainstream denominations and as preachers became more interested in preaching ethical and life situation sermons, especially with the introduction of Harry Emerson Fosdick's popular project method, homileticians in Presbyterian seminaries reacted strongly at first. By the mid-1920s, courses that confronted students with the history of preaching and the great preachers began to appear in the curriculum to remind students of former models.[41] Union Seminary in Virginia published an "Introductory Statement" to the Homiletics section of their 1929–30 catalog declaring that it had "no sympathy . . . with the modern cry against what some people speak of as the 'menace' of the sermon," defending preaching as "the central and foremost part of worship" and as the "pre-eminent function of the minister," and defining such preaching as expository in method.[42] By and large, homiletical departments were bastions of conservatism on Presbyterian seminary campuses.

By the early 1930s, however, seminary curricula were somewhat more open to a growing interest in the human, ethical, and pragmatic aspects of preaching and the influence of the behavioral sciences. In 1930, Andrew Blackwood at Princeton Theological Seminary introduced a course in the "Psychology of Preaching" and a parallel course in the "Psychology of Worship." Benjamin Rice Lacy at Union Seminary in Richmond introduced in 1930 a course in pastoral preaching entitled "The Preacher's Use of His Materials." In 1940, Blackwood introduced a course in "Modern Preachers" in which students could analyze the preaching of well-known twentieth-century preachers, including those who preached "ethical sermons" or who used topical or "project" methods. Students were exposed to sermons by Karl Barth, John Sutherland Bonnell, Walter Russell Bowie, Emil Brunner, George Buttrick, Harry Emerson Fosdick, Clovis Chappell, Arthur John Gossip, Clarence Macartney, and William McCallum Clow.[43]

Because of the increasing need for the preacher to "earn" authority instead of assuming it, the topical, life-situation method of preaching found a ready audience among Presbyterian preachers. Harry Emerson Fosdick taught homiletics between 1911 and 1946 at Union Seminary in New York, was preacher at First Presbyterian Church and later at Riverside Church, and was widely heard on the radio. His preaching method had a profound influence on Presbyterian preachers, especially in the Northeast. Rather than beginning with the Bible, preachers learned to begin with a problem or question to be solved or answered. The biblical text then informed the sermon only indirectly as the sermon developed.[44]

With the introduction of university-trained faculties in the 1940s and 1950s, the Greek and Hebrew biblical texts supplanted the English Bible in Presbyterian seminary curricula. Students were no longer engaged in an extensive process of becoming exposed to the whole of scripture. Instead, they were trained to do historical-critical exegesis of the biblical texts.

At the same time, biblical and homiletical departments in seminaries parted company. Preaching remained in practical theology departments. The departments were growing in size through specialization into subdepartments of homiletics, pastoral theology, Christian education, and church administration. The number of required courses in preaching shrank to one course, usually with a companion practicum in which students practice-preached before small groups of students and instructors.

Rather than training students to outline texts mechanically around theological points as had been done in the early decades of the century, students were encouraged to find a unified theme within the text which could then be preached using a variety of rhetorical strategies. Lutheran homiletician H. Grady Davis's book *Design for Preaching* was a milestone in homiletics, proposing this more organic, idea-centered approach to homiletical theory. His book supplanted Broadus's *On the Preparation and Delivery of Sermons* as the basic textbook in most Presbyterian seminaries, and it remained the basic text until the mid-1970s.[45]

The introduction of the biblical languages and more organic methods to preaching had great potential to keep students interested in more biblically centered models of preaching. Students, however, began to feel the strain in trying to find unified themes while engaged in the process of rigorous exegesis. Exegetical work sheets became standard preliminary work to preaching. Many students despaired of finding acceptable themes to preach in a climate of close scrutiny and criticism. Hermeneutical problems and issues had undermined traditional methods of interpretation, and students found it more and more difficult to bring the ancient biblical text into an acceptable interaction with the modern world. At the same time, biblical criticism was seriously challenging the authority of scripture in the church in an era in which the authority of the preacher was already under close scrutiny.[46]

By 1965, interest in preaching was on the wane on seminary campuses. Donald Macleod, professor of preaching at Princeton Seminary during the 1960s and 1970s, noted that "the average homiletics class is not bursting to learn to preach; most of them have to be convinced of the viability of the preaching office today."[47]

The publication of *The Miracle of Dialogue* by Episcopalian Reuel L. Howe in 1963 was a watershed for mainline preachers and students.[48] The word "dialogue" became a catchword on seminary campuses and in the parish. If preaching was to be truly a nonauthoritarian form of communication, it needed to become dialogical. Students and preachers began to experiment with preaching, instituting talk-back sessions, conversational preaching, walk-around sermons, rap sessions, and "teachings." Being dialogical was no longer an important *principle* for preaching. In many cases, it was elevated to the status of a *method* of preaching altogether.[49]

Interpersonal communication theories and the suspicion of monological forms of communication influenced the parish pulpit. Some Presbyterian preachers left behind established and accepted methods of sermon preparation and delivery, experimenting with new, creative methods. Oratorical or persuasive models of communication were traded for conversational and interactive models. Sermon structure was not tailored to either the points within the text or to the organic continuity of a theme but to the unique communication style of the particular preacher in relation to his or her congregation. Field-based education flourished during this period, and supervisory models of teaching preaching increased, focusing on this more interactive method of sermon preparation.[50]

In the late 1970s and 1980s there was a resurgent interest in preaching both among parish preachers and on seminary campuses. A rediscovery of the performative power of language to shape worldviews brought narrative, inductive, and linguistic-performative (phenomenological) methods into the seminary classrooms and continuing education seminars.[51]

The concept of biblical preaching also saw a revival in the 1970s and 1980s. The *Common Texts Lectionary* received wider use in the parish. Challenges to the historical-critical method by biblical theologians such as Walter Wink led to new methods of exegesis that invite the discovery of a postcritical subjective dimension in the exegetical process.[52] Canonical exegesis reemphasized the church's witness of faith as vital to exegesis.[53] Preachers began to feel less intimidated by the historical-critical process and freer to explore the literary, performative, and transformative aspects of biblical exegesis for preaching.

Questions regarding an adequate method for preaching in a postmodern environment continue to plague mainstream academic homileticians. Many of these questions are rooted in the postmodern debate concerning the nature and function of religious language. Narrative and phenomenological models of preaching have been promoted by academic homileticians in response to postmodern challenges to the denotative and referential functions of religious language.[54]

Whether the current trend toward narrative and phenomenological models is adequate to issues of the authority of preaching or the integrity of the message of preaching is under debate, and Presbyterian homileticians are at the center of that debate. Both narrative and phenomenological approaches in which the preacher becomes the storyteller of a congregation's "lived world," or "world in language," are under scrutiny as potentially inattentive to both the contingent realities of human experience which cannot be "storied" and to historical-critical dimensions of the biblical text which lie "behind" rather than "in front" of the text.[55]

Empirical methods are also being explored, in which the preacher becomes a practical theologian who interprets human experience using the language and perspective of a particular biblical-theological tradition. This approach, however, continues to suffer from lack of theory, theological rigor, and an adequate pedagogy.[56]

Doctoral programs in homiletics have been instituted in seminaries and universities around the country in the last thirty years.[57] The introduction of Ph.D.-trained faculty in homiletics into the life of seminaries has already brought about a more careful and systematic study of the theory of preaching, the theology of preaching, and the pedagogy of preaching. A relatively new Academy of Homiletics, founded in 1965, has become a yearly convocation for the sharing of perspectives and new insights among mainstream preachers and homileticians.[58] This is already offering a forum for homileticians to reflect on the essential problems that face mainstream preachers today and to strategize for new methods of preaching to meet these problems.

The Changing Theological Message
of Presbyterian Preaching

While assessing the basic differences between the 1931 and 1933 Preaching Conferences in Boston, Methodist Bishop G. Bromley Oxnam observed that at the 1931 conference there was general agreement on the fundamental theological message to be preached from the American pulpit while at the 1933 conference "some insisted that the social gospel was first and others insisted the personal gospel was first."[59]

This dividing line between factions of mainstream preachers in 1933 was indicative of the conflicting and often antagonistic way in which Presbyterian preachers, especially in the North, spoke about their "message" since the early 1920s when the fundamentalist controversy repolarized the denomination. In 1924, when the Auburn Affirmation was circulated for signatures in opposition to the fundamentalist five-point "deliverance" of 1910, there were signs of significant support in the Presbyterian Church for a "liberal evangelical" theological perspective.[60] This perspective was not a full-blown modernism. It was an attempt to bring the evangelical message alive in the modern context. A passage from a sermon by William P. Merrill, pastor of the Brick Presbyterian Church in New York City and strong opponent of the fundamentalist five-point deliverance, illustrates this liberal-evangelical perspective:

> To one who views the conditions of to-day with open eyes and honest mind, there comes a tremendous call for a revival of true Protestantism; not the Fundamentalism that walks backward with its eyes on the past; not the Modernism that rushes forward, careless whether it keeps the path; but true Protestantism, the religion of the free soul and the open Bible, the religion of the spirit, the religion that is bold and broad and ever moving on.[61]

By 1925, the liberal-evangelical message from the pulpit was gaining strength, especially in the northern Presbyterian church. Liberal evangelicals were concerned above all else with "offering the Gospel in a convincing manner to contemporary thinking persons."[62] Several theological themes of liberalism were heard from Presbyterian pulpits during the 1920s and 1930s. One of these themes was the continuity between humanity and God and an accent on human potential and self-esteem rather than on human depravity and unworthiness.[63]

> Let us look into our own hearts, to see if we are one of the prophets among men, to see if the prophet born of God within us is still alive and active. Did not each of us start with a prophet in our being? He should still be the commanding figure within. . . . Yes, verily, there is the prophet within us; that part of our nature that loves right and hates evil.[64]

There was more of an evolutionary optimism regarding the human ability to change history and improve the world situation. Preachers preached progressive revelation or the idea that there is continuity between God's self-revelation in the past and now and thus the idea of an ongoing progress toward a realizable kingdom of God.[65]

> In fact, instead of having settled upon us the discouraging gloom and chill of a coming night of godlessness, we should be able to understand that God's Kingdom keeps coming on earth like an everlasting dawn, as the glowing light of the righteous "that shineth more and more unto the perfect day."[66]

The message of liberal-evangelical preachers contained hints of the social gospel. Many preached that "the object of Christianity is human welfare; its method is character building; its process is evolution, and the secret of its power is God."[67]

> Our country calls for men, Christ-converted, spirit-filled, conviction-moved, patriotic men, who will step out into the arena of our modern conflict and help to usher in the new era of individual integrity, social purity, industrial honesty, national democracy, and world-wide peace.[68]

Fundamentalist themes largely reacted to liberalism: the salvation of individuals, the evils of evolutionism and the historical criticism of scripture, the inerrancy of the Bible, premillennialism and a pessimistic historical apocalypticism, apologetic messages on the essentials of fundamentalist doctrine, and messages on principles of correct behavior and opinion in the face of an ungodly humanist generation. One of the basic messages of the fundamentalist was a dramatic and often militaristic attack on liberal theological opponents. In a sermon entitled "The Virgin Birth of Jesus" Mark Allison Matthews states:

> If the statements as to the birth of Jesus are not infallible and if he was not born of a virgin, then it is impossible for one to be saved. . . . While we were asleep Satan sowed tares in Christendom, and there are those in the visible organization, known as the church militant, who are unsaved. They are, no doubt, rationalists, direct agents of Satan. If they want to fight God, and if this doctrine is the battleground, then, when we have finished with them, if they have any conscience at all, we hope they will leave the visible ecclesiastical organization and go out into the world of Satan and stay there, for they most assuredly have no place in the real church of Jesus Christ.[69]

A large group of Presbyterian preachers remained "moderates" in the fundamentalist-liberalist controversy. These preachers, "possessing some theological affinity to the (fundamentalist) group, tended to stress the corporate work of a united church."[70] According to Lefferts Loetscher, this group, "while welcoming every movement that promised to aid in the struggle against liberalism, did not identify themselves completely with interdenominational fundamentalism at the double price of abandoning distinctive Calvinism and accepting premillennialism."[71] They were against theological and ecclesiastical controversy and, while sustaining a traditional evangelistic rhetoric, kept most of the rhetoric of the fundamentalist-liberalist controversy out of their sermons. They usually preached noncontroversial messages. Charles Goodall in the foreword to *Southern Presbyterian Sermons* (1929) described their messages as "eternal verities," "a dateless religion, one that is the same yesterday, today and forever."[72]

By the mid-1940s many of this large group of moderate conservatives, as well as some disaffected liberals and fundamentalists in the Presbyterian Church became neo-orthodox in their perspective. While retaining some of the liberalist concern for social change, the neo-orthodox message from the pulpit was informed by a more realistic view of human nature conditioned by two world wars, economic depression, and significant changes in the moral climate of American society. Neo-orthodox preachers denied continuity of any kind between God and humanity. By 1950, some formerly liberal Presbyterian preachers were preaching against liberal optimism about the human ability to better the world. In its place was a call to persistent social involvement coupled with constant self-critical realism and reliance upon the grace of God. A sermon entitled "No Two Ways," written in 1948 by Rev. Lowell R. Ditzen of First Presbyterian Church, Utica, New York, illustrates this self-critical theological realism, addressing the social problem of racial prejudice.

> Oh, Americans, must it not be said of us in the light of such accusations "the people answered not a word"? For while we have paid tribute to the God under whom this nation is established, we have followed the practice of Baal, and we stand condemned as false Americans. . . . Be on guard lest the acolyte of Baal, known as Conceit, cloak itself with empty pomposity and usurp the throne of real merit and honest worth![73]

Neo-orthodox sermons deflated the historical and social optimism of liberal preaching and turned the mainline churches upon themselves with a powerful and unrelenting self-criticism, convicting the churches of prejudice, parochialism, and complicity in a host of social sins. Sermon titles such as "Which Way Lies Wisdom?," "Modern Pharisees," "Blind Spots," "We Are All Guilty," "They Preach but Do Not Practice," and "Prejudice and Its Cure" reflected this change in message in the mainstream Protestant pulpit.[74]

The existentialist theologies of Tillich and Kierkegaard and the categories of modern pastoral psychology signaled a significant new theological turn inward which captured the imagination of preachers who wanted to address the personal dynamics of faith but who did not want to return to the fundamentalist categories of depravity, conversion, and individual salvation. Some Presbyterian preachers, especially in the 1960s, introduced themes of alienation/reconciliation, negation/affirmation, estrangement/reunion, anxiety/courage, sickness/health, fragmentation/wholeness, destruction/creativity, into their thematic repertoire. In a sermon entitled "Negation and Affirmation in Life," Rev. William Baillie Green invokes the names of Sartre, Kafka, O'Neill, Tennessee Williams, Arthur Miller, Freud, and Stravinsky, observing that

> Men in every discipline have peered into the depths of life. They have seen its deserts and jungles. And they have had the courage, in the face of an unrestrained Yes, to pronounce a despairing No.[75]

In a powerful existentialist sermon entitled "The Face in the Mirror," Clayton E. Williams uses psychology to make a case for existential alienation.

> Indeed, modern depth psychology tells us that deep down in our hearts there lies hidden a part of us that we do not really know, and that you and I are not in fact the persons that we think we are. Not only do we hide ourselves from others but we hide ourselves from our own selves.[76]

More recently, William Sloane Coffin in his sermon "The Courage to Love" accents the existentialist theme of the courage it takes to be radically free and therefore radically responsible in today's world.

> What I am driving at is, I think, the central problem of the Christian Church in America today: most of us fear the cure more than the illness. Most of us prefer the plausible lie that we cannot be cured to the fantastic truth that we can be. And there is a reason: if it's hell to be guilty, it's certainly scarier to be responsible—*response-able,* able to respond to God's visionary, creative love. No longer paralyzed, our arms would be free to embrace the outcast and the enemy—the most confirmed addict, the reddest of communists. . . . Everything is possible for those whose eyes, no longer fixed on some status symbol, are held instead by the gaze of him who is the eternal dispenser of freedom, the eternal dispenser of life.[77]

In the late 1970s and 1980s Black, feminist, and liberation theologies had some effect on the Presbyterian pulpit.
Liberation theologies have been taught in Presbyterian
seminaries since the early 1970s, and books bearing on
preaching from liberationist perspectives have been written by Justo L. González and Catherine G. González and
Robert McAfee Brown.[78] Themes that focus on social and
political empowerment, the nature and structure of social
and political evil, the partiality of God toward the poor,
the historical character of revelation, and the hidden
voices of the powerless in biblical texts have found an increasing voice in the Presbyterian pulpit.[79] In this preaching the pessimistic self-critique of the mainline church
begun by neo-orthodoxy has increased in intensity while
the neo-Marxist vision of achieving liberation for the
world's poor and socially marginalized peoples has been
freed from the restrictions imposed upon it by the critique
of neo-orthodox theologians like Reinhold Niebuhr.[80]

Although a variety of theological models have influenced the theological message of the Presbyterian pulpit,
making it less than uniform theologically, the most significant influence on the message of the Presbyterian pulpit in
the twentieth century has been the rise of the empirical
sciences and the adoption of a modern scientific
worldview[81] by those in the culture and in the church.
Many Presbyterians were educated in secular institutions
by the turn of the century.[82] These institutions taught students the scientific method and promulgated the scientific
worldview. Between 1920 and 1940 especially, there was a
"vast literature of popularization in magazines and newspapers" and "substantial works, often in book form, coming from various intellectual and scholarly traditions"
which promoted the scientific worldview with ideological
fervor.[83] After World War II, the technological revolution
brought the benefits of science into homes and workplaces
making its influence more pervasive than ever.[84]

It is largely a worldview that controls the shape that a
message will take in its communication. This shaping of
messages to accommodate them to a particular worldview

has a significant impact on both the final content of the message and the "hearing" a message receives.

By 1920, it was difficult to preach objective principles of the Christian faith to a congregation whose worldview contained a mixture of pragmatism and empiricism which insisted that truth was subjective, situational, and verifiable only through the five human senses. This emerging worldview created yet another division among Presbyterian preachers: between those who saw their messages as often unverifiable religious truths, and those who saw their messages as religious truths verifiable through generalization to the experience of common humanity. Where the former were criticized as "Puritan absolutists," with "pretensions to special knowledge," the latter were criticized as "seeking for as much common ground as is possible with 'enlightened opinions' outside the church,"[85] and throwing the distinctiveness of Christianity away in the process.

For the most part, Presbyterian preachers, especially in the North, joined the movement away from objectivism and abstraction. What resulted in the 1920s was, in many instances, the preaching of apologetic or "philosophy of religion" messages in order to explain how certain ideas about God were to be reasonably reached in the twentieth century. These messages were followed by the preaching of ethical or life situation messages in order to apply those ideas and demonstrate that "Christianity is a life."[86] William P. Merrill and Harry Emerson Fosdick were exemplars of these early efforts to accommodate the modern scientific worldview.[87] Sermons on topics such as "What Religion Is and Does," "Why I Believe in God," or "Christianity Can Make a Difference," "What Is a Religious Life?," "Incontestable Fact and Indispensable Truth," and "What Is Religion?" were legion during this period.[88]

Whereas liberal preaching sought for ways to bring about a credible integration between theology and modern science and philosophy, neo-orthodox preaching, in its reaction to liberalism, evaded and at times ignored any effort to be credible "in the face of the onslaught of modern secular thought."[89] Neo-orthodox preachers often failed to engage and interact with modern science and philosophy. They spent most of their time attempting to "restore elements of the religious tradition lost during the liberal era."[90] Rather than carrying forward the task of generating a realistic understanding of Christian hope and a new theology of history, the result of neo-orthodox's critical "realism" by the 1960s was what Benton Johnson calls its "dour legacy" in the church, the "aura of pessimism, judgment, and guilt."[91]

As the modern scientific worldview became more entrenched in the 1950s, practical theologians in mainstream seminaries were developing methods of correlation between theology and human experience which were more sophisticated. Preachers discovered that the language and categories of the behavioral and social sciences provided a common currency they could use in the parish.

In 1951, William Howard Kadel solicited eight hundred Presbyterian preachers in both the northern and southern Presbyterian churches regarding their homiletical themes. He noted that although "historically, there was little of this kind of preaching . . . , our generation particularly has given rise to what may be called the psychological message."[92] According to Kadel, "the practical application of the message of the Christian Gospel to everyday life" was "without a doubt the largest emphasis" of the Presbyterian preachers he polled.[93] At the same time, a new therapeutic function for preaching arose alongside of classical prophetic, didactic, and proclamatory functions in popular homiletical texts.[94]

In many psychological sermons and social sermons the theological content was largely missing or secondary. Some preachers used methods of correlation, raising existential or social questions and then answering them using biblical and theological resources. For the most part, however, preachers "had strong convictions about social issues" and about the psychological needs of their congregations, "but they were uncertain about theology."[95]

The modern scientific and secular worldview continues

to exert a controlling influence on the shaping of the "message" of the Presbyterian pulpit. This worldview is not altogether accommodating of any of the previously mentioned theological message systems. Certainly the liberal and existentialist models are more at home in this worldview, but even their ultimate claims are not easily accommodated in this framework. This may be one reason why there seems to be no coherent and consistent theological message system at work in much of Presbyterian preaching today.[96]

It is not easy to speak of a single theological "message" or of a unified theological "message system" for the Presbyterian pulpit in the twentieth century. The messages of the Presbyterian pulpit in the twentieth century are characterized by theological conflict, pluralism, and more recently by what seems to be incoherence and inconsistent theological content.

The conflict between worldview and theology promotes ad hoc theologizing on the part of some.[97] A group of Presbyterian preachers recently acknowledged that they tend to interpret texts and experiences from a mixture of psychological, sociological, philosophical, and theological perspectives as they find themselves in a given situation in the parish or working with a particular kind of biblical text.[98] In some instances this was held to be the meaning of "pastoral preaching." In most cases there was little conscious reflection on the relationships and/or contradictions between various perspectives. Given this approach to arriving at messages for preaching, it is probable that no consistent theological hermeneutic emerges either in preaching or in parish life.

Given the theological pluralism in the Presbyterian denomination at this time, it is doubtful that it would be possible to arrive at some kind of denominational theological consensus that would provide a coherent platform for a positive and assertive "Presbyterian" form of theological communication. The last denominationally identified theology to significantly influence the Presbyterian pulpit was the Princeton theology of the late nineteenth century. Most major Protestant theological movements before and since that time have transcended denominational affiliation.

What seems to be missing in Presbyterian preaching now, which was present in nineteenth-century postmillennialist preaching[99] and in twentieth-century liberal-evangelical preaching is a consistent and assertive theological message. Since there is no theological consensus among Protestants in America today and a wide range of theologies from which to choose, what Presbyterian preachers need to do if they are to recover consistency and strength of message in their preaching is to stand within their own confessional tradition and the community in which they preach, and make clear, committed, and critical theological choices.

Since preachers today tend to pick up bits and pieces of their theological commitments here and there, preachers first of all need to learn to recognize the theological ideas to which they are already committed in their preaching. Then they need to study and critique these ideas in order to integrate them into their own broader Reformed and Presbyterian confessional tradition. In order to preach these ideas with strength of purpose, they will need to decide that these ideas are important and in some sense necessary for the life of the church and world today. Finally, they will need to learn how to communicate these ideas to congregations whose theological commitments may be equally eclectic and pluralistic.

4

Themes in Southern Presbyterian Preaching, 1920 to 1983

Beverly Ann Zink

Preaching can be regarded as a barometer of theological and cultural changes in the nature of the church. To examine the preaching of a particular denomination over an expanse of history is to discern many of the forces which have shaped the life and witness of that church as well as the evolution of the society in which it exists. This study focuses on the content of selected preaching in the Presbyterian Church in the United States from 1920 to the reunion with the United Presbyterian Church in the United States of America in 1983. More than 150 sermons representing sixty southern Presbyterian preachers were reviewed as found in published sermon collections and journals of the PCUS. It exhibits as broad a survey of published materials as possible with attention to wide geographic coverage but recognizes that such a method of determining sources weighs heavily toward large, urban churches. While it does not intend to generalize for the whole of the PCUS, it seeks to identify homiletical themes and how those themes reflect the massive changes that have occurred in southern culture ana southern Presbyterianism over the twentieth century and perhaps open the way to a deeper investigation of this denomination's rich homiletical tradition.

"A Life of Its Own": Religion in the South

To understand the theological development of the Presbyterian Church U.S. is to understand the South as an identifiable religious, cultural, and political entity. The existence of the Confederate States of America "symbolizes and confirms the reality of the South as a cultural unity. For a half-century before its formation and more than a century since, a human complex called southern society has had a recognizable life of its own."[1]

The identity forged in the South through the Civil War was preserved in the attitude of the "Lost Cause," the linking of religion, culture, and history in an effort to perpetuate the political hope lost in the war by means of a regional mind-set.[2] With a strong emphasis on personal piety and an equally strong resistance to the intermingling of church and state, churches in the South have maintained an identity clearer than that of most of their northern counterparts. The PCUS ranked behind several other denominations in size but played an important role in Southern life, greater than its numbers might suggest. Its influence upon education and culture made it a powerful voice in the South,[3] and that voice may have been heard most clearly through the proclamation of the Word.

The sermons of PCUS preachers reviewed in this study exhibit a remarkable reiteration of common themes across the century. They represent theological and doctrinal issues, social and political issues, ecclesiastical and personal issues. Some of the most prevalent themes and those which echo through the decades include: the sovereignty of God; God's omnipresence and pursuit of God's people;[4] the shape of Christian discipleship; the promise of eternal life; the assurance of Christian hope through personal and corporate tragedy; the nature and role of the church; the human longing for fulfillment and search for truth; the struggle to reconcile faith with the modern worldview; the motivation for and extent of participation in the social realm; the dangers of secularism and materialism; and the sanctity of the nation and home. Sermons delivered later in the century add to these themes others informed by the development of the social sciences and new theologies as well as contemporary issues of race, poverty, oppression, substance abuse, world peace, and the environment. In the end, the themes that rise from the proclamation of many southern Presbyterian pulpits evidence a church fighting to maintain its historic confession of faith while confronted by the questions of modern society.

Into a New World: The 1920s and 1930s

The decades following Reconstruction brought opportunities as well as challenges to the South. Despite the persistence of old problems, a new state of mind was evident. "The New South!" became a rallying cry, joining forces to promote industrial, educational, and social development so that the South might "be again a part of the nation."[5] As a result of this eager embrace of progress, the South seemed open as never before to the infiltration of new ideas such as evolutionary theory, biblical criticism, the threat of communism, secular materialism, and the social gospel.

Much southern Presbyterian preaching of the 1920s and 1930s acknowledged the dawn of this new age and its resultant social turmoil. "The age of comfortableness has gone," proclaimed Retiring Moderator Harris E. Kirk of the Franklin Street Church of Baltimore in a sermon entitled "The Presbyterian Mind," delivered at the opening of the General Assembly in 1929. "Society everywhere is characterized by profound instability."[6] Sermons by James I. Vance of the First Presbyterian Church of Nashville reiterated this theme of instability. "Religion is not fighting for its perquisites and privileges. It is fighting for its life," he asserted in a sermon that asked the question, "Is Religion Worthwhile?"[7] In a commencement address given at Austin Theological Seminary, George L. Bitzer of the Presbyterian Church in Holly Springs, Mississippi, declared, "We are living in a difficult time for the evangelical minister, a time of change. . . . It is impossible for the Presbyterian Church to remain static in the midst of a changing world."[8]

In response to that changing world, many sermons coun-
tered with a Christian apologetic in reaction to the secular
influences which sought to destroy personal faith, calling
for salvation through Jesus Christ and a reaffirmation of
the traditional doctrines of the church. These preachers
addressed the fact that the new theories of the day attempted to replace Christianity as alternative "religions."
"Most men are willing to be religious, if they are allowed
to pick their God," proclaimed Vance.[9] Rather than relying on dogmatic proclamation to be accepted without
question, however, preachers now were challenged to present the gospel as the only true alternative to the modern
worldview.

Most southern preachers reiterated the sovereignty of
God and the need for God in human life. Many used familiar stories of the Old Testament in a didactic way, citing
examples of individuals who had turned from God in
search of more promising things. In *One Generation to Another,* Harris Kirk compared modern idealists to Jacob,
who sought success at the price of moral compromise.[10]
Another series of sermons by Kirk explored the faith and
discipline of Moses as an example of the acceptable way to
bring about change within the church and society.[11] In describing "Humanity's Birthright" to accept or reject the
presence of God, Thomas W. Currie of Austin, Texas, cited
the fates of several characters from the opening chapters of
Genesis as examples of those who lived "as though God
did not exist" as opposed to those who attempted "to seek,
find and follow God."[12] These examples of faith were
meant to demonstrate that, in spite of all philosophies and
discoveries, the "presence and power of the Holy Spirit at
the heart of every man . . . has constantly reminded him
of the futility of life without God."[13]

The primary pursuit which distracted individuals from
their spiritual emptiness was economic prosperity. Many
preachers of the 1920s focused on rampant materialism
and its inadequacy as a substitute for faith, proclaiming
that the "ruling principle of the age" was "largely one of
material values," while the "fatal lack" of the time was

"ignorance of God."[14] They cautioned those who were busy "moving heaven and earth to make money," disregarding their need for worship and private prayer.[15] They acknowledged the human search for contentment but warned that we "cannot quench our longings with the material things of life, however abundant."[16] "There are many who have well nigh run the gamut of experience but have not found rest unto their souls," said J. A. McClure of the First Presbyterian Church, St. Petersburg, Florida. "They acquired wealth only to find that riches do not satisfy."[17] J. S. Lyons of the First Presbyterian Church, Atlanta, expressed an "apprehension that the mad passion for pleasure and gain now rampant in America . . . will lead us logically as a nation to spiritual death and misery."[18]

How prophetic Lyons's words proved to be, for in the midst of this newly discovered materialism, the Depression dealt its crushing blow. Many preachers took the opportunity to posit a correlation between the economic crisis of the nation and its spiritual decline. "How far are our financial troubles the result of decadence in the moral and spiritual?" asked Vance.[19] "Man has not yet learned that he cannot find rest for his soul in material things," proclaimed Robert F. Campbell of the First Presbyterian Church of Asheville, North Carolina.[20]

With such affirmation of Christian faith, most PCUS preachers challenged more than condemned the modern theories. Even evolution, which had the most profound effect on southern religion and culture of all the new ideas,[21] did not appear to pose a major threat. The church knew where it stood and continued to preach the sovereignty of God which transcends any human philosophy. As a result, rather than a clear condemnation of the new theories, many preachers offered a defiant challenge to those who would find in them the solace and hope of the Christian faith:

> We have tried science, and we have lost our souls. We have tried electrons and chromosomes and ductless glands, and

scrapped morality. We have tried the world, the flesh, and the devil, and laughed at religion. Is there anything else to try? It might not be a bad plan to go back to Calvary and try the religion of Jesus.[22]

The movement which did evoke a more obvious response from the southern Presbyterian church, however, was the social gospel. While there is some disagreement among historians as to the extent of influence it had on this denomination, it is generally felt that "no more hostile environment could be found for the social gospel than the Presbyterian Church in the United States."[23] Beyond its conservative outlook, two specific ideological stances peculiar to the PCUS and markedly present in its preaching can be identified as the roots of this hostility: the distinctive doctrine of the spirituality of the church and the belief in personal regeneration as the prerequisite for social transformation.

The doctrine of the spirituality of the church, articulated best in the nineteenth century by James Henley Thornwell, declared, "Where God has not commanded, the Church has no jurisdiction."[24] The church's only mission was spiritual; it should, therefore, refrain from speaking on political and social issues. Coupled with this historic stance was an understanding of salvation that focused on individuals rather than institutions. Even Walter L. Lingle, president of the General Assembly's Training School in Richmond and regarded as a PCUS "liberal" of his day, reiterated the primary task of every church "to be a soul-winning church. That is the great purpose for which the church was founded."[25] The church was called to speak to the hearts of people who in turn would translate their faith into civic responsibility and acts of Christian compassion. Said J. V. Johnson of the Westminster Church in Memphis, "These are the ends that Jesus would ordain for us: to love our fellowmen and, loving them, move heaven and earth to win them for the Lord."[26]

Nevertheless, southern churches could not ignore the changed conditions of their members and communities which resulted from the economic and social transformations generated by the industrial revolution. D. Clay Lilly, pastor of the Reynolda Presbyterian Church in Winston-Salem, North Carolina, departed from the traditional southern Presbyterian stance in advocating the mutual support of the spiritual and social realms: "The spiritual cannot be neglectful or forgetful of the burdens borne by our fellows in their industrial and economic life. . . . God is concerned with all life."[27] Other preachers did not fear to call people to responsible participation in society. "[It] is one of the best indications of the moral health of these times that multitudes of well favoured people are beginning to awake to their responsibility for the social and spiritual condition of men," proclaimed Kirk.[28] "If America and the world are to be delivered from the sin and curse of war and illiteracy and preventable poverty and liquor and the broken home," said Bitzer, "Church and State must find a way of working together for the common good."[29] He went so far as to question the denomination's tenacious hold on the doctrine of the spirituality of the church as an impediment to the church's witness in the face of moral questions.[30]

The majority of preachers in this study, however, were content to encourage some form of social ministry so long as it issued from and was directed toward personal regeneration. "Now, there is no word we hear more of to-day than service," agreed Kirk. "We must serve each other . . . but service is an effect, not a cause. . . . The power to make service effective comes from another region, namely, this mystical spiritual communion with God."[31] These preachers again relied on biblical examples. This time many challenged their listeners to emulate the life of Christ through sermons with titles such as "The Supremacy of Christian Love," "Follow Thou Me," and "What Is It to Be a Christian?"[32] Some traditionalists continued to oppose efforts cloaked in social gospel language or methods, but the prevailing attitude was that of James Vance, who affirmed the twofold nature of the church's mission.

> A great many foolish things have been written and spoken by good and well-meaning people in criticism of the social mis-

sion of the church. As if there could be any real contradiction
between personal regeneration and social service! The two be-
long together. The social Gospel is worthless unless preceded
by individual regeneration, but personal conversion is woefully inadequate unless followed by social service.[33]

No area of society, least of all the church, remained un-
touched by the pervasive effects of the scientific pragmatism, social dislocation, theological controversy, and moral
and economic turmoil characteristic of the 1920s and
1930s. The "new world" created by this transformation of
the South challenged the church to make its proclamation
relevant to the lives of its members as they sought to mold
a meaningful faith out of timeless truths and contemporary
knowledge. These early decades appear to have set the
agenda of issues for the witness of the church in the twentieth century.

Keeping the Faith: World War II

The Great Depression tempered the spirit of optimism
which characterized the 1920s. Although the worst of the
Depression was over by the end of the 1930s, it left its mark
on the church in the form of lingering debts, reduced programs, and enduring ministries to broken bodies and shattered souls. By 1938, the "disastrous retrenchment" of the
PCUS which resulted from the economic situation came to
an end, and the work of the church moved on.[34] It was not
long, however, before the effects of another, more pervasive
intrusion were felt: the beginning of World War II.

The personal and national crises precipitated by the war
drove many people back to church. What they heard frequently from pulpits when they returned was a call to hold
fast to the promises of Christian faith as the only source of
comfort and hope. Once again, faith in God was shaken to
its foundations. This time, however, the cause was not scientific achievement or intellectual pursuit but a breakdown in human relationships which threatened lives and
freedoms. In response, most preachers presented a clear
and simple proclamation of the gospel: there is "no hope

for man apart from God."[35] No longer did preachers have the luxury of debating theological issues or commenting on the latest trends of the day. They had to preach the essential relevance of the gospel in the face of individual and corporate tragedy or not preach at all.

Some of the sermon collections published during the war such as *Keep Your Faith* by Teunis E. Gouwens of the Second Presbyterian Church in Louisville, Kentucky, and *Our Fighting Faith* by J. Blanton Belk of St. Giles Church in Richmond indicate the extent to which personal Christian faith was put to the test by the exigencies of war. The struggle to hold on to faith became a battle in itself, and the metaphorical use of militaristic imagery often pervaded sermon titles such as "Our Fighting Faith," "Spiritual Re-Armament," "Steady Souls in Troubled Times," and "The Bible as a Sword." The war threatened the national and personal security taken for granted by many in America. "Our world is being flooded with impurity," said J. Kenton Parker of Mount Mourne, North Carolina. "It is sapping the very foundations of our country."[36] Those "very foundations" of American society—God, country, and home—became the focus of much wartime preaching.

As in earlier decades, the sovereignty of God appeared to be the most significant theme of the church's preaching. Individuals were "on a quest for personal peace" in the midst of the confusion engendered by war.[37] As they experienced the loss of lives, loved ones, and possessions, they reached out "for something strong, serene and sure beyond us and above us. . . . It is either God or endless confusion."[38] "Our best is insufficient," proclaimed Samuel Glasgow of the Independent Presbyterian Church in Savannah. "If we are protected and kept, provided for and given peace, God must do it."[39] "Is there anything more needed than a great turning to God?" asked Edgar Woods of Statesboro, Georgia.[40] "Many of us are feeling the hands of God upon us as we grope into the darkness of the night, giving us guidance, security, peace," asserted Ansley C. Moore, pastor of the Government Street Church in Mobile, Alabama.[41] "We have tried everything we can think of," said Robert A. Lapsley, Jr., of the First Presbyterian Church, Roanoke, Virginia, in a sermon that asked, "Why Not Try God?" "God will give us something to hold to in our darkest hours."[42]

Evident in many sermons is the implication that the war was a judgment upon the United States. In response, some preachers sounded a call to repentance and accountability in the sight of God. At the opening of the General Assembly in 1943, Chaplain Benjamin L. Rose preached "A Call to Humility." "America at this moment stands in crisis," he said. "A great choice is before us . . . to be greatly used of God or to be destroyed by God."[43] "We are not at war because of Hitler or Tojo," said J. Kelly Unger of the First Presbyterian Church, West Point, Mississippi. "We are at war because of doing without God."[44]

Also inherent in much of this preaching is the suggestion that the prosperity of the nation had lulled its people into a false sense of security: "Our gods have been, intentionally, false gods, and now we are getting exactly what false gods give man."[45] John Allan MacLean of the Ginter Park Church in Richmond blamed the decline of the Western world on the "emptiness of material progress" and the need for repentance and a spiritual and moral readjustment of society.[46] In a similar vein, J. Blanton Belk saw the war as an opportunity to call the country to a "new life of moral soundness," suggesting that "the one thing that will give us our second chance is the breakdown of our materialistic philosophy of life."[47]

In addition to the sovereignty of God, the sovereignty of America was proclaimed from many pulpits. Patriotic themes often pervaded wartime sermons, bolstering the idealistic concept of America that had been tarnished by the ravages of war. "America has a destiny," said Belk, to lead in the remaking of the world under God's direction.[48] In a sermon entitled "Patriotism Plus," MacLean presented historical examples of American patriotism and concluded from them that the love of God and the love of country cannot be separated.[49]

Even many of the preachers who asserted the sovereignty

of America nevertheless recognized a sense of judgment upon the nation inherent in the war. This sense of corporate failure and responsibility introduced a unique aspect to the doctrine of salvation present in some of the preaching of this study. While individual salvation through Jesus Christ remained the ultimate goal of the church's proclamation, salvation as portrayed in these sermons took on more of a corporate dimension than in the preceding decades. Not only did individuals stand in need of salvation; the nation itself must be saved. The entire country labored under the "disease" of sin.[50] L. A. Gebb of the First Presbyterian Church in Tyler, Texas, challenged hearers to "be bold in the Spirit and with divine tactics break the black-out of sin in (so called) Christian America."[51]

Many of these preachers believed that the church was called to take the lead in the moral and spiritual awakening of America. "The trends of world events make it imperative that the church of Jesus Christ gird herself to do in a spiritual way for America what the factories, shops and shipyards are doing in a material way," proclaimed Joseph B. Overmyer of the Bream Memorial Church in Charleston, West Virginia.[52] "Patriotism is not enough" to solve the problems of the world, said MacLean. "The solution will require the realization of the Fatherhood of God and the practice of the brotherhood of man and the universal recognition of the teachings of Jesus Christ."[53] In the opening sermon of the General Assembly of 1944, Retiring Moderator Donald W. Richardson confirmed that "the Church of Christ is to function as a light in the spiritual confusion and moral darkness of the contemporary world."[54] "We have the Word . . . ," said Parker. "It is ours not to keep to ourselves but to speak to a world that is perishing."[55] "The world is looking to the church in this hour of crisis. If the church fails, we are lost."[56]

The third foundation of American society, the home, figured prominently in much preaching during the war. As early as the 1920s, some sermons included references to the decline in morality and neglect of responsibility which were causing homes to crumble. During World War II, however, there appears to be a marked increase in sermons which denounce the fragmentation of homes and propose the stability of the family as a means to restoring world peace. In his sermon "Building Sound Homes," Belk recounted the decline in the importance of home life through America's history and compared the war on the battlefield to the "war" in homes against such enemies as divorce, abortion, and juvenile delinquency.[57] Glasgow condemned those who had gone AWOL from their home and family obligations.[58] "All sorts of direct and indirect attacks have been made on the sanctity of the hearth," said Gouwens. "If the home collapses, the chief fortress of our social solidarity falls."[59]

The fears and uncertainty of a world at war tested America's faith and institutions as wartime conditions impinged upon congregations and their members. The preaching of the PCUS represented in this study expressed a concern for the alienation existent at all levels of society, from the individual to the international, during the war. Nevertheless, these preachers sounded a note of hope: hope generated by the reaffirmation of the healing presence of God in the midst of human despair. It was on that hope that the church was able to begin to rebuild and move forward.

"Out of the Back Waters": 1946–1961

World War II represented a turning point for the South in many ways. It demanded a national effort which helped to end consideration of the South as a separate region. From the beginning of the war, there was "a blending of general national and southern regional concerns, problems, programs, peoples, and cultures. The 'solid South' was breaking up not only politically but also culturally."[60] This new mind-set influenced Southern cultural history in general as well as the direction of the PCUS as noted by Ernest Trice Thompson.

> Since World War I the church has been buffeted by winds of change—theological, ethical, and ecumenical. At first hesi-

tantly, and then—particularly after World War II—more decidedly, the church, despite strain and stress, has begun to move out of the back waters into the mainstream of American Christianity.[61]

The southern Presbyterian church could not have chosen a more opportune time to move into the mainstream of American religion. From the end of the war to the celebration of its centennial in 1961, the denomination organized an average of one new church a week under its Home Mission program as a result of the postwar expansionism.[62] Population increased by one million people a year during the 1950s in states where there was a southern Presbyterian presence. Once again, the church was challenged to address the changes imposed by economic and social upheaval. In a postwar sermon entitled "Preaching to Men of the Twentieth Century," R. Wilbur Cousar of the Central Presbyterian Church in Chattanooga reflected, "We seem to have come to the end of an old era and the beginning of a new one. . . . We stand aghast at both the perils and the possibilities that lie ahead of us."[63]

"Perils" and "possibilities" appropriately encompass the themes of much of the church's postwar preaching. The possibilities were evident in the growth and heightened authority of the church. A sense of optimism pervaded the titles of many sermons, such as these in a collection by William M. Elliott, Jr., pastor of the flourishing Highland Park Church in Dallas: "God Is at the Door!," "Lift High That Banner!," and "Can You Stand Prosperity?"[64] As the intensely rural South gave way to rapid industrialization following World War II, the population tended to shift from rural to urban and, eventually, suburban areas. For the first time in the century, the term "evangelism" appeared frequently in sermons. It seemed to hold the key to church growth as well as the answer to the quest for human fulfillment. The church's task, according to Massey Mott Heltzel of the Ginter Park Church in Richmond, was to "make disciples of all nations, persuading men everywhere to accept this Manger Babe, this Prince of Peace. . . . This is the world's hope, and there is none other."[65] "How will this muddled generation ever find the new and better way," asked Elliott, "if we do not lift high the banner of Christ?"[66]

The possibilities of the age were accompanied by an equal number of perils, however. Despite the prosperity of the time, a lingering emptiness haunted those who sought fulfillment in material comforts. Ernest Lee Stoffel of the First Presbyterian Church of Charlotte, North Carolina, expressed the sentiment of many preachers when he proclaimed, "For all the revival of interest in religion, ours is still a secular age."[67] Russell Cartwright Stroup, pastor of the Georgetown Church in Washington, D.C., compared the hedonism of people of the 1950s to that exemplified by Omar in *The Rubáiyát:* "Without hope of joy, they seek escape. Without hope of pleasure, they seek oblivion from pain."[68]

An acknowledgment of the human search for meaning and fulfillment appears to be characteristic of every era of preaching, but a new peril was introduced following World War II: the reality of atomic weaponry. The horrors of Hiroshima and Nagasaki obliterated the sense of innocence and challenged the belief in the essential goodness of humanity which had once been guiding principles of life. "The great search for security and peace of mind stems from fear," said Stoffel.[69] To look to armaments for peace of mind was futile: "Our age will not be saved with swords, but with ideas and the men who embody them. . . . The real strength of the age will not be in guided missiles and gadgets for comfort, but in people who are sworn to Christ."[70] "I am becoming more and more convinced," said Cousar, "that biblical preaching is the need of our day."[71]

The call to "biblical preaching," however, did not seem to be as clearly defined as in earlier years, for by this time much of the PCUS exhibited a shift in theological stance occasioned by the wave of neo-orthodoxy which swept across American Protestantism in the mid-twentieth century.[72] The denomination was more theologically monolithic and bound to traditional Calvinism than its northern

counterpart and thus did not often give evidence of changing theological winds. By mid-century, however, the rigid
Calvinism which had characterized the PCUS gave way to
a Reformed theology tempered by the influence of contemporary thought.[73] This enlightened theology made its way
into southern theological institutions and, eventually, into
many southern pulpits.

The discovery of neo-orthodoxy seemed to occur at an
opportune time, in the midst of the nation's loss of innocence and growing concern for social ills. It enabled many
preachers to call their hearers to a faith rooted in both
traditional doctrines and enlightened biblical interpretation without embracing either of the extremes of fundamentalism or liberalism. These preachers did not hesitate
to use the language of faith and, particularly, to challenge
their people to discover God's self-revelation in the person
of Jesus Christ rather than in the "infallible" words of
scripture. Massey Mott Heltzel wrote a collection of sermons *The Invincible Christ* with titles such as "The Fascinating Christ," "The All-Sufficient Christ," and "The
Disturbing Christ."[74] His aim, he said, was "to show what
Christ was and is, what he has done, and what difference
this should make in our lives."[75]

In addition to a new perspective on Christology and biblical authority, the other significant legacy of neo-orthodoxy inherent in the preaching studied was an acceptance
of human sin and the need for divine intervention to ac-
complish social progress. "We can change the world . . . ,"
proclaimed Walter Dale Langtry of the Prytania Street
Church in New Orleans, "but many things in it we must
accept."[76] One of the things to be accepted was the reality
of human sin in the light of God's judgment and grace.
The task of the church was to encourage people to "resist
temptation and overcome the evil in themselves" through
the proclamation of "the matchless gospel of the Lord Jesus Christ."[77] The realization of the kingdom of God
would come not as the result of human efforts but "as the
result of divine achievement; not as man working out his
own destiny in the world, but as the gift of God bursting

through from outside the world."[78] All the best social crusades "are sure to peter out unless individuals are being made into new creatures."[79]

The single greatest issue among the perils and possibilities for the postwar church, and one to which a neo-orthodox view of social progress could be applied, appeared to be the issue of race. Despite the abolition of slavery, racism continued to plague the New South, especially in the form of segregation. While race had been a nagging concern within the church since its formation and an item on the agenda of early social reformers, it was brought to the fore of the church's attention following World War II in response to the participation of Blacks in the war, civil rights activities, and the beginning of desegregation. This coincided with the church's increasing acceptance of a neo-orthodox theology along with a willingness to address social concerns. The latter came as the result of a gradual move which had been occurring since the 1930s when the church responded to the economic injustices stemming from the Depression. The 1934 General Assembly established a Permanent Committee on Moral and Social Welfare which, while pledging loyalty to the denomination's historic doctrine of the spirituality of the church, acknowledged responsibility for preaching the gospel to society as well as the individual.[80] In 1946, a Department of Christian Relations was created which declared, in a 1954 document concerning "The Church and Segregation," that "the Church, in its relationships to cultural patterns, should lead rather than follow."[81]

The results of a poll conducted in 1940 indicated a notable absence of discussion concerning race relations in the southern Presbyterian pulpit, with the vast majority of ministers admitting that they "rarely or never discussed these matters with their people."[82] Twenty years later, in the midst of the struggle for civil rights, there was still little word evident on the issue. A few prophetic voices, such as Paul Tudor Jones of the Idlewild Church in Memphis, challenged the silence of the church. He likened those who impeded progress on the racial issue to Pharaoh in a sermon entitled "Let My People Go."

> Now there are some who hold, even today, that the problem of a minority racial group living in the midst of a majority of another race is a social and political problem and not religious at all. Let the church stay out of it, they say. But folks of that persuasion find themselves lined right up with Pharaoh.[83]

Others, such as Ernest Lee Stoffel, appealed to the judgment of the individual conscience concerning the issue of race, declaring that every Christian "must undergo the discipline of facing this problem, and of deciding out of his own convictions what he must do and how he must conduct himself."[84]

Even when these preachers addressed the issue of race, however, there remained disagreement as to whether the problem was to be met on an individual or institutional level. In a 1951 study of preaching in the PCUS and UPCUSA, William Howard Kadel cited the "ticklish race problem in America" evident among the themes of social ethics preaching. The example he presented was a sermon that suggested "three ways of helping the Negro: Treat the Negro as a person and not as a problem; Deal honestly and fairly in every contact with him; Help him to develop his highest life."[85] Other preachers, such as Jones, saw the only lasting resolution of racial tensions in social transformation: "God is concerned . . . and lifting up his powerful right arm of judgment to break the arm of the oppressor in the very historic events of our day."[86]

Indeed, as Ernest Trice Thompson noted, the PCUS had moved "out of the back waters into the mainstream of American Christianity."[87] The era of expansionism and favorability toward religion in American society was reflected in the denomination's prosperity. New and revitalized emphases on Christian education, the ministry of the laity, local and world mission, and ecumenical cooperation characterized the denomination by the time of its centennial. Many preachers captured in their sermons this spirit of enthusiasm and hope. In a book written in observance of the centennial, T. Watson Street remarked on the church's move into the mainstream during the second half of its first century: "With new vigor [the church] sought to apply the gospel to all of life. . . . And it showed itself willing to think prayerfully and seriously of what it means to be the Church in the modern world."[88]

"The Winds of Change": 1962–1983

Being "the Church in the modern world" was not an easy proposition. It necessitated the release of much of the southern Presbyterian church's distinctiveness in exchange for a vital role on the stage of American religion. Despite the positive climate which marked the end of the denomination's first century, the church continued to wrestle with monumental questions concerning its purpose, theology, and participation in the wider world. The second century of the PCUS began at what proved to be a critical turning point for the nation, as well, as the Kennedy inauguration ushered in a new era which questioned the assumptions that had shaped America's identity. As Paul Tudor Jones concluded, "The winds of change are blowing a stiff gale in our time. Rapid and radical changes are insistently demanded in every facet of contemporary life."[89]

A hopeful spirit pervaded the PCUS at the beginning of the 1960s, but that spirit did not always culminate in tangible results. The denomination had capitalized on the postwar prosperity by expanding the work of its Permanent Committee on Evangelism and appointing to it a full-time secretary. The major thrust of the plan of evangelism was "to secure decisions for Christ and membership for the Church."[90] These evangelistic efforts came to a climax in a major campaign planned in conjunction with the denomination's centennial celebration. Despite significant publicity and preparation, including sensitivity to the calls for social ministry and to an understanding of human nature informed by the social sciences, the campaign proved to be a major disappointment.[91] The PCUS, along with many other denominations, appeared to be suffering from the waning of the religious revival which characterized American Christianity at mid-century.

Such disappointment may have, in the end, served to move the denomination to a more realistic perspective. Several years later, Frank H. Caldwell, Retiring Moderator of the 1967 General Assembly, reminded the church that "the scope of evangelism is not just geographical or numerical in terms of people. . . . The task of redemption, of reconciliation, is a cosmic enterprise."[92] The church had begun to recognize this as early as 1962 when the General Assembly adopted "A Brief Statement of Belief," which reaffirmed the historic doctrines of the church while indicating a broadened theological stance which challenged the distinctive doctrine of the spirituality of the church: "Christians as individuals and as groups have the right and the duty to examine in the light of the Word of God the effects on human personality of social institutions and practices" and "are under obligation . . . to shape and influence these institutions and practices."[93]

Most pressing of the "institutions and practices" to be influenced were those related to the issue of race. Some of the preachers in this study realized the church had erred in emphasizing growth while ignoring the more tangible expressions of Christian faith which were desperately needed in many communities. Like their counterparts earlier in the century, preachers of the 1960s and 1970s identified human sin as the root of modern problems, particularly the problem of race. "The sin of putting yourself in the place of God not only causes estrangement from the divine presence, but it causes trouble between you and other people," said John A. Redhead of the First Presbyterian Church, Greensboro, North Carolina. "When you stop to think about it, here is the basis also of our race problem."[94] "So the pressing problems of our cities in this split-second is in essence the ancient problem of man—his sin, his rebellion against God, his refusal to acknowledge God's sovereignty and his own obedience," agreed Paul Tudor Jones.[95] In the sermon "The Forgiveness of Sins," James

O. Speed of the First Presbyterian Church, Marietta, Georgia, declared:

> For, you see, sin is the problem. It is *the* problem. It has always been *the* problem. We may define the problem as a political problem or an engineering problem or a chemical problem; but, basically, all of the things we have to solve are human problems, and human problems have as their root: sin.[96]

These preachers seemed to place greater emphasis upon "sin" as an existential state of alienation from God than upon the moral "sins" denounced by many earlier preachers. Redhead asserted that "our human condition is that we are estranged from God."[97] The "deepest longing of every human heart" is to be "saved from all life's deadly destroyers," said Jones. Hope of human reconciliation depended upon "knowing God, experiencing his mercy, and having one's heart reconciled to God's will in all man's relationships with his fellow men."[98] Many sermons reaffirmed the truth of God's saving work in Jesus Christ but moved beyond a simplistic call to faith to probe the depths of human emotions that could be transformed by grace. Speed declared that the "solution to sin is forgiveness, and the result is freedom": freedom from guilt, freedom from the fear of exposure, freedom from cynicism, freedom to love, freedom from the fear of death.[99] Jones identified "life's deadly destroyers" as "sin and death and self and anxiety and fear and meaninglessness."[100] Representing a marked deviation from traditional homiletical themes, this concern for specific and personal emotions had come about through the advent of modern psychological theory and the new discipline of practical theology, giving rise to what William H. Kadel referred to as the "psychological sermon."[101]

The psychological sermon proved to be an appropriate and necessary response in this era of "America's search for soul."[102] Many preachers across the theological spectrum decried the chaotic condition of society. Vance Barron of the University Presbyterian Church, Chapel Hill, North

Carolina, asked, "[W]hat reasons are there to make us feel hopeful about our world? The world is a mess, and we know it."[103] In a sermon honoring the memory of Dr. Martin Luther King, Jr., Elias S. Hardge, Jr., of the West End Church in Atlanta asserted, "This nation is afflicted with several illnesses which undermine its general health."[104] Some believed the state of the church reflected this confusion. Said Walter Rowe Courtenay of the First Presbyterian Church of Nashville, "The church in the twentieth century is restless, secular, guilt driven, vacillatory, unsure of its existence, untrue to its inheritance, distrustful of its purpose, and fearful of its future."[105]

A number of preachers identified the perennial themes of secularism and materialism as causes of this turmoil. The church needed to face the fact, said Holmes Rolston of the West Avenue Church in Charlotte, North Carolina, that "a vast secularism has permeated modern society, a secularism in which the basic presuppositions of a Christian society are no longer assumed."[106] "[T]here is a whole family of popular idols bearing the general name of 'secularism' at whose shrine modern men (including many churchgoers) regularly worship," declared Jones.[107] "Things are big idols in this country—" proclaimed Diane Tennis of the PCUS staff, "carved gods or other expensive art, cars, machines, land, furniture. . . . The world's luxuries become our necessities."[108]

Each era of preaching in the twentieth century brought its own condemnation of materialism as noted throughout this study. In times of prosperity, such as the 1920s and 1950s, many preachers warned their listeners of the danger of losing sight of their need for God inherent in the comfort of their material possessions. In times of adversity, such as the economic depression and the war, many preachers posited a direct relationship between the people's preoccupation with material gain to the detriment of their spiritual well-being and the corporate suffering which beset them. Evident in all eras, however, was the pervasive message that people yearn to fill the emptiness inside them, an emptiness which can be filled falsely by transient possessions or genuinely by the recognition of the grace of God.

People of the modern era continued their search for fulfillment in material possessions, but the idolatry of wealth had new consequences. Whereas earlier preachers condemned materialism as an impediment to the relationship between humanity and God, many modern preachers added to this its resultant discontinuity between humanity and God's creation. Christians have become sensitized to their participation in the global village, and many preachers have acknowledged the culpability of America for environmental and world concerns. "We can demonstrate life everlasting by taking up less room in the physical life we live now," said James E. Andrews, Stated Clerk of the PCUS. "Christian people are beginning to realize that there is just not enough food, not enough fuel, not enough wealth, for everyone to have an American standard of living."[109]

Despite this heightened awareness of the needs of the world community, some PCUS preachers remained divided over the terminology of evangelism and social witness. "What we really need is more evangelism, not more socialism," said Courtenay. "What we really need is the Gospel of Christ, and not the Manifesto of Karl Marx."[110] He blamed the church's emphasis on social action rather than salvation for the decline in membership and giving.[111] A more moderate word came from Frank H. Caldwell, who declared that there is "no such thing as an 'individual Gospel' *and* a 'social Gospel.' There is one Gospel for the whole man . . . throughout the whole world."[112]

The "whole world" increasingly became a concern for many southern Presbyterians as progress brought them into closer association with the rest of the nation and the world.[113] The purpose of the church was to preach salvation, but that proclamation was put into a wider context. "What is the will of God?" asked Barbara Campbell of the Synod of Red River. "We are told, 'Go into all the world and preach the gospel.' Come see, go tell, is the mission of the Christian church."[114] "The saved Christian can never be an isolationist salvationist," said Jones, for "my salvation is included in and a part of [God's] salvation for the whole world."[115] Caldwell challenged his denomination to take the basic principles of the gospel "and apply them to the complex and far-reaching relationships and the complicated actions of life in a space age."[116]

Christian unity represented the last and greatest step of the PCUS into the mainstream of religious and social witness.[117] Throughout the century, many southern preachers had condemned the actions and pronouncements of the Federal and then National Council of Churches because of its emphasis on social action which, they believed, resulted in "a decline in biblical preaching and teaching, a decline in evangelism, and a decline in the presentation of Christ as Redeemer."[118] Others insisted that it was the church's task "to recover that unity in Christ which is the Christian's rightful heritage, and which is so desperately needed to strengthen its evangelistic missionary function."[119] "It is not the quality or the perfection of our ideas or practices that establishes our identity as the church," said Speed, but "our response in faith to the Lord Jesus Christ."[120]

The ultimate wind of change to blow across the PCUS was the move toward organic union with the UPCUSA. Despite opposition from various factions, the approval of union presbyteries in 1969 and the consummation of reunion in 1983 confirmed the termination of the isolationism which had characterized the PCUS for much of the century. The complexity and ambiguity of life at the close of the twentieth century demands a word of hope from the church, and a united Presbyterian body perhaps can speak with greater voice and vision.

Conclusion: The "Rise to New Life"

In the Stone Lectures delivered at Princeton Theological Seminary in 1943, Ernest Trice Thompson set out to demonstrate how preaching "emphasizes neglected truth at the expense of old truth that will in the end inevitably rise to new life."[121] This survey of preaching in the PCUS during the twentieth century illustrates the continual and inevitable "rise to new life" by old truths of the gospel inherent in the church's proclamation despite the passing of time and changing of circumstance.

This study concludes that preaching in the PCUS has changed very little over the course of the century when considering the dominant homiletical themes. The sermons reviewed herein exhibit a consistency of perspective and content that reflects the significant concerns of the twentieth-century church while adhering to the "coherent theological tradition" which defined the "solid South," a tradition of preaching "centered in the themes of man's depravity, Christ's atoning death, and the assurance of salvation."[122] Some preachers of each era addressed the compelling issues and questions of the day, be they moral or ethical, theological or sociological, global or individual, but all were brought into the context of personal salvation transcending their theological and political points of view.

In addition to the concern for spiritual regeneration, the doctrine of the spirituality of the church echoes faintly through the decades of the southern Presbyterian preaching reviewed. Most preachers have demanded that the church be the church and find its purpose in "the basic style of southern evangelicalism," which is "to rekindle, constantly rekindle, vital faith in every person and generation."[123] These concerns for personal salvation and maintaining the spirituality of the church seem to have served as the dynamics which sustained the PCUS through the pervasive changes of the century and resulted in the critique of secular society as well as the clarity of purpose unique to the denomination.

The rich homiletical tradition of the Presbyterian Church U.S. is now a part of the reunited Presbyterian Church (U.S.A.). No one can say what its unique contribution to the new denomination will be. But perhaps a hint of its value can be found in its concerns for spiritual regeneration and the spirituality of the church. These unique characteristics have generated a creative tension which has challenged the work and witness of the denomination and kept it faithful to the intention of the church. As the re-united Presbyterian Church enters the third century of its ministry in the United States, its leaders are calling for a return to the essential imperatives of the gospel and a renewed emphasis on evangelistic efforts. This challenge offers the new denomination an opportunity to recapture the significant homiletical tradition characteristic of many Presbyterians in the South. Perhaps the "old truth" which sustained and defined the PCUS through the perils and possibilities of the twentieth century will once again rise to new life.

5

Challenging the Ethos:
A History of Presbyterian Worship
Resources in the Twentieth Century

Ronald P. Byars

During the láte nineteenth century, there began to be stirrings in both the American and the Scottish Presbyterian churches toward a reconsideration of current worship practices, prompted in both cases by a sense that something of more than minor significance was lacking. In both Scotland and the United States, there were thoughtful Presbyterians who deplored the state of divine worship, in which people were left to the mercy of ministers of varying talent and sensitivity, who not infrequently made up in quantity of words what they lacked in quality. American Presbyterians, particularly with the dawning of nineteenth-century romanticism, began to suffer losses of both ministers and members to the Episcopal Church. Scottish Presbyterians were challenged by the Oxford Movement. For those drawn to Anglicanism, not even the sense of the awesome majesty of God, so characteristic of Presbyterian worship, was sufficient to compensate for its terrible austerity and its avalanche of clerical words.

At the age of twenty-seven, Charles Baird, an American who had been chaplain to English-speaking Protestants in Rome, produced a volume that marked a major milestone in American Presbyterianism. *Eutaxia, or the Presbyterian*

Liturgies, published anonymously in 1855, did the unthinkable when it juxtaposed "Presbyterian" and "Liturgies." This volume drew the attention of Presbyterians to
the fact that they had a liturgical heritage that preceded the
rise of Puritanism.[1] Others with similar interests followed
Baird with published liturgies and prayer books for Presbyterians throughout the remainder of the century.[2]

Early Books of Common Worship

In March 1897, meeting at Brick Presbyterian Church in
New York City, a group of Presbyterian ministers, following the example of Scottish colleagues, organized the first
American Church Service Society.[3] It appears to have met
no more than one time, although it did survey a selected
group of ministers to inquire about modes of worship in
their congregations. When the General Assembly of the
Presbyterian Church in the U.S.A. (PCUSA) set up a committee in 1903 to prepare a "book of simple forms and
services," six of the committee members, including the
chairperson Rev. Henry van Dyke, had been active in the
short-lived Society.[4] The prestige of the committee was no
doubt enhanced by the fact that Van Dyke, pastor of the
Brick Church, had been Moderator of the Assembly the
previous year.

As a result of the committee's labor, the 1905 Assembly
approved the first *Book of Common Worship* (*BCW*) "for
voluntary use," but not without bitter opposition, chiefly
from antiliturgical laymen who sought to have the committee discharged.[5] Claiming to have followed instructions of
the Directory for Worship (DW) and the 1903 Assembly,
the book was published in 1906.[6]

The 1788 Directory for Worship in use at the time gave
only general instructions for the morning service. The
1906 *BCW* incorporated all the elements required by the
DW, but went beyond it when it provided a Prayer of Confession to be prayed by minister and people together, when
it specifically directed that scripture be read, and in the use
of the Apostles' Creed and the Lord's Prayer. The *BCW*

service showed the influence of John Knox's service from the 1556 *Book of Common Order* (*BCO*), although Knox's service, following Calvin, had placed the Sermon nearer the middle of the service rather than at the end.

There was only one order for a morning service in the 1906 *BCW.* The "Order for the Celebration of Holy Communion" was not printed as a complete service, but was rather intended to be inserted after the Sermon in the regular "Order of Morning Service" on Communion occasions. The rubric quotes the DW to the effect that the Lord's Supper "is to be celebrated frequently."[7] The Communion service was a remarkable example of the traditional "shape" of the liturgy. Following usual Reformed practice, the Words of Institution were read as a Warrant before the Prayer of Consecration. A Salutation ("The Lord be with you . . . ") and Sursum Corda ("Lift up your hearts . . . ") introduced the Prayer of Consecration, which included a Sanctus ("Holy, Holy, Holy, Lord God of Hosts . . . "), and the ancient forms characteristic of the traditional eucharistic prayer: an anamnesis (memorial of the Passion), epiclesis (invocation of the Holy Spirit), and a concluding ascription to the Trinity, as well as oblations of praise and of selves. The rubric directed that the bread be broken, and the cup elevated.

All in all, for a church that held antiliturgical biases of such long standing, and for whom interest in recovering its pre-Puritan Reformed heritage was of such recent origin, it is no less than amazing that a book of this quality should have been produced. The committee chaired by Dr. van Dyke had shared the interest of the Scottish Church Service Society in studying specifically Reformed liturgical sources with the purpose of challenging the antiliturgical patterns and biases that had prevailed for many years. While certainly influenced by the *Book of Common Prayer* (*BCP*), they found ample Reformed precedents for reforming worship according to a liturgical model. Thus the initial impetus for liturgical reform, fueled both by dissatisfaction with the relative barrenness of existing worship patterns and by a wistful admiration of Episcopal forms, nevertheless was able to appeal to a Reformed liturgical tradition for justification. Perhaps to reassure those who feared moving too fast, the committee declared that the book would be profitable "only to those who are careful not to make it a means of formal or restricted worship."[8]

When the 1906 *BCW* began to appear dated, the General Assembly of 1928 appointed a committee to revise it.[9] Henry van Dyke was again appointed chair. It demonstrated a considerable change in attitude within the preceding quarter century when the General Assembly accepted the 1932 revision without significant opposition.[10] The changes in the 1932 revision were few. The most notable was the optional use of the Doxology after the Offering. This usage soon became standard in Presbyterian churches. There were no important changes in the 1932 service of Holy Communion, except that a new rubric preceded the service advising that the minister have a large cup of wine "to be raised and exhibited" and a piece of bread large enough "to break in the sight of the people." According to David Bluhm, "the rubric arose from the recent act of substituting small individual pieces of bread and small individual glasses for the large pieces of bread and large cups formerly passed in the pews."[11] Perhaps the most interesting development in the 1932 *BCW* was the new emphasis on the Christian year and the addition of a rudimentary lectionary.

Not only did the General Assembly of 1931 accept the revised book without controversy, but the Assembly of the Presbyterian Church in the United States (PCUS) accepted it "for the optional and selective use of our ministers." The publishing house of the southern church printed it, and that church's journals reviewed it favorably.[12]

During the second and third decades of the twentieth century, a romantic interest in ecclesiastical aesthetics developed. The first and most notable manifestation of this interest took the form of a neo-Gothic revival in church architecture. New England Congregational churches replaced their Communion tables with elevated "altars," complete with tall candlesticks. The sentimentality associated with the imitation of medieval architecture extended also to a growing concern for the "enrichment" of Protestant worship generally. Processions and split chancels became the rage. Professors in Protestant theological seminaries taught courses in worship based on psychological and aesthetic principles.[13] Von Ogden Vogt published his Lowell Institute Lectures in which he listed "aesthetic canons" as the basis for what he called "the art of liturgies." In deciding, for example, between an altar and a Communion table, Vogt argued that "artistically, no other device has been invented, and one might dare to say nor can be, so effective as the altar."[14]

The enrichment movement, based on psychological or aesthetic norms, sought beauty in architecture and ritual, but was not itself liturgical in nature because it was not theologically based. Nevertheless, it had an enormous influence on American Protestant worship, including worship in Presbyterian churches. While the movement away from austere Puritan norms may have been useful in some respects, the lack of a sound theological and liturgical basis permitted the development of a ceremonialism which, though sometimes interesting, was often inappropriate, inconsistent, or even gauche. For example, consider the effects of the enrichment movement as it influenced several of the service books produced for use in various Protestant denominations between 1923 and 1953. A book published by the General Council of the Congregational Christian Churches in 1948 stated that either a table or an altar was appropriate in churches of that tradition, and then offered directions for the placement of an altar. "An altar commonly stands close against the end wall or reredos, and Communion is served from before it, the minister standing either with his back to the people or facing them from one end."[15] Directions told these descendants of the Puritans how to cover the altar: frontal, fair linen, and superfrontal. While the Congregationalists incorporated alien and undigested liturgical dressing into their service book, the Methodists turned psychological in theirs. The Methodist

Book of Worship (1944) said that "the experience of forgiveness should bring a mood of exaltation."[16]

It may be that some who are least receptive to a genuine liturgical renewal today may harbor a lingering revulsion to the pretentiousness of the enrichment movement. And yet, enrichment and liturgical renewal are in fact profoundly antithetical. The enrichment movement, like much of American evangelicalism, found its roots in the desire to be moved or inspired. In contrast, the liturgical movement based itself on the pursuit of theological integrity in worship quite as much as in doctrine, preaching, and mission. As James Hastings Nichols has said, "Liturgical reforms which are not theologically self-conscious and responsible are a menace."[17]

While Presbyterians were no doubt also participating in and influenced by the enrichment movement, their published worship resources reflected those interests less than the influence of the developing Reformed, ecumenical, and liturgical scholarship. This may have been because Presbyterians had deeper ties to European churches than did Congregationalists, Methodists, and others. It was certainly true that American Presbyterians admired the 1940 edition of the Church of Scotland's *Book of Common Order* (*BCO*).[18]

From Voluntary Use to Official Status in the PCUSA

In 1941 the General Assembly of the PCUSA authorized the establishment of a permanent committee on revision of the *BCW*.[19] The work of this committee culminated in the 1946 edition of the *BCW*.[20] The 1946 *BCW* owed a debt not only to its American predecessors but also to the 1940 Scottish *BCO*. There is no doubt that the 1946 book also drew upon the American Episcopal *Book of Common Prayer* (*BCP*). From 1937 until 1948, the two denominations had been involved in conversations looking toward possible union, and this courtship, which had been initiated by the Episcopalians, had an effect on the Presbyterian committee.[21]

Harry Ernest Winter, a Roman Catholic priest of the Oblate order, has written an insightful study of the 1946 *BCW* as well as later developments.[22] Winter's study devoted attention to the special role of William Barrow Pugh, the Stated Clerk of the General Assembly, in the elevation of the 1946 *BCW* to "official" status, in contrast to earlier editions in which the emphasis had fallen on "for voluntary use." Claiming many "typographical errors" in the 1932 *BCW*, Pugh brought two important recommendations to the 1941 General Assembly. The first was "that *The Book of Common Worship* be recognized as an official publication of the Presbyterian Church in the United States of America, and that its supervision be lodged in the Office of the General Assembly," and the second was that a committee "be appointed to act in collaboration with the Stated Clerk of the General Assembly in the supervision of this book and to bring to the General Assembly at stated intervals any suggested changes for approval that it deems advisable."[23]

Recognizing the *BCW* as an "official publication" was an enormous step. Pugh's reason for such action was that the service for ordination of ministers, included in the *BCW*, was an official service permitting no variation. Because of its presence in the *BCW*, the *BCW* could "be added to those official books in the library of the Stated Clerk and thereby receive a peculiar significance."[24] Pugh believed that this was the only way for the *BCW* to become the asset to the church that it ought to be. Although Pugh and the committee emphasized that the forms other than the ordination service were "for voluntary use," that phrase disappeared from the title page and was replaced by the far stronger words, "Approved by the General Assembly of the Presbyterian Church in the United States of America." This action was accomplished, Winter observes, without going through the usual process of consideration by the presbyteries. Winter argues that the committee which prepared the 1946 *BCW* was clearly dominated by Hugh T. Kerr, Sr., and J. Shackelford Dauerty, both of whom he describes as of "catholic" sympathies.[25]

The 1946 *BCW* differed from the earlier editions in several respects. For the first time in an American Presbyterian liturgy, the service offered the Nicene Creed as an alternative to the Apostles' Creed.[26] "The Lord's Supper or Holy Communion" was for the first time printed as a complete order of service. Unfortunately, it was tucked away in a separate section called "The Sacraments and Ordinances of the Church," set apart from the several morning and evening services. Following the American *BCP* as well as the Scottish *BCO,* the 1946 *BCW* began the Communion service with the familiar Collect for Purity. Then followed the optional use of the Ten Commandments, which practice Calvin had introduced in a liturgy of 1540. The service then called for the Kyrie Eleison, as in the *BCP*—another innovation for American Presbyterians. There were other Anglican touches throughout the service. The Prayer of Consecration introduced the use of a Proper Preface for the first time, and included the Agnus Dei as found in both the *BCP* and the *BCO.* The text of the services displayed much verbal dependence on the *BCO,* and some on the *BCP.* The rubrics from the DW, common to both the earlier editions, have been removed. The 1946 *BCW* adopted a two-year lectionary from the Scottish *BCO.* Since a psalter was available in the denominational hymnal, there was none in the *BCW.* It is of interest that two months after the 1946 *BCW* came from the press, it was adopted by the PCUS General Assembly "for optional use in our churches."[27] But even as the 1946 *BCW* achieved an official status not granted to its predecessors, some Presbyterians charged it with being "too Episcopalian." No less a figure than Stated Clerk Eugene Carson Blake wrote to a correspondent in 1954:

> You have put your finger on one illustration of a tendency in this latest revision of [*The*] *Book of Common Worship* to move toward a liturgical emphasis not present in the earlier editions. It would appear to me, therefore, that the crucial matter is going to be in the personnel of the Special Committee on [*The Book of*] *Common Worship.*[28]

Joint Efforts to Revise the Liturgy

When in 1955 the PCUSA appointed new people to that Special Committee to consider revising the *BCW*, the committee returned with a proposal that the Assembly first give it permission to revise the DW.[29] As actual Presbyterian worship practices changed, it became more and more evident that the 1788 DW had become outdated. It made sense to create a new directory which would clearly state the principles that should underlie a revised *BCW*. With the revision of the DW in mind, the 1957 General Assemblies of the United Presbyterian Church of North America (UPCNA) and the Presbyterian Church in the United States determined to join in the project.[30] The Assemblies formed the Joint Committee on Worship, which continued to work even after the 1958 union of the PCUSA and the UPCNA, and in 1959 produced the draft of a new directory.

Members of the Joint Committee on Worship had accepted assignments to do research in particular areas of worship and write papers on assigned subjects. Dr. Robert McAfee Brown had been retained to write the initial draft of the directory. The committee asked Dr. George S. Hendry of Princeton Theological Seminary to write a memorandum on the relation of the drafted DW to the doctrinal standards of the church, the Westminster Confession of Faith (CF) and Larger and Shorter Catechisms. Hendry wrote that the Westminster documents had been produced at a time "when the understanding of the meaning and function of worship in the life of the church was at a low level, and they reflect this in their teaching."[31] He added that "the treatment of worship in the [Confession of Faith] is one of the weakest and most unsatisfactory features of it."[32] Hendry commented that prayer was not once mentioned in CF XXV, 5. Rather, attention focused on that aspect of worship which moves toward human beings rather than toward God.

> This emphasis reflects the tendency, which is deeply rooted in the Reformed tradition, to conceive of the church after the

pattern of the synagogue rather than the temple; it is not so much a place of worship as rather a school, or a gymnasium, where spiritual athletes are trained for "the practice of true holiness."[33]

The General Assembly of the UPCUSA approved the new DW in 1961.[34] The PCUS had withdrawn from the project and drafted its own Directory for the Worship and Work of the Church (DWW), which its General Assembly approved in 1963.[35] The revised DW of 1961 bore the strong imprint of neo-orthodoxy. The document was beautifully written, uncluttered, and succinct. It set forth a doctrine of the Word and sacraments which, as Hendry pointed out, was a departure from the earlier directories (1645 and 1788), neither of which had gone into matters of doctrine at all.

The new directory set forth a service which, even when the Lord's Supper was not celebrated, took the service of Word and sacrament to be the norm. In reference to the Lord's Supper, the directory said that

it is fitting that it be observed as frequently as on each Lord's Day, and it ought to be observed frequently and regularly enough that it is seen as a proper part of, and not an addition to, the worship of God by his people.[36]

The directory set forth a high Calvinist doctrine of the Eucharist, insisting that

the sacrament is more than a memorial to, or reminder of, God's love set forth in Christ. It is a means, appointed for people by Christ, through which is demonstrated the present power and reality of Christ in the hearts of those who gather around his table, and which lifts them into communion with him who is the source of their common life together.[37]

The 1961 DW marked a firm departure from the Westminster Directory and its American revision of 1788. The earlier directories had reflected the triumph of a Puritan form of pietism which obscured the earlier liturgical tradition of the Continental and Scottish Reformed churches, and, some would say, blighted the worship of English-speaking Presbyterians for centuries. Ready for a revital-

ization of worship along lines compatible with their love of
the scriptures and their sense of a holy awe, American
Presbyterians found in the liturgical models of Martin Bu-
cer, John Calvin, and John Knox new directions for liturgy
which would be both ecumenical and Reformed.

The 1963 PCUS Directory for Worship and Work
shared many of the theological assumptions and view-
points of the UPCUSA directory, but turned out to be a
much more cautious revision of the earlier standard.
While both directories conceived of the church's worship
as a people's service, the PCUS directory was much less
specific than the other. By adding "and Work" to the title
of its directory, the PCUS extended the scope of the DWW
beyond gatherings for worship, continuing a trend begun
in the PCUS revision of 1894, when it included the Sabbath school in its directory.

Having completed the task of revising the directory, the
Joint Committee on Worship was ready to move on to the
next task: the revision of *The Book of Common Worship.*
At this point, the Cumberland Presbyterian Church joined
the project. In revising the *BCW,* the intention was, of
course, to incorporate the insights of the new directories.
This proved somewhat more difficult than first imagined,
primarily because the two new directories were quite different. Lewis A. Briner, who had drafted an introduction
to the new Lord's Day service and lectionary, reported:

> This was no easy assignment. The considerable disparity be-
> tween our Directory and the one the southern church has just
> adopted has hounded me throughout. I tried to reflect the
> elements in the service that could find support in both Direc-
> tories, and this is probably an impossible task.[38]

Fr. Winter believes that there was a steady competition
for influence throughout this period among representatives
of loosely defined groups which he calls "catholics,"
"evangelicals," and "evangelical-liberals."[39] The "catholic" Presbyterians had successfully shaped the 1946 *BCW.*
Another generation of the "catholic" party, in which Winter includes Scott Brenner, Lewis A. Briner, and others

responsible for the work of the Joint Committee, had a significant influence on the new Service for the Lord's Day (SLD), which would appear for publication in 1964. However, Winter believes that the neo-orthodox members of the Joint Committee played the most significant role in that they created a bridge that made possible a rapprochement between catholics and evangelicals. It helped the cause of liturgical renewal that the esteemed Reformed father of the neo-orthodox movement, Karl Barth, whom no one could accuse of neglecting the Word in scripture or sermon, had written in favor of liturgical renewal. Barth had said that "with regard to the Sacrament the Evangelical church has made a grave mistake. There is undoubtedly a connection between the neglect of the Sacrament and Protestantism becoming modernist."[40]

The Joint Committee on Worship engaged the services of Rev. David G. Buttrick, then on the faculty of Pittsburgh Theological Seminary, "to carry out certain tasks of research, writing, and editing."[41] Winter describes Buttrick as "catholic" in sympathy, but he appealed strongly to the neo-orthodox and the evangelicals because he held the Word (biblical preaching) in such high esteem. In fact, Buttrick became the principal writer of the new "Service for the Lord's Day."

Fr. Winter's description of competition for influence among parties in the church no doubt has some truth to it, but the labels imply a far more distinct party consciousness than is really evident. In fact, the lines tended to blur and sympathies overlap, particularly between catholic and neo-orthodox, and neo-orthodox and evangelical. Many of those Winter would identify as belonging to one category or another would resist such a rigid confinement.

The fact is that the twentieth century has witnessed an enormous flowering of creative energies among both Protestant and Roman Catholic churches. The ecumenical movement, the renewal of interest in biblical theology, the attempts in both Europe and North America to recover a doctrine of the church, efforts to reconnect worship and daily work, and renewed interest in the role of the laity have all released energies which have a bearing on liturgical renewal. Efforts at liturgical renewal emerged out of multifaceted interests and passions. It is not a movement with a single origin, nor is it merely the esoteric hobby of a few aesthetes, although the U.S. enrichment movement may contribute to such an impression. A good example of the kind of soil from which liturgical renewal sprang is the experiment of the Iona community in Scotland.

> By founding a community based on twin foci of Iona and the industrial slums of Glasgow, [Lord George] Macleod joined Social Gospel to the strong worship interest he always manifested. Peacemaking, the weekly Lord's Supper, and a unity of life, worship and mission soon became the hallmark of the Iona community.[42]

The Taizé community in France, with its Reformed origins, grew out of a similar concern to relate liturgy and life. The formation of the World Council of Churches in 1948 increased contacts between American Presbyterians and continental Reformed theologians such as Max Thurian of the Taizé community, and Josef Hromádka, of Czechoslovakia, whose situation as a Christian in a Marxist society raised new questions about the identity of the church. At the First Assembly of the World Council of Churches in Amsterdam, the papers presented all focused on the nature and mission of the church.[43] The World Student Christian Federation also directed attention to this question. The renewed interest in biblical images of the church and the church in a disordered world also raised questions about worship and about mission. Many young Presbyterians who later advanced to leadership responsibilities in the denomination had been influenced by their contacts with European renewal movements. Horace T. Allen, Jr., the first director of the Presbyterian Joint Office of Worship, had been a member of the Iona community. And so in the 1960s, the Joint Committee on Worship was not controlled by a few with high-church tastes who maneuvered for influence. Rather, its concern and its work grew out of this enormous ferment, the impact of which had been felt with particular excitement in the postwar period and had been supported by the work which had been done since before the turn of the century to recover the liturgical heritage of the Reformed churches.

The Service for the Lord's Day

In 1964, the Joint Committee published *Service for the Lord's Day and Lectionary for the Christian Year.* The UPCUSA General Assembly had in the meantime also appointed a committee to draw up a new Confession of Faith for the reunited church. In October 1964, David Romig, then chairperson of the Joint Committee, was instructed to consult with Edward Dowey of Princeton Seminary and others "to make sure that there were no conflicts between the doctrinal confession of the church and its liturgical practices."[44]

The 1964 Service for the Lord's Day used traditional, King James "churchly" language. Its order followed closely the order suggested by the 1961 Directory for Worship. A number of versicles and responses bridged the parts of the service. The prayers departed from the pattern of one long "comprehensive" or "pastoral" prayer and introduced the use of a series of petitions, after each of which the people responded, "Amen." The rubric then stated that "properly, the Lord's Supper is to be celebrated every Lord's Day."[45] The Invitation to the Table included no exhortation or fencing (that is, the traditional warning to the unworthy or unprepared not to commune). The Offering might include bringing forward the bread and wine. This followed Scottish, early Genevan, and some ecumenical practice, but was not common among American Presbyterians. The Words of Institution from 1 Corinthians 11 used as a Warrant introduced the Prayer of Consecration. There was also a verse from the Gospel According to Luke, chapter 24: "When he was at table with them, he took the bread and blessed, and broke it, and gave it to them. And their eyes were opened and they recognized him."[46] This was a significant departure from earlier Presbyterian Communion services, because it focused on the present rather than limiting the references almost exclusively to a past event. The Prayer of Consecration was unusual for Presbyterians in that it referred to "Jesus Christ, who was born of Mary."[47] The Words of Institution were repeated within the body of the prayer, which is the usual ecumenical placement but not common to Reformed worship.[48] They were used again at the breaking of bread and the pouring of the wine.

The language of the SLD is simpler and also less elegant than that of the 1946 *BCW.* The order and basic contents were nearly the same. The remarkable thing, reflecting the 1961 DW, is that a service of Word and sacrament was set forth as the norm for Sunday worship. Even when the sacrament was not celebrated, the same service, the Ante-Communion, served as the norm. And, perhaps most significant, the entire tenor of the service had been altered so that the accent fell not so much on Jesus' death as on his resurrection, his contemporary presence, his coming again, and the Messianic banquet. "Men [*sic*] will come from east and west, and from north and south, and sit at table in the kingdom of God."

The lectionary itself was not an innovation, since one had appeared in the 1946 *BCW,* and in rudimentary form in the 1932 *BCW.* However, the use of a lectionary is not the traditional Reformed practice. The Reformed way was more likely *lectio continua,* which is a sequential reading of whole blocks of scripture over a course of Sundays, with a sermon preached on whatever portion came up on a particular day. For generations, however, neither a lectionary nor a *lectio continua* commended themselves to Presbyterians. The far more usual practice was either an expository sermon based on a passage chosen by the preacher for the occasion, or certainly more frequently at least in the twentieth century, topical preaching. Topical preaching and liturgical renewal seldom go together in Presbyterian circles. James Hastings Nichols insisted that

occasional and topical sermons cannot be really integrated with any liturgy, and where they dominate the service, noth-

ing done with the prayers will really help much. The service
will break apart at the sermon.[49]

While not strictly Reformed in precedent, the use of a
lectionary was certainly Reformed in that it proposed a
method of preaching which began with scripture. The
Joint Committee understood that in the Reformed tradition the sermon must be an integral part of the liturgy, and
that to be Reformed and truly liturgical, the sermon must
be intimately related to scripture. Surely here also there
was a responsible reflection of the 1961 DW.

Howard Hageman, a liturgical scholar from the Reformed Church in America, asks, "If the history of Roman
Catholicism demonstrates that a Church which loses the
Word must finally lose the sacrament, is there not evidence
in our history that a Church which loses the sacrament
must finally lose the Word?"[50] The SLD could unequivo-
cally affirm both Word and sacrament in the confidence
that to do so was to stand solidly with John Calvin.

There were a good many responses, both favorable and
critical, to the 1964 Service for the Lord's Day. The Joint
Committee examined all those sent to it, and took them
seriously. Some critics charged, as they had regarding the
1946 *BCW,* that the SLD was "too Episcopalian."[51] Many
opposed celebrating the sacrament every Sunday and the
suggestion that such should be the norm. Many did not
like the idea of a lectionary. Some thought the service "too
modern," while others questioned the traditional "thees"
and "thous." Some thought the versicles and responses
and the people's "Amens" "too heavy a dose." A few preferred the more familiar placement of the sermon at the
end of the service. There were objections to the use of the
colors of the liturgical seasons. One questioned the appro-
priateness of a Prayer of Confession. There were criticisms
of the lack of a psalter or responsive readings. Nevertheless, James Appleby of Union Seminary in Virginia, a representative of the PCUS on the Joint Committee, reported
that they had received four or five favorable letters for
every one that was hostile.[52]

There were also comments from critics of particular sophistication in liturgical matters. James Hastings Nichols made a generally positive affirmation of the effort, but expressed serious reservation about weekly Communion as the norm. Although not objecting to a weekly celebration in principle, Nichols argued that the typical Presbyterian congregation was not adequately prepared to approach the Lord's Table with repentance, reverence, and holy awe "in the sense contemplated in our traditional confessions and service books."[53] Under such circumstances, he thought a weekly Communion a "desperately risky expedient," and expressed preference for a monthly norm. Nichols preferred the *lectio continua* to the lectionary, particularly during the long season between Pentecost and Advent. Spoken responses, he argued, had rarely been received enthusiastically in the Reformed tradition. "And are we to be delivered into the hands of the ecclesiastical milliners and the Ladies' Altar Guild with the 'colors of the season'? . . . Surely these are borrowed feathers."[54] Nichols and others also lamented the virtual abandonment of the psalms, the use of which had been particularly treasured among Reformed people.

While Nichols preferred the Reformed practice of using the Words of Institution exclusively in the form of a Warrant, William D. Maxwell, the renowned Scottish liturgist, affirmed their optional placement within the Prayer of Consecration because such use conformed to ecumenical practice both east and west.[55]

Other criticisms were less balanced. George E. Sweazey, pastor of the Webster Groves church in suburban St. Louis, made bitter charges against the new service. He charged that

> the "pristine purity" of the "sources" which are cited with such reverence mean no more and no less than "from a long time ago." . . . The D. A. R. state of mind in the church skirts dangerously close to superstition.[56]

Sweazey added that "forms and rituals offer those who are groping some support," and concluded, "for many reasons we might shrink from worship which threatens a direct experience of literal Christian reality."[57]

In 1966, the Joint Committee published *The Book of Common Worship: Provisional Services and Lectionary for the Christian Year (BCW-PS).*[58] In it, the Service for the Lord's Day appeared in two forms: traditional language and a contemporary language service. The changes in the traditional language service since 1964 were minor. The contemporary language service, however, was not just a paraphrase of the other, but used new texts. The Words of Institution from 1 Corinthians were removed entirely in favor of the Luke 24 passage which directed attention to the experience on the road to Emmaus. In both services, the language was direct and simple but lacked the soaring gracefulness of the 1946 *BCW.*

The Worshipbook

When *The Worshipbook—Services* was published in 1970, there was only one Service for the Lord's Day, and it was in contemporary language.[59] This service was basically similar to the traditional language service in the 1966 *BCW-PS.* The Words of Institution, using Luke 24 exclusively, served as a Warrant. There was no longer provision for their optional use within the Prayer of Consecration. Reference to Jesus as "born of Mary" had been removed. The Agnus Dei, considered too penitential in a service that accented the resurrection, had been eliminated.

In the Preface, the Joint Committee explained the change of the name of the book by saying that "the old and well-loved title of the former book, *The Book of Common Worship,* has been sacrificed because the word *common* is no longer used as it was in times gone by."[60] In an interesting note, the Joint Committee also explained that since they were the same committee that had prepared the 1961 Directory for Worship, they had followed that as their standard, taking care "not to trespass against the Constitutions of the other two Churches."[61] The lectionary, organized on a three-year cycle, followed a post–Vatican II Roman Catholic lectionary with a few alterations.[62]

It is not surprising that the Joint Committee decided in the end to provide a contemporary language service, although it was the first denominational service book to do so. There had been a proliferation of new Bible translations beginning with the Revised Standard Version in 1952, which meant that King James English no longer enjoyed hegemony. Also, the Second Vatican Council's *Constitution on the Sacred Liturgy* earlier in the decade had required that the Mass be celebrated in the vernacular. Presbyterians could hardly feel comfortable worshiping in an archaic English while neighboring Catholic parishes used contemporary language.

The language of *The Worshipbook* was simple and direct. In an interpretive document, the director of the Office of Worship and Music explained that words with Anglo-Saxon stems had been used more often than polysyllabic Latin stems. The prayers had been kept short.[63] In some respects the simplicity of the language may have been an advantage in deflecting the usual opposition which can be expected to evaluate each new service as too "high church" or "too Episcopal." However, some found the very directness of the language to be a problem. Howard Hageman commented:

> Successful as it may be at provoking us to a new awareness of our horizontal obligations as Christians, it fails notably to provoke us to a similar awareness of our transcendental relationships. The language, with a few lapses, is efficiently expressive, but it fails to be equally evocative.[64]

Hageman believed that the problems in the language of *The Worshipbook* arose precisely from the terms which the committee set for itself, that is, "the straightforward use of words and language in current, contemporary use in the last third of the twentieth century."[65] The last third of the twentieth century "has not been celebrated for any speech about the transcendental dimension of human existence. . . . Does that mean that this aspect of human existence must simply be dropped?"[66] Hageman held that there were alternatives to falling back on archaisms and unintelligible liturgical jargon.

David Buttrick, the chief writer and editor of *The Worshipbook,* had not taken lightly the problem of language. He had been struggling with the question of how to frame a language for worship when the language of the culture was not hospitable.

> Language always embodies cultural assumptions, and our language tends to express the rational assumptions of the Enlightenment. Thus, we are expected to phrase liturgical meaning in a language that is essentially anti-liturgical; to convey faith with secular words.[67]

Citing an article in *The New Yorker* magazine which discussed changing language, Buttrick commented:

> In a time when language is changing and meanings are "slippery," we must employ the simple, basic words of our vocabulary in liturgy, avoiding both the archaic and the transient modern.[68]

He pointed to a recent French Reformed liturgy as a model. In the same essay, Buttrick argued against acculturation, trendiness, and "faddism."[69]

While Buttrick and the Joint Committee made a thoughtful and conscientious attempt to find a new liturgical language, in retrospect the effort seems to have fallen short. Somehow reminiscent of the iconoclasm of the 1960s, the very simplicity of the phrasing of the language in the SLD now seems dated. In a 1985 essay, J. Randall Nichols cited the work of Victor Turner, a cultural anthropologist, who argues that worship serves as a temporary retreat from the "structured" world of competition, hierarchies, and statuses. This retreat is not escapism, but a brief experience of "communitas." Having seen a vision of a reality that transcends the usual distinctions and obligations among human beings, people find energy to return to the structured world and participate actively in it. Worship as a kind of temporary "sanctuary" need not be conservative or retrograde, but it may in fact very well be essential to a prophetic or service ministry. If Turner's insights are correct, then those very things that make worship uninteresting or irrelevant to some are the things that give it its essential power. "If we are trying to create an environment in which communitas can occur, purging the liturgy of its archaic symbols can be counter productive."[70] In other words, the very efforts to make worship "relevant" can destroy it. It may be that the attempt to find a new liturgical language has unintentionally undermined the power of the liturgy to evoke that communitas which is essential to it.

Unfortunately, *The Worshipbook* appeared in a time of cultural upheaval. There is, in American culture, an endemic anti-institutionalism, antiformalism, and antihistoricism. In the 1960s these latent prejudices were triggered once again by the frustration felt by many Americans at the stubbornness and impotence of government, universities, churches, and other institutions in the face of acute social injustices. Hostility to institutions, formalities, and tradition has a great deal in common with the basic temper of Puritanism, which shares a "throw the rascals out" kind of mentality. Puritanism, reacting against the coldness and indifference of the established Church of England, longed for a "heartfelt" religion, and in search of that opted for a worship that appears to be invented on the spot, from scratch, at the inspiration of the Spirit. At first novel and even moving, Puritan worship becomes tedious, a burden to be borne, an appearance of ardor to be kept up. It is a worship without resonances, antihistorical and antiecumenical. There is neither "communion of saints" nor "holy catholic church." The 1960s reinvoked some of these Puritan themes, not entirely latent in Presbyterianism. Decked out with balloons and guitars and themes of cultural subversion, the churches of the 1960s did not even have the benefit of that theological confidence which gave Puritanism its original strength. It was not a good time to recover a liturgical tradition.

The Worshipbook soon ran into problems when almost

overnight there began to be a new consciousness about gender-inclusive language. Ironically, in a 1970 item in *Presbyterian Life* anticipating the publication of *The Worshipbook,* a writer claimed that "a positive effort is made throughout the *Worshipbook* to avoid masculine assumptions in the use of pronouns."[71] In fact, the very attempt to be universal had led to the frequent use of references to "man." These made *The Worshipbook* seem to be more gender-exclusive than its predecessors.

Does the Service for the Lord's Day in *The Worshipbook* challenge the prevailing Presbyterian ethos, perhaps diminish the distinctive character of Presbyterian worship? On the one hand, it simply carries on a tradition that began with the 1906 *BCW,* an attempt to recover the liturgical heritage of the Reformed churches when it had been obscured or disfigured by Puritanism. On the other hand, the SLD does challenge the prevailing Presbyterian assumptions about worship, but even in this it follows in the footsteps of its predecessors. The SLD goes beyond its predecessors in challenging the prevailing ethos primarily by moving away from a medieval piety, shifting the accent of the Communion service from the funereal and toward joy in the risen and present Lord, with whom people will sit at table in the kingdom. It also distinguishes itself by making the weekly celebration of the Lord's Supper the norm, using the Ante-Communion service even when the Supper is not celebrated. This was a move to recover the essential unity of Word and sacrament, as Calvin himself had desired it, and it accurately reflected the theology of the 1961 DW. The SLD also reemphasized the Christian year and the use of a lectionary as a means of underscoring the Reformed bias toward expository preaching. Following the 1961 DW, the SLD thus challenged not only the Puritan legacy in the church but also the practice of topical preaching, closely associated with that species of Protestantism that Karl Barth had called "modernism."[72]

In 1970, the 182nd General Assembly of the UPCUSA amended its DW to empower sessions to permit baptized children to receive the Lord's Supper when their families "deem it appropriate."[73] The 190th Assembly amended the 1970 amendment when in 1978 it removed the condition that tied the admission of baptized children to the Lord's Table to the specific approval of their families.[74] Then in 1980 the 120th General Assembly of the PCUS acted to amend its DWW to admit baptized children to the Lord's Table.[75] While rooted in the Reformed conviction that baptized children are members of the church, the practice of admitting such children to the Lord's Supper before such time as they are ready to make a personal profession of faith has no specific Reformed precedent. This action was rooted in ecumenical theology, and several other American denominations took similar action at roughly the same time.

Resources for a Reunited Church

New Directory for Worship

In 1983, the UPCUSA and the PCUS reunited. Upon reunion, a new *Book of Order* and *Book of Confessions* were adopted to become the Constitution of the Presbyterian Church (U.S.A.). The new Directory for the Service of God was basically a revision of the 1961 DW, with additions and revisions coming from the 1963 DWW.[76] There was a reordering of the sequence of the material. The addition of Ch. VI, "The Service of God Through Ministry to Others," derives in large part from the DWW and attempts to broaden the definition of worship.

The 201st General Assembly (1989), having received an affirmative vote from the majority of the presbyteries, adopted a new Directory for Worship.[77] The new directory is a long document, comprehensive to the point of being repetitious, and written in a rather prosaic language that typifies a bureaucratic rather than a churchly style. It follows the example of the 1963 DWW in that it broadens the definition of worship to include such matters as "Mutual Ministries in the Church," "Christian Nurture," "Pastoral Care," and "The Ministry of the Church in the World."

One possible objection to so extending the definition of worship is that it is by no means clear where to stop.

The new directory reflects many concerns and developments in both Presbyterian and ecumenical liturgical and theological thought in recent years. The directory differs from its predecessors in the following ways: reference to the use of symbolic language; inclusive language; daily public worship; the arrangement of liturgical space; and the use of material things in worship. It differs also in its call for review and oversight of a congregation's worship life as a responsibility of presbytery; mention of the use of drama, dance, and other art forms; enacted prayer, for example, raised hands, clapping, anointing; and three readings from scripture as the norm for the SLD. The new directory permits forms of proclaiming the Word other than the traditional sermon, provides for sponsors at baptism, and places an even stronger emphasis on eschatology in the section on the Lord's Supper, with special accent on the Messianic banquet. The Lord's Supper is to be celebrated "regularly and frequently," at least *six* times a year, but appropriately "as often as each Lord's Day." The directory lists topics that are appropriate for inclusion in intercessory prayers in the SLD. There is permission for healing services, and for praying in tongues "as a personal and private discipline."[78]

With these innovations, the proposed directory both reflects some actual Presbyterian practice and challenges the traditional ethos. It also exhibits a remarkable ecumenical convergence. While the so-called mainline Protestant churches in America have followed roughly the same trajectory in the development of their published liturgical resources in the past sixty years, it is less easy since Vatican II and subsequent Roman Catholic liturgical reforms to distinguish a Presbyterian service book from one used by Methodists, Roman Catholics, Episcopalians, or Lutherans. In part this convergence is due to ecumenical conversation—sometimes as formal as the Consultation on Church Union, sometimes informal—which leads to mutual respect and imitation. More often, this convergence can be traced to the common experience of the twentieth-century church in its recovery of a sense of community, of "people of God," and of that community's mission to challenge the conventional wisdom of the prevailing culture. In the search for theological integrity and authenticity, churches all across the denominational spectrum have turned to the sources of faith and life and begun to recover pieces of their heritage which had become lost. Roman Catholics learn to preach; Presbyterians recover the Eucharist.

Supplemental Liturgical Resources

In the 1980s, Presbyterians produced five paperback volumes called Supplemental Liturgical Resources (SLR). The first, SLR 1, published in 1984, is a revision of the Service for the Lord's Day.[79] In response to requests frcm pastors, this resource includes a number of options for each element of the service. There are eight eucharistic prayers. The first six include the Words of Institution within the prayer, bowing to ecumenical consensus rather than to specifically Reformed practice. They are used as a Warrant in two of the prayers, and in the first three, it is possible to use them that way. The Great Prayer of Thanksgiving C is revised from the 1946 *BCW,* and appeared originally in the 1906 *BCW.* From the 1661 *Book of Common Prayer,* it is one of the most widely used and best loved among Presbyterians.

Supplemental Liturgical Resource 2 is called *Holy Baptism and Services for the Renewal of Baptism.*[80] Chiefly notable, in addition to a service for the sick and dying which permits anointing with oil, is that the baptismal service itself includes the traditional renunciations of evil and the signing of the cross on the baptizand's forehead, which may be done with oil.

Christian Marriage, SLR 3, gives alternate rites and a rite for recognition of a civil marriage.[81] SLR 4 is *The Funeral: A Service of Witness to the Resurrection* and SLR 5 is *Daily Prayer.*[82] *Daily Prayer* is just that: a resource for daily, noneucharistic morning and evening worship. It includes a daily lectionary; psalms and biblical songs, some with musical settings; midday and night prayer; and variations for the Christian year.

Because the SLR materials offer so many options, it poses a problem for those trying to use these books directly in public worship. A loose-leaf binding might have been a more useful format. The language in the Supplemental Liturgical Resources is gender-inclusive. Pronominal references to God are eliminated, and although references to God as "Father" and "Son" are reduced, there is a commitment to maintain the traditional Trinitarian language. The SLR materials use contemporary English, of course, with some success in restoring the cadences and grace of traditional liturgical prayer. In a time when so much new liturgical material needs to be written, and when it seems no longer adequate simply to revise classical prayers, not everything produced will be of equal quality or prove enduring. The unevenness of the quality of the Supplemental Liturgical Resources, then, does not come as a surprise.

The Convergence of Ecumenism and Reformed Liturgical Renewal

Since the first *Book of Common Worship* in 1906, the prevailing ethos of Presbyterian worship, which has itself evolved over time, has been continually and repeatedly challenged by a sequence of published resources for worship. Presbyterian worship has changed—not only in published resources but also in actual practice. What would have seemed a "normal" Presbyterian service in 1905 would now seem to most Presbyterians exceedingly bare, and excessively clergy-centered. What would have seemed bold or even esoteric in 1905 is taken for granted now. The corporate Prayer of Confession, rare in 1905, is today nearly ubiquitous. While typical practice cannot be ascertained simply by studying official liturgical publications, impressionistic evidence is sufficient to indicate that the typical Presbyterian service has followed the publications in moving toward the pre-Puritan Reformed patterns. In that movement, they have also come nearer ecumenical norms.

The same stimuli that caused Presbyterians to rethink their worship patterns as they prepared new resources have also influenced other Christian communities. The recovery of the sense of "church," dissatisfaction with the prevailing rationalism, a resurgence of interest in biblical, theological, and historical studies were common stimuli among ecumenically inclined Christians in many denominations. If, in becoming more like other denominations in actual worship practices, Presbyterians have lost a sense of denominational distinctiveness, with a corresponding decrease in denominational loyalty, then so also has there been a similar loss of denominational distinctiveness and loyalty in other church bodies. If it is relatively easier for Presbyterians to feel at home in a nearby Methodist or Lutheran church, so is it relatively easier for Methodists and Lutherans to find a compatible worshiping community in a convenient Presbyterian congregation. Remarkably enough, the reduction in denominational loyalty seems to have affected Roman Catholics at least as dramatically as others. As Presbyterian worship has grown closer to an ecumenical norm, so has it become less inhibiting to Roman Catholics who consider crossing over. Some other study than this would be required to provide a statistical report on whether Presbyterians gain or lose more from this new denominational mobility. It would seem reasonable, however, that in the long run the Presbyterian Church ought to benefit as much as it may suffer from the situation.

The original impulses for liturgical renewal among Presbyterians had grown out of a sense of something missing. Topical preaching; the earnest but often lacking compositions of pastors whose liturgical prose was unsuccessful in evoking the transcendent; a heavy, penitential, and even somber approach to the Lord's Supper which contributed to its marginalization—all these led to a yearning to reexamine the theology and traditions of worship. Neo-orthodoxy, the biblical theology movement, historical studies, and the ecumenical movement served as stimuli which encouraged efforts to recover a worship that resonated with the language of scripture and a communal piety. Given such stimuli, those who searched patiently had no difficulty finding more than adequate Reformed precedents for a communal worship rooted in Word and sacrament.

For Presbyterians, liturgical renewal has meant reconsidering the sources: both explicitly Reformed sources and those dating from the undivided church. It has also meant invoking the Reformed definition as a church which is "always being reformed." From its earliest roots, the Reformed tradition at its best has refused a narrow sectarianism and nurtured its connections with other Christians. The twentieth-century liturgical renewal among Presbyterians might have taken a somewhat different direction were they a people who cultivated a splendid ecclesiastical isolation, but such isolation is not in character for them. Even though Presbyterians have, to some extent, crossbred with other Christians in the search for a recovery of worship both communal and touched by a holy awe, liturgical reform among them is not an alien imposition, but follows logically from the best Reformed premises.

6

Hymnody: Its Place in Twentieth-Century Presbyterianism

Morgan F. Simmons

Central to Christian worship is music, and the essence of that centrality is hymnody, the corporate voice of congregants. Strongly affirmed by reformers of all generations, it is a matter that still commands our attention. This tenet was particularly salient in the sixteenth century when Martin Luther and John Calvin projected different aspects of congregational song. In succeeding generations, most Reformed churches have strayed widely from Calvin's restrictive judgment: the only permissible texts for corporate musical expression were the Psalms, the Ten Commandments, and the Nunc Dimittis—and those to be sung in metrical vernacular without the benefit of harmony. Under Calvin's careful eye the *Genevan Psalter* evolved into a rich treasury of word and music; at its completion in 1562, 110 different meters and 125 discrete tunes were available for the 152 texts.[1]

As early as 1564 a revision of the *Anglo-Genevan Psalter* appeared in Scotland and contained only 105 tunes and a reduction in the variety of meters. These changes were a portent of things to come. For instance, texts of *The Ainsworth Psalter* (1612), which the Pilgrims brought with them to Plymouth, could be sung to a meager eight tunes.

In the seventeenth century, internal as well as external forces in the Church of Scotland were at work to widen the scope of congregational expression through Christianizing the Psalms or introducing hymns of "human composure." Officially, these efforts had no effect, but cracks in the armor of psalmody appeared in 1745 and 1781 with "Scottish Paraphrases." Those introductions reflect the powerful influence of Isaac Watts, whose *Psalms of David imitated in the language of the New Testament* (1719) reached far beyond his nonconformist church in England.

Early American Presbyterianism was largely a reflection of Scottish practice, and the most commonly used psalter was of Scottish origin: *The Psalms of David in Meeter: Newly translated and diligently compared with the originall Text, and former Translations: More plaine, smooth and agreeable to the Text, than any heretofore* (1650). Referred to as "Rous' Version," it was often bound together with the parishioners' Bibles. But the American church was more open to change than its parent body. As early as 1729, Watts's *Psalms of David* was published under the aegis of Benjamin Franklin, and those paraphrases as well as Watts's hymns entered Presbyterian worship with but reluctant resistance.

Of great significance for the future of worship music is the fact that the historic Directory for Worship, which was a product of the Synod of New York and Philadelphia in 1788 (the first General Assembly), included a chapter entitled "Of the Singing of Psalms." The first admonition read: "It is the duty of Christians to praise God, by singing psalms, or hymns, publicly in the church, as also privately in the family." Not only was the way opened for the inclusion of hymns and psalms, but the directive went further to encourage the expansion of music in services: "The proportion of the time of public worship to be spent in singing is left to the prudence of every minister; but it is recommended that more time be allowed for this excellent part of divine service than has been usual in most of our churches."[2]

As we look at hymnody in twentieth-century Presbyterianism in America, we are mindful of influential phenomena outside the denomination which frame the time span of our consideration. During the last quarter of the nineteenth century, there were, among others, these polemics: the full flowering of the Oxford Movement and the burgeoning of revivalism led by Dwight L. Moody and Ira D. Sankey. One of the strongest forces of liturgical revival and a product of the second generation of the Oxford Movement was the publication in England of *Hymns Ancient and Modern* which had gone through four editions by the end of the century (1861, 1868, 1875 and 1889). Another evidence of matters liturgical was the expanding interest in manuals of worship among "free" churches, an interest that began in Great Britain and followed in America.[3]

As with all great movements in the church, music has played a central role, and this was certainly the case with the revivals of the nineteenth century. It has been said that "Moody and Sankey found themselves not only salesmen of salvation . . . but also indirectly salesmen of books of gospel hymns."[4] The impact of the gospel hymn upon the worship life in America was considerable, and as we shall see, it has presented a continuing dilemma for hymnal editors regarding the balance between "standard" hymns of the church and "songs of salvation." The question remains: Does an editor or a committee make the judgment as to what the worshiper "needs" or what the worshiper "wants"? Will congregations spurn a collection that does not fit their desires and thus affect the economics of a publication? Which takes precedence, expediency or integrity? These are questions that have always plagued the church and are issues that will be reflected in the following survey.

The 1895 Hymnal: A Prelude to the New Century

By the end of the nineteenth century, the Presbyterian Church in the U.S. and the Presbyterian Church in the U.S.A. had essentially abandoned their psalm-singing heritage, and the hymnals reflected the eclecticism which began to characterize most denominational collections. Exceptions to this trend were the psalm books used by the

United Presbyterian Church of North America, the Associate Reformed Presbyterian Church, and the Reformed Presbyterian Church of North America.

Representative of such inclusive works were two collections, one of the southern church: *Book of Hymns and Tunes comprising The Psalms and Hymns for the Worship of God, Approved by the General Assembly of 1866, arranged with appropriate tunes, and an Appendix, Prepared by the Presbyterian Committee of Publication, by Authority of General Assembly of 1873* (Richmond: Presbyterian Committee of Publication, 1874), and the other of the northern church: *The Hymnal published by authority of the General Assembly of the Presbyterian Church in the United States of America* (Presbyterian Board of Publication and Sabbath-School Work, Philadelphia, 1895).

This latter publication was of great importance not only because of its high level of integrity, inclusiveness, and scholarship, but also because it launched the significant hymnological career of its editor, Louis F. Benson. He is still recognized as America's leading hymnologist. His magnum opus *The English Hymn* (1915) was the outgrowth of two series of lectures delivered in 1907 and 1910 at Princeton Seminary, which has housed his extensive library since his death in 1930.

Describing the approach that was taken in preparation of the 1895 book, Benson wrote:

> The whole field of Hymnody was freshly studied with the resources of the new Hymnology; the hymns were chosen in the interests of devotion as distinguished from homiletics, and their text was determined with a scrupulousness that had been more common in literature than in Hymnody. In setting the hymns a large use was made of the Anglican music, and of the American composers developed in connection with the musical editions of the Protestant Episcopal *Hymnal* of 1892.[5]

He continued his description:

> It sought to bring forward a backward Church to the van of progressive Church Song, and to prepare a church book unexcelled for utility, beauty and editorial carefulness.[6]

That it fulfilled this aim is affirmed by Henry Wilder Foote, who judged that "it was the first official hymnbook of the Presbyterian Church to stand in the front rank with other hymnbooks of its day."[7] This is the hymnal that would see the northern church into the twentieth century and the book by which all subsequent collections would be measured.

Its character is marked by clarity in both style and format. The first stanza of each of the hymns is interlined with the music, and full credit is given to author, composer, or sources along with tune names, meters, and pertinent dates. Standard authors such as Isaac Watts, Charles Wesley, John Newton, and James Montgomery are well represented as are many later nineteenth-century English and American hymnodists. Obvious by scarcity are psalm versions.

The musical editor was Dr. William W. Gilchrist, assisted among others by George William Warren and Rev. William P. Merrill, later to become known as hymn text author and pastor of the Brick Presbyterian Church in New York City. Although the book included many older tunes from various sources, there was a very large number by nineteenth-century English composers; for instance, forty-eight by John B. Dykes, thirty-nine by Joseph Barnby, and twenty-four by Sir Arthur Sullivan. These inclusions reflect the strong influence of *Hymns Ancient and Modern.* At the back of the collection are "Ancient Hymns and Canticles" set to Anglican chant. One might describe the book as "high church." It is virtually free of gospel hymns, tipping its hat in that direction with the inclusion of "He Leadeth Me" and "I Love to Tell the Story."

Although it was officially sanctioned by the General Assembly, this book had its rivals in non-Presbyterian publications, as have all hymnals that have received the imprimatur of the denominations. One such collection was *In Excelsis,* published in 1897 by the Century Company of New York. Serving on the committee that prepared this collection were several prominent Presbyterians, among them Maltbie D. Babcock, pastor of the Brick Presbyterian

Church in New York City. In format and content this hymnal was on a par with the 1895 book and could hardly be described as a "popular" alternative.

By the time of its revision in 1911, *The Hymnal* was used by 1,880 congregations and had a circulation of 322,000.[8] In the forty-sixth printing of 1928, it was reported that 491,000 copies had been run. Before the end of the century, the Board of Publication issued two collections which were complementary to the 1895 hymnal: *The Chapel Hymnal* (1898) and *The School Hymnal* (1899), both edited by Dr. Benson. The latter work was prepared for those who wished a smaller book for personal devotional use and for prayer meetings. It did include more gospel hymns than the parent collection, as did *The School Hymnal,* which was intended for use in Sabbath schools.

These two volumes reflect a double standard that has often prevailed in the churches: modes of praising God differ between formal morning worship and informal worship at church school, on Sunday evenings, and at midweek prayer meetings. It has been a common practice for many churches to have two hymnals—a tradition that has conveyed a mixed message to worshipers that speaks of the "otherness" of God in a formal setting and of an anthropomorphic God in an informal one. It is little wonder that many parishioners have a clouded theology.

The First Hymnal
of the Twentieth Century (U.S. Church)

The first hymnal of the twentieth century with denominational scope was *The New Psalms and Hymns Published by Authority of The General Assembly of the Presbyterian Church in the United States A.D. 1901.* This book, which contained a compilation of 715 psalms and hymns, was an outgrowth of overtures presented to the General Assembly of 1889 which appointed a committee to undertake the task of preparing a collection to "meet the demands of our Church, the product of her own life and effort." Assisting in its preparation was once again the northern Presbyterian, Louis F. Benson. This cooperative endeavor is a happy incident where political and regional differences were put aside for the sake of the worship of God. The editor for this hymnal was Rev. J. W. Walden, and the musical editor was Professor Joseph Maclean, assisted by John P. Campbell.

The preface to this book acknowledges the heritage of psalm singing and states: "A large number of the versions of Psalms has been distributed through the book, under appropriate classification. An index of these, at the beginning of the book, puts them within as easy reach as if arranged separately, after the old way." Each text was printed with its own tune, and there were no "Amens" appended for any hymns.

Gospel hymnody had gained strength within the denomination, and it became a force to be reckoned with. On the one hand, these hymns had great appeal for those who longed for a word of comfort which could be had for small demands on the intellect and musical ability. On the other hand, they presented a predicament for those who felt that they were truncated vehicles for proclaiming the gospel. Assessing the phenomenon that nurtured gospel hymnody, Erik Routley was prompted to write:

> One of the distinguishing marks of Revivalist technique is the emphasis in its preaching on judgment, together with the emphasis in its singing on peace. And singing played, on the whole, a greater part than preaching, certainly a greater part than reason, in the success of the movement.[9]

A more stinging assessment was made by H. Wiley Hitchcock, who said of gospel hymnody: "It is at its best . . . a kind of religious pop art almost irresistible in its visceral appeal; at its worst, an embarrassingly trivial sacred counterpart of the sentimental 'songs of heart and home' of the same era."[10]

The southern church yielded to the appeal of the gospel hymn, and the 1910 General Assembly of that denomination authorized the Publication Committee to prepare a book slanted toward that genre of hymn.[11] That same year

Assembly Songs for Use in Evangelistic Services, Sabbath School, Young People Societies, Devotional Meeting, and the Home was issued by the Presbyterian Committee of Publication, Richmond, Virginia. Of the 238 items included almost all were gospel songs.

A similar collection, *Life and Service Hymns,* was published by the same group in 1917, and it was followed in 1926 by *Premier Hymns: Selections for the Church, the Sunday School, Young Peoples Meetings, Evangelistic Services and Great Religious Conferences, Assembled with a Happy Balance.* B. D. Ackley was the music editor of this gospel song collection and was the composer of many of its tunes.

The Revision of 1911

The northern church was not immune from similar pressures for a more popular form of hymn, and so the 1911 revision of Benson's monumental collection of 1895 reflects the move toward a wider range of hymnic literature. At the back of the hymnal was a section of twenty-nine hymns for Evangelistic Services, which went no further than some of the more familiar texts by Fanny Crosby such as "Pass Me Not, O Gentle Saviour," "Safe in the Arms of Jesus," and "Rescue the Perishing."

This 1911 book was more than a simple revision; there were substantive changes with a large number of deletions and additions. Among these changes was an acknowledgment of the social gospel begun in the previous century by Washington Gladden (1836–1918), author of the hymn "O Master, Let Me Walk with Thee." The movement's leading prophet and writer was Walter Rauschenbusch (1861–1918), whose book *Christianity and the Social Crisis* was published in 1907.[12] Gladden's hymn was included in the 1895 hymnal, but a specific social emphasis may be seen in the following which were included in the 1911 book: " 'Thy Kingdom Come,' on Bended Knee the Passing Ages Pray" by Frederick L. Hosmer (1891), "Where Cross the Crowded Ways of Life" by Frank Mason North (1903), and "The Light of God Is Falling" by Louis F. Benson (1910), the third stanza of which read:

Where human lives are thronging
In toil and pain and sin,
While cloistered hearts are longing
To bring the Kingdom in,
O Christ, the Elder Brother
Of proud and beaten men,
When they have found each other,
Thy Kingdom will come then!

This language with sexist overtones is questioned in many circles today, but at its inception the hymn was a bold step toward emphasizing the church's responsibility for social justice. In the year of the hymnal's publication, Rauschenbusch criticized Gladden's hymn as too patient for workers who "don't want 'a trust that triumphs over wrong,' but a religion of action which will annihilate the wrong."[13]

The same high standards of Benson's meticulous scholarship that characterized the 1895 collection remained a hallmark and placed this 1911 book at the forefront of Protestant hymnals. Just as the earlier hymnal had reflected strong British influence from *Hymns Ancient and Modern,* this revision showed an awareness of the highly respected *English Hymnal* (1906), which had been edited by Percy Dearmer and Ralph Vaughan Williams. Included were a text by Dearmer, "Father, Who on Man Dost Shower," with a German tune arranged for the British collection and also a hymn by Arthur C. Ainger, "God Is Working His Purpose Out." None of the magnificent tunes by Vaughan Williams or texts which Robert Bridges had written for the *Yattendon Hymnal* (1899) was included in this 1911 collection.

Among the important new hymns by Americans was "Joyful, Joyful, We Adore Thee" by Henry van Dyke, which had been written in 1907, but omitted was his more socially oriented text, "Jesus, Thou Divine Companion," first written in 1889 and revised in 1909 for Henry Sloane Coffin's *Hymns of the Kingdom of God* (1910).

In 1917 a supplement of items was included in the printing of the 1911 hymnal. These additions reflected the fact that the nation was at war and included Rudyard Kipling's "God of Our Fathers, Known of Old," "The Star-Spangled Banner," and "The Battle Hymn of the Republic."

Before his death in 1930 Benson was to edit two more hymnals for the Presbyterian Board of Christian Education: *Christian Song* (1926) and *The Smaller Hymnal* (1928). In the preface to the latter he wrote, "The use of the hymnal as a companion of our private devotion, its place in the home circle, the thought of it as a book to be owned and loved and read, seem almost to have passed away." In 1926 he delivered the Stone Lectures at Princeton Seminary in which he criticized the growing custom of placing all stanzas between the music staves—"the latest menace to the integrity of our hymns." (In all the hymnals that he edited only the first stanza was printed between the staves.) He devoted considerable space to his objections to this practice.[14] His principal fear was that worshipers would be unable to read or sing the hymns with comprehension if the texts were printed between the staves rather than as poetry.

The Psalter Tradition Maintained

The psalm-singing tradition was maintained by certain branches of the Presbyterian Church. In 1887 the United Presbyterian Board of Publication in Pittsburgh published *The Psalter.* In this rather unusual collection, the standard texts from the past—the *Scottish Psalter,* Rous's version, Tate and Brady, and the versions of Watts—were passed over for metrical translations which appear to be peculiar to this book. Two exceptions are the Scottish form of Psalm 23 and William Kethe's version of Psalm 100, "All People That on Earth Do Dwell." There is no preface, and no credits are given for the translations. For certain psalms there are several different renderings; in some they are in different meters. The texts are separate from the music.

There is a preponderance of nineteenth-century tunes

with many by Lowell Mason, William Bradbury, and Thomas Hastings. Some of the marriages of text and tune seem ill fitted, to say the least. Consider singing the following to the tune "Antioch" ("Joy to the World!"):

> Praise God. From heavens praise the Lord,
>   In heights praise to him be.
> O all his angels, praise ye him;
>   His hosts all, praise him ye.
>
> *(Psalm 148:1)*

Other tunes that are associated with hymn texts were used: "Woodworth" ("Just as I Am") to Psalm 139, "Coronation" ("All Hail the Power of Jesus' Name") to Psalms 72 and 150, and "Sweet Hour of Prayer" to Psalm 149. This was the vehicle of congregational song that accompanied a large segment of the Presbyterian family into the twentieth century.

A successor to this book was published in 1912, again by the United Presbyterian Board of Publication in Pittsburgh. Its preface states:

> The prime distinction of this Psalter is its use of the metrical version of the Psalms approved September 22nd, 1909, by a Joint Committee from nine Churches of the Presbyterian family in Canada and the United States. These churches are as follows: the Presbyterian Church in the United States of America, the Presbyterian Church in Canada, the Reformed Church in America, the United Presbyterian Church of North America, the Reformed Presbyterian Church, Synod, the Reformed Presbyterian Church, General Synod, the Christian Reformed Church, and the Associate Reformed Presbyterian Church, and the Associate Presbyterian Church.

The impetus for this book began as early as 1893 and continued with a series of joint meetings every two or three years, but the final work was completed by a committee from the United Presbyterian Church which consisted of David A. McClenahan, chairperson, David R. Miller, William E. McCulloch, John McNaugher, William J. Reid, and William I. Wishart. The assistance of Edward A. Collier of the Reformed Church in America and Charles E. Craven of the Presbyterian Church in the U.S.A. was acknowledged. Their work resulted in "practically a new metrical translation of the Psalms." The musical editor was Charles N. Boyd, instructor in church music at Western Theological Seminary, Pittsburgh.

Like its predecessor, the early metrical versions were almost totally avoided with the exceptions of Psalms 23 and 100, mentioned above. This version did include Watts's "O God, Our Help in Ages Past" (Psalm 90), but it was not set to its well-known tune "St. Anne." The first stanzas of the psalms were printed between the staves of music and many popular hymn tunes were continued and others introduced. For instance, Psalm 77 was set to "Auld Lang Syne" and began, "I thought upon the days of old, The years departed long," Psalm 24 to "Adeste Fidelis," and Psalm 99 to "Nicaea" ("Holy, Holy, Holy!"). Two Genevan tunes in addition to "Old Hundredth" were added: "St. Michael" and "Old 124th." It appears that the use of many well-known tunes was offered as a sop for the singing of what in many cases was nothing more than doggerel; a case in point may be seen in an excerpt from Psalm 55:

> O had I wings, I sight and say,
>   Like some swift dove to roam,
> Then would I hasten far away
> And find a peaceful home.

In neither of these collections was there an attempt at Christianizing the Psalms or of including scriptural paraphrases. In 1927 the United Presbyterian Church of North America published *The Psalter Hymnal,* which included 295 metrical psalm versions from the 1912 collection and appended another 163 items which included mostly standard hymns and responses. The chairperson of the committee that prepared this book was John McNaugher, a committee member for the previous book; others from the past committee were William J. Reid and William I. Wishart.

The U.S. Hymnal of 1927

That same year the Presbyterian Church in the United States published a successor to the hymnal of 1901. This 1927 collection was titled *The Presbyterian Hymnal Published by Authority of the Presbyterian Church in the United States.* A committee of eight men was appointed by the General Assembly in May of 1925 and consisted of Walter L. Lingle, C. T. Caldwell, Claude T. Carr, Samuel McP. Glasgow, James Lewis Howe, R. E. Magill, G. G. Sydnor, and W. Taliaferro Thompson. To the detriment of the collection there was no informed hymnologist and no musician on the committee, and apparently the committee did not have benefit of professional consultants. The result was a very mediocre hymnal. It was the first book of this denomination in which the texts were printed within the music score, as directed by the General Assembly, which also stipulated "that Amen should be added to each hymn and that Scripture selections for responsive reading should be included."

There is little or no evidence that the committee was in touch with the heritage of the Reformed tradition, the great hymnic legacy from Luther, the wealth of Latin texts, or the more recent strong influence of the Anglican Church. Such standard hymns as "Praise to the Lord, the Almighty," "Now Thank We All Our God," and "O Come, O Come, Emmanuel" were omitted, and "O Sacred Head, Now Wounded" was set to "St. Christopher" ("Beneath the Cross of Jesus") rather than to the "Passion Chorale." Dr. James R. Sydnor reports that more than one third of the music plates contained errors which were never corrected.[15] There were not a large number of "gospel hymns," but the book included what one might describe as "gray hymns," those without significant character either musically or textually. There were five hundred items in this book, including choral responses.

Fortunately only thirteen years passed before there was a supplement or an alternative smaller volume, *Hymnal for Christian Worship,* published in 1940 by John Knox Press and edited by James R. Sydnor. It was described as an "inexpensive [60 cents, postpaid, for a single copy] book of praise . . . designed primarily as a Sunday school hymnal," which "may be used by churches as a general hymnal for the regular services of worship." An eclectic compilation, it included things as disparate as Luther's "Ah, Dearest Jesus, Holy Child" and William P. Merrill's "Not Alone for Mighty Empire" to "There's a Church in the Valley by the Wildwood." It was amazingly comprehensive for a collection of 340 entries. It reflects Dr. Sydnor's training as a church musician and demonstrates his knowledge of the hymnic field, offering to the church many excellent choices that were omitted from the 1927 book. It paved the way for *The Hymnbook* of 1955.

A Landmark Hymnal, 1933

In 1933 the Presbyterian Church in the U.S.A. issued a new hymnal, "published by authority of the General Assembly." It was in the noble tradition of the work begun by Louis F. Benson in the 1895 book. The editor was Dr. Clarence Dickinson and the assistant editor was Dr. Calvin W. Laufer. Dr. Dickinson was a church musician of international stature, having been trained at Northwestern University and in Germany and France. In 1909 he began a long tenure at the Brick Presbyterian Church in New York City, and in 1912 he was named instructor of church music at Union Theological Seminary in New York. Along with his wife, Dr. Helen A. Dickinson, and Dr. Henry Sloane Coffin he founded the prestigious School of Sacred Music at Union in 1928. He had also been a founder of the American Guild of Organists in 1896. Although Dr. Helen Dickinson's name does not appear anyplace in the hymnal, those who were acquainted with this remarkable couple are aware of her involvement in all areas of her husband's work. She was the first woman to receive the doctor of philosophy degree from Heidelberg University and had a prodigious knowledge of art, languages, literature, and music. Although it is impossible to document her work on the hymnal, it is very probable that she influenced the musical and textual selections.

The assistant editor, Dr. Calvin W. Laufer, has been described "as a church musician, devotional poet, and writer of hymns for special occasions as well as for general use, who has rendered a distinct service to the Church at large."[16] An ordained Presbyterian minister, he began work with the Board of Christian Education of the Presbyterian Church U.S.A. in 1913, later becoming editor of musical publications. He was associated with Dr. Louis F. Benson in the preparation of several hymnals.

An indication of the level of sophistication—one might even say erudition—that governed the selection of hymns is found in this statement in the book's preface: "Old hymns which through the years of association have become fixed in the affections of many people have been retained, even though they may, in some cases, fall below the general standard set for the Hymnal." The tilt toward "hymns by popular demand" is slight and goes no further than "He Leadeth Me," "What a Friend We Have in Jesus" and "I Love to Tell the Story." On the other hand, a large number of texts and tunes from the Genevan and Scottish psalm-singing tradition were introduced, as well as the Lutheran chorale heritage and even some Latin hymns with plainsong melodies. The influence from British sources is considerable, particularly from *The Church Hymnary* (1927), published for the Church of Scotland and her sister churches. There are also materials from the *Yattendon Hymnal* (1899), *The English Hymnal* (1906), and *Songs of Praise* (1925). The preface states:

> Considerable new poetic material has been added to give expression to certain new emphases in the religious thought of the present day, which concerns itself in such large measure, on the one hand, with social service, the brotherhood of man and world friendship, and, on the other, with the inner life, that mystical conception of the Christian life as "hid with Christ in God."

The strength of this fine hymnal is affirmed by the fact that after a fifty-six-year history and two more hymnals, there are churches which continue its use for worship. Naturally, with all the trends in contemporary hymnody—matters of inclusive language, a deepening social awareness, renovation of archaic language—as well as a spate of new texts and tunes in the last two decades, it is outdated, but certainly not useless.

In 1935 the *Handbook to the Hymnal* was published by the Board of Christian Education, edited by William Chalmers Covert, assisted by Calvin W. Laufer. It includes notes on each of the hymns: biographical data on author and composer and backgrounds of the texts and tunes. Compared to companions for other denominational hymnals, it is mediocre at best and does not measure up to the caliber of discriminating scholarship that marked its parent volume.

Adjunct Collections

Under the editorship of Calvin Laufer, the Westminster Press published *The Church School Hymnal for Youth* in 1928. A comprehensive volume of 386 hymns, this was the first in a rather long series of hymnals for children and youth. In addition to the hymns which, for the most part, were standard hymns of the church, there was a selection of instrumental music and a section devoted to worship materials. This hymnal was replaced by *The Hymnal for Youth* in 1941, and its revision was overseen by Laufer until his death when he was succeeded by Frank D. Getty; its music editor was Lawrence Curry, who was to have a long association with the Westminster Press. Like its predecessor, it consisted mostly of standard hymns of the church and reflected some of the emphases of the 1933 denominational collection.

In the preceding year, 1940, *Hymns for Junior Worship* was published by the Westminster Press, and in 1946 *Hymns for Primary Worship* appeared. Among other hymnals for young people were *Songs for Early Childhood* (1958), *Hymnal for Juniors in Worship and Study* (1966), and *Worship and Hymns for All Occasions* (1968). The latter volume was not sanctioned by the General Assembly and was designed as a companion to the Service for the Lord's Day. In 1966 John Knox Press issued *Songs and Hymns for Primary Children.*

The Hymnbook, 1955

The first hymnal authorized by the undivided church was published in 1831 under the title: *Psalms and Hymns adapted to public worship and approved by the General Assembly of the Presbyterian Church in the United States of America.* It was not until 1955 that another such volume would be issued. The initiative was taken in 1950 by the General Assembly of the Presbyterian Church in the U.S. when it charged its publication committee to "proceed with the compilation of a new hymnal, if possible in cooperation with other Presbyterian bodies for use of all Presbyterians in America, but, if not, then for our own church."[17] The invitation was accepted by four other denominations: Associate Reformed Presbyterian Church, Reformed Church in America, Presbyterian Church in the U.S.A., and United Presbyterian Church of North America. A committee of twenty-four men was formed from the five groups, with the U.S. church having the largest representation of ten, including the chair, Albert J. Kissling. The editor was David Hugh Jones, who served for many years as director of music at Princeton Theological Seminary. This group's diligence resulted in *The Hymnbook* (1955).

The preface of this book states:

> The interweaving of the strands of worship from five denominations, each with its own peculiar and precious heritage, has added immeasurable richness to the book. It has been responsible for the inclusion of many of the psalms in meter, a happy recovery of one of the great sources of strength of both the Genevan and the Scottish tradition. With the exception of a few metrical psalms taken directly from the Scottish Psalter of 1650, the version used in this hymnbook is the revision prepared in 1909 by a joint committee representing

nine Churches. . . . This concerted effort of five Churches has also secured the admission of a representative body of so-called "gospel songs," which properly have a place in the devotional life of the Church.

The inclusion of gospel songs had a mixed effect on the book's acceptance. Their presence was the deciding factor for many churches that had turned elsewhere for their church hymnal; but for others, particularly those in the U.S.A. churches, who used *The Hymnal* (1933), *The Hymnbook* appeared to be a backward step. Those assumptions aside, the collection had much to commend it, and it was certainly a vast improvement over the hymnals used by most of the cooperating denominations.

Among the committee there were at least three hymnological scholars: George Litch Knight, Austin C. Lovelace, and James R. Sydnor, all of whom had been influenced by the work of Clarence and Helen Dickinson when they studied at Union Theological Seminary in New York. The book reflects the same kind of scholarship that had begun with Louis F. Benson, and introduced to the churches a number of fine texts and tunes which had not appeared in the 1933 collection, including some folk and indigenous hymns. It was the first American Presbyterian hymnal to include all the various indexes at the back of the volume; it made a serious attempt to lower keys to more singable ranges; and the scripture readings are particularly noteworthy for their readability. This collection continues to serve many churches well.

The Worshipbook, 1972

Another joint venture followed in 1972 with *The Worshipbook.* Denominational support included the Cumberland Presbyterian Church, the Presbyterian Church in the U.S., and the United Presbyterian Church in the U.S.A., the latter reflecting the merger of two denominations which had participated in preparing the 1955 book. The title of the collection is indicative that it was more than a hymnal, and some might add, it was less than a hymnal! Actually it was issued in two forms: *The Worshipbook—Services* (1970) and *The Worshipbook—Services and Hymns* (1972). The first form was seen as a successor to *The Book of Common Worship* (1946), but went well beyond the concept of that earlier volume, expanding the services and prayers and centering around the three-year lectionary cycle. At the heart of the book is the Service for the Lord's Day, and in the 1972 book there are three musical settings for congregational responses included in that service. An early intention of *The Worshipbook* committee was to append one hundred hymns that would support this service. By the time of its completion, there were 363 hymns included, arranged alphabetically by title.

Many people agree that the book—both the texts of the worship materials and the hymns—suffers because of the turbulent time in which the committees functioned, and those who were charged with its preparation served more as reflectors of uncertainty rather than as prophets of the coming age. Society in general was reeling from political and emotional turmoil sparked by the Vietnam war and the civil rights crisis, and the ecclesiastical world was still sorting out the implications of Vatican II. It was a challenging time that called for bold action in the face of declining memberships, attendance, and influence. What those committees produced was disappointing and generally ineffectual. Some of the alterations of archaic pronouns and verbs appear to have been hastily made and violate rules of euphony. Sensitivity to feminists' concerns was not widespread at that time, and as a result there were no changes in language related to gender or male imagery. The alphabetical arrangement of the hymns reflects the sense of drift that was prevalent. The resulting pagination significantly weakens the book's usage because it is sometimes necessary to turn the page while singing a hymn. In its favor are the fresh materials that are included—some older hymns that had not found their way into Presbyterian collections and other newer hymns that widen the church's repertory of contemporary expression.

The weaknesses found in *The Worshipbook* were not peculiar to Presbyterians. *The Hymnal of the United Church of Christ* (1974) was a large step backward from its predecessor *The Pilgrim Hymnal* (1958). Both collections had a rather large number of materials prepared especially for them, and these items do not appear to be destined for long life.

Toward the Future

As the church looks toward the twenty-first century, it is encouraging to note that a brighter day for hymnody appears to be dawning. Just as *The Worshipbook* was published, there began a decade of lively interest in hymnological matters—a phenomenon that has been described as the "hymn explosion." This movement began in Great Britain with the work of hymn writers such as Fred Pratt Green, Erik Routley, Brian Wren, Fred Kaan, and Timothy Dudley Smith. The vitality and forcefulness of their writing has been widely appreciated on both sides of the Atlantic, and it has caused concerned church people to assess the whole gamut of hymnody, both these newer, provocative texts and older hymns that had been taken for granted. Most of these writers and many others have addressed the question of sexist language and have also grappled with outmoded imagery for God and Jesus Christ.

This recent legacy is already being shared in new hymnals such as *The Hymnal 1982* (Episcopal) and *Worship III* (Roman Catholic, 1986), and it has had a strong impact on the committee charged with the preparation of a new hymnal for Presbyterians—*The Presbyterian Hymnal: Hymns, Psalms, and Spiritual Songs,* published in 1990.

Among the facts gleaned by the committee's questionnaire to churches was this startling statistic: 32 percent of the pastors reporting said that their congregations had replaced their primary hymnbook within the last ten years. Almost half selected books published by non-Presbyterian concerns. It has been previously noted that conformity in using the denominational hymnal has never prevailed within the Presbyterian family. Such noncompliance is not peculiar to this denomination, but more liturgically oriented communions, including Episcopalians and Lutherans, are much more likely to use their official hymnals. This conformity is also applicable to the United Methodists who have had difficulty in filling orders for their new hymnal. Two of the most popular non-Presbyterian hymnals in current use are *Hymns for the Living Church* published in 1974 by Hope Publishing Company and edited by Donald P. Hustad and *Hymns for the Family of God* published two years later by Paragon Associates and edited by Fred Bock. Both of these hymnals include a far larger proportion of hymns that express personal piety than would be found in any of the denominational books. The latter book has an unusually large number of contemporary texts and tunes of the same ilk begun by Ira D. Sankey: theologically thin and musically vapid. It is beyond the scope of this study to determine the effect of these and other numerous examples of narcissistic religion, but one wonders how the mission of the church or the commands of Jesus Christ can be accomplished when congregations are offered such solipsistic fare as one finds here.

Defining a denomination's character and resolve by the hymns that it sings is a task of enormous depth. Here one can only make general suppositions about the impact of congregational song. Most observers of church music have determined empirically for generations that people judge or accept a hymn by its music rather than by its text; that fact remains to the present. For this reason it is incumbent upon those who select hymns for worship to give careful consideration to the theological content of the text without being seduced by the music. At the same time, one must judge the soundness of the music as an appropriate vehicle for a strong text.

The eclecticism of most hymnals declares loud and clear the tenet of the creed: "I believe in the holy catholic church." It is in our hymn singing that we affirm our ecumenism. James F. White, whose denominational affiliation is Methodist, comments on this growing trend: "Freed from old inhibitions, everyone shamelessly borrows from everyone else. Denominational hymnals, for example, have become an anomaly, the contents becoming more and more identical with each revision. If one's only criterion is finding the best hymnody available, denominational labels are no longer important."[18]

We are the richer for sharing in the wealth of expression that comes from all branches of Christendom, and to shy away from this practice would be a giant step backward. At the same time it is a healthy refreshment to take a serious look at the Reformed tradition of psalmody and to understand the attraction of those 150 poems which have sustained the Judeo-Christian community for centuries. The whole gamut of human emotions and God's involvement in those feelings is reflected there. To understand this fact is to gain a new appreciation of John Calvin's elevation of these texts. This revived interest in the Psalms is evident in the new Presbyterian hymnal of 1990 as well as the United Methodist hymnal which has recently been issued. Other current hymnals to bring fresh breath to the psalm-singing tradition are *Rejoice in the Lord* (1985) (Reformed Church in America) and the *Psalter Hymnal* (1987) (Christian Reformed Church in North America).

It is presumptuous to make sweeping forecasts about the future, but all signs point to a strong sense of resolve in the areas of music and worship for the Presbyterian Church, which shows signs of a deep commitment to excellence and faithfulness in these areas of the church's life. The Presbyterian Association of Musicians (PAM), which was founded in 1970 under the auspices of the Joint Office of Worship for the Presbyterian Church in the U.S. and in the U.S.A., continues as a vital link between worship leaders and congregations. Their work is supported by *Reformed Liturgy & Music,* a quarterly journal of high caliber, and through the sponsoring of national and regional workshops.[19]

As one reflects on almost any segment of history, it becomes apparent how strong individuals mold that history.

In this survey there are two names that come to the fore: Louis F. Benson and Clarence Dickinson. Both men viewed the past with discernment and approached the future with vision. The hymnals they edited became models not only in the Presbyterian fold but also for those in other denominations. Each was respectful of sentiment, but neither had time for sentimentality. The solidity and inclusiveness of their approach appears alive and well among the committee that has prepared the 1990 hymnal, a collection that should "equip the saints" for service well into the new century.

Following the lead of other recent collections, the committee of seventeen—Melva W. Costen, chairperson, and LindaJo McKim, hymnal editor—has been faithful to the directives of the General Assemblies of 1980 and 1983 to develop a hymnal "using inclusive language and sensitive to the diverse nature" of the church. Pluralism is reflected not only in the constituency of the committee but also in the inclusion of a number of ethnic and indigenous hymns. Texts and tunes are drawn from a wide variety of sources: a large body of time-tested European and American hymns; recent hymns from the spate of offerings of the last fifteen or twenty years; hymns of ethnic origin, including many of African-American background; and a moderate number of gospel hymns. Of particular interest are texts in languages other than English: Spanish, Korean, Chinese, Philippine, Tai, German, Latin, and Native American (The first stanza of "Amazing Grace" appears in five Native American languages). These selections reflect thoughtful balance and careful attention to diversity, not mere tokenism or faddism.

This is the first Presbyterian hymnal of denominational scope that reflects inclusive language, but the approach has been neither rigid nor radical. References to God as "Father" or "King" have been retained in many instances: "Father, We Praise Thee, Now the Night Is Over," "O Worship the King, All Glorious Above." And the word "mankind" remains in "Dear Lord and Father of Mankind." "Great Is Thy Faithfulness" carries an asterisk with the note that "my Father" may be sung "Creator." A bolder result may be seen in Henry Francis Lyte's version of Psalm 150, which now reads: "Praise the Lord, God's Glories Show" instead of "Praise the Lord, His Glories Show."

Offensive stanzas were dropped from hymns as in the case of "Be Thou My Vision" where these words appear: "Thou my great Father, I Thy true son." But alterations were made in other hymns: "Who serves my Father as a son is surely kin to me" sing "All children of the living God are surely kin to me." Two versions of Psalm 23 are included: the traditional text from the *Scottish Psalter* (1650) and a contemporary one by Christopher L. Webber in which there is no male imagery.

Responsible moderation are the definitive words for this collection which the committee hopes will serve the church for at least a generation.

The Presbyterian Hymnal: Hymns, Psalms, and Spiritual Songs (1990) includes Aids to Worship: Service for the Lord's Day, Apostles' Creed (English: traditional, ecumenical; Spanish and Korean), and Lord's Prayer (in the forms just cited). Hymns are arranged in three categories: Christian Year (Advent, Christmas, Epiphany, Baptism of the Lord, etc.); Psalms, and Topical Hymns (God, Jesus Christ, Holy Spirit, Holy Scripture, Life in Christ, Church, Morning and Opening Hymns, Sacraments and Ordinances, etc.). Service music and comprehensive indexes complete the collection.

One of the features of the hymnal which will characterize it as a Presbyterian collection is the special emphasis that is placed on psalmody. In a separate, designated section there are settings of seventy-three different psalms, most of which appear in metrical versions, but some of which are intended for chanting or responsive reading. Many of them are given more than one version; Psalm 23, for instance, has six different settings. A variety of historic periods is represented: the Scottish and English Reformation, the work of Isaac Watts, the joint Reformed-Presbyterian psalter of the early part of this century, and contemporary translations. The Genevan Psalter tradition is honored by the inclusion of several tunes from that famous collection. These seventy-three psalms correspond to the three-year lectionary cycle and provide a rich resource for deepening and enlivening the worship experience for congregations.

No hymnal can be judged ultimately until it has stood the test of congregational use, but it can be said with a large measure of confidence that this collection with its strong commitment for balance, a serious regard for the Reformed tradition, its clear, readable format, and overall intention to address the worship needs of the whole church will serve the church for many years to come. It stands in worthy succession to the work of Louis F. Benson and Clarence Dickinson.

Although the current hymnic scene reflects movement from the sanctuary to the world outside cloistered walls, it does not refute the magnetism of the *mysterium tremendum.* The heightening of social consciousness that began in the early decades of the century has broadened considerably, and hymns that deal with urban blight, the environment, peace, justice, and racial equality have multiplied to good effect. As the dichotomy between spiritual and social facets of humanity fades, we can only hope that the gap between the language of Sundays and the verbiage of other days narrows. Hymnody, no doubt, will play a major part in closing the breach that has existed far too long.

7

The Language(s) of Zion: Presbyterian Devotional Literature in the Twentieth Century

Mark A. Noll and Darryl G. Hart

To study comprehensively the devotional materials used by twentieth-century Presbyterians would be a profoundly rewarding task. It would also be a task beset with great difficulties. This essay, which draws on selective reading from books produced by the Westminster Press and John Knox Press, can only scratch the surface of a protean subject. A thorough study would go much further. It would have to determine, not just what official Presbyterian boards and publishers issued, but what Presbyterians actually read, and so would probably be as much a study in the influence of Walter Rauschenbusch, Henry Drummond, C. S. Lewis, Billy Graham, Harvey Cox, and Henri Nouwen as of distinctly Presbyterian authors. It would have to make a much more sophisticated determination of what counts as "devotional literature" than we have done, which was to peruse books cataloged as "devotional" in major Presbyterian libraries or designated as "devotional" by the Presbyterian publishers.[1] Popular biblical exposition, week-by-week Sunday school material, periodicals in an infinite variety, novels, poetry, hymns, published sermons, reprinted spiritual classics, social commentary, books directing daily meditation, and even more—all may properly be "devotional," if the word is defined simply as writing designed to draw common audiences into closer fellowship with God.[2]

A comprehensive study of devotional materials would also examine the mechanics of publishing and the networks of dissemination: What have Presbyterian publishers designated as "devotional"? Who are the authors of this material—pastors, seminary professors, lay people, denominational officials, or yet others? How widely does such material circulate in comparison with other kinds of Presbyterian literature and in comparison with devotional literature from non-Presbyterian sources? And important structural questions touch the content of the works themselves. For example, are there shifts over time in the portions of scripture featured most prominently in these writings? Again, does the reading level of the books become simpler or more complex over the course of the century?

Finally, a thorough study would have to situate devotional literature in the larger story of the Presbyterians, a story shaped by depression and prosperity as well as by discipleship and preaching; a story intertwined with radio, television, and the satellite dish as well as with Sunday school, the Lord's Supper, and seminary education; a story sharing the history of the Republican Party, the growth of professionalization, and a rise of geographic mobility as well as the history of General Assemblies, denominational publications, and the Revised Standard Version. These and other venues compose an immensely fruitful, but also immensely complicated, research agenda. To repeat, this essay is not such a comprehensive study. It is rather a preliminary probe, offering only preliminary observations about officially sponsored Presbyterian devotional publications in the twentieth century.

One last, important caveat to keep in mind is that books from John Knox Press and Westminster Press have always reflected the presses' ecumenical character. Therefore, some of the works mentioned below actually were written by non-Presbyterians, though published by publishing houses sponsored by the two major Presbyterian denominations.[3]

Presbyterian Attitudes Toward Piety

In the fall of 1911, Benjamin B. Warfield, professor of didactic and polemic theology at Princeton Seminary, was asked to address the student body at the start of an academic year on a devotional subject, "The Religious Life of Theological Students." This Warfield did, first by stressing the compatibility of inner spirituality and mental exertion, then by recommending the importance of common worship for the one who would be a minister of the gospel, and finally by describing what he called "the foundation-stone of your piety," which was "to be found, of course, in your closets, or rather in your hearts, in your private religious exercises, and in your intimate religious aspirations." He ended his speech with a ringing challenge that contrasted the drift of American values with a notable example from America's Reformed heritage.

> In the tendencies of modern life, which all make for ceaseless—I had almost said thoughtless, meaningless—activity, have a care. . . . Do you pray? How much do you pray? How much do you love to pray? What place in your life does the "still hour" alone with God take?
>
> I am sure that if you once get a true glimpse of what the ministry of the cross is, for which you are preparing, and of what you, as men preparing for this ministry, should be, . . . your whole soul will be wrung with the petition: Lord, make me sufficient for these things. Old Cotton Mather wrote a great little book once, to serve as a guide to students for the ministry. The not very happy title which he gave it is *Manductio ad Ministerium.* But by a stroke of genius he added a subtitle which is more significant. And this is the sub-title he added: *The angels preparing to sound the trumpets.* That is what Cotton Mather calls you, students for the ministry; the angels, preparing to sound the trumpets! Take the name to yourselves, and live up to it. Give your days and nights to living up to it! And then, perhaps, when you come to sound the trumpets the note will be pure and clear and strong, and perchance may pierce even to the grave and wake the dead.[4]

Three quarters of a century after Warfield's address, the Westminster Press in Philadelphia published a symposium on a similar theme entitled *Spiritual Dimensions of Pastoral Care.* One of the contributors to this volume, John Patton, chose to write on "The New Language of Pastoral Counseling." Patton recommended that pastors heed important recent trends in "the psychological sciences." These trends were "attempting to move toward new theories that are closer to human experiencing." The theories stressed "empathy" as the prime virtue in spiritual direction and made much of the usefulness of "symbol and story." Patton was indeed "committed to the importance of Christian theological meaning" in pastoral work, but also was sure that "the problem of theological language" had become acute. That is, overtly theological reflection on the human condition had only limited usefulness because most who now sought pastoral counseling did not share "membership in the same religious community," and very often the person being counseled did not want "to think of life in Christian theological terms." Patton regretted this absence of shared theological concepts, but was not too discouraged, since his experience had taught him a more important lesson. As he put it, "Perhaps the most important thing about the language of pastoral counseling is its awareness of the limits of language." Better to pursue the special character of the counseling situation, he seemed to say, than to rue in vain the lost theological consensus. "We have been taught in our clinical work," Patton noted, "to resonate with the affect in a situation—to go after the feeling." He ended his essay by noting how the new language of pastoral counseling stresses *"relational humanness."* "Pastoral counseling is, most importantly, the offering of relationship . . . and using that relationship to help the counselee learn a more satisfying way to deal with all the relationships of life." Finally, the authorities whom Patton cites are twentieth-century figures, including other pastoral theologians, psychologists like Heinz Kohut, Roy Shafer, and Carl Rogers, and more general figures like Walker Percy.[5]

Warfield's address of 1911 and Patton's essay of 1985 are not devotional works, strictly considered. They do, however, illustrate graphically the changed circumstances of officially sponsored Presbyterian devotional writing in the twentieth century. Warfield, the self-conscious theologian, looked to the history of the Christian church for examples of devotion. For him devotion was a response to revelation from a transcendent God. In addition, it was axiomatic that piety be nurtured *"of course"* in the solitary exercises of the prayer closet. Patton, the self-conscious clinician, looked to the history of modern psychotherapy for examples of human flourishing. For him, devotion grew as humans experienced God immanently in their circumstances. In addition, it was a bold new discovery that this human flourishing could be found in "relational humanness." The contrast between Warfield and Patton is so striking that it hardly seems possible that the two could be part of the same ecclesiastical tradition.

The dramatic contrast between the address of Warfield and the essay of Patton is heightened, moreover, when some note is taken of wider contexts. Those wider contexts concern general Presbyterian assumptions about piety. To oversimplify the situation, at the start of the century Presbyterians seemed to enjoy a common framework of expectations and a common set of assumptions about piety. By the mid-1980s, by contrast, Presbyterian attitudes toward piety had become as pluralistic as Presbyterian theology and Presbyterian social attitudes.

It may come as a surprise, but for most of the twentieth century, Presbyterians shared a common language of piety. This commonality was manifest, for example, when in 1906 the northern Presbyterians issued a *Book of Common Worship.* The chair of the committee that prepared the book was Henry van Dyke. Those who have studied Presbyterian history know that Henry van Dyke's theological disposition opposed B. B. Warfield's in many particulars. Yet the preface to *The Book of Common Worship* could as easily have been written by Warfield as by Van Dyke. That preface assumed that the life of devotion would focus on the actions of a transcendent God, that the scriptures were the touchstone of piety, and that the resources of church history offered the fullest treasure for the cultivation of spirituality in the present. As the compilers of *The Book of Common Worship* put it,

> We have studied earnestly to embody the truths of our Holy Religion in the language of orderly devotion, to the end that by the Sacraments, the stated Ordinances of the Lord's Day, and all the ordinary and occasional offices of the Church, men may be both instructed and confirmed in the faith of Jesus Christ. We have searched the Holy Scriptures, the usage of the Reformed Churches, and the devotional treasures of early Christianity, for the most noble, clear, and moving expressions of the Spirit of Praise and Prayer; and we have added to these ancient and venerable forms and models, such others as might serve, under the guidance of the same Spirit, to give a voice to the present needs, the urgent desires, and the vital hopes of the Church living in these latter days and in the freedom of this Republic.[6]

A decade after the northern Presbyterians issued their *Book of Common Worship,* Harry Emerson Fosdick, at that time a homiletics professor at Union Seminary, but soon to be installed as the pulpit supply of New York's First Presbyterian Church, published a book of daily readings called *The Meaning of Prayer.* In it Fosdick offered daily devotionals consisting of a passage of scripture, a brief meditation, and a prayer taken from a figure in church history. It says a very great deal about the commonalities of piety in a day of fragmenting theology that Presbyterian conservatives, who soon would see Fosdick as the epitome of decadent modernism, appreciated the book and felt its piety was much like their own.[7]

Seventy years later the consensus on piety had clearly dissolved. Another essay in *Spiritual Dimensions of Pastoral Care* explains and illustrates that dissolution. Wayne E. Oates, in whose honor this book was published, contributed an essay that differed sharply from John Patton's celebration of "The New Language of Pastoral Counseling." Oates's theme was "The Power of Spiritual Language in Self-understanding." Like Patton, Oates had also experienced the increasing problem in using traditional theological language, but unlike Patton, this was to Oates a matter for grave regret.

> The wholesale branding of spiritual language as unintelligible God talk, the increasing secularization of American education, the severing of technological education from the humanities, and the intensive specialization of professional education . . . have shattered the English language itself into as many dialects of sophistication in the helping professions as there were dialects in England before Wycliffe's translation, Caxton's work, the King James Bible, and Shakespeare's writing. We are a people "without one language and few words." We leave off building a common self-understanding of our spiritual selfhood, of our healing in time of suffering, and our redemption in the face of our mortality and death.

Given this situation, Oates called, not for a simple acceptance of the new jargons, but for a studied effort to translate, as he put it, "the dialects of the secularized value systems of the behavioral sciences into the wisdom, words, and power of the good news of God in Jesus Christ." To that end, Oates called upon voices of the Christian past, including John Calvin and Martin Luther. To reinforce the need for confession, he aptly put the Bible to use in confronting the problems of modern men and women, and he was as eager to challenge the conventions of this age as to renovate the insights of the past. While appreciating what he called "psychiatric categories," he also warned that "these categories . . . can easily become a yoke of bondage, just as other religious rituals and prescriptions. They can become vested interests of power, idols in themselves. They can prompt the necessity for a return again and again of a Spirit that offers a yoke that is easy and a burden that is light, a faith imbued with joy."[8]

The contrast between Oates's assessment of pastoral counseling and Patton's—at least as revealed in these two essays—is almost as striking as that between Warfield, Van Dyke, and Fosdick early in the century and Patton at the end. With those earlier Presbyterians, Oates finds piety, devotion, and human flourishing grounded in scripture, theology, and the history of the church. He is more impressed than his predecessors earlier in the century with what psychology and other social sciences may offer to the pastoral counselor, but with them he shares the belief that transcendence, the Bible, and church tradition are the wellsprings of piety. Voices like Oates's testify, therefore, to substantial continuity throughout the twentieth century in descriptions of piety sponsored by Presbyterians, even as his differences with contemporaries like Patton illustrate powerfully the divide among modern Presbyterians concerning the nature of Christian devotion.

Emphasis on the Bible

Before World War II the predominant note in Presbyterian devotional literature was the Bible. In 1925 the southern Presbyterian's Committee of Publication issued M. Ryerson Turnbull's popular *Studying the Book of Exodus* in which brief reference to contemporary religious figures like Dwight L. Moody and introductory deference to theological themes like the covenant rapidly gave way to a concentration on the content of the biblical book. Turnbull took for his motto "Apply thyself wholly to the text, apply the text wholly to thyself."[9] The same note loomed large in Howard Tillman Kuist's *How to Enjoy the Bible,* published by John Knox Press in 1939. Kuist, who taught English Bible at Princeton Seminary, advised those who would find God to read the Bible more than books about the Bible and, above all, to "listen for the Voice" to be found in the scriptures.[10] In 1942 the northern church's Board of National Missions issued a booklet entitled *Great Peace Have They* for women anxious about loved ones in combat. The first chapter showed how to read the Bible, with special concern for its personalities and its attitudes toward world affairs. Most of the rest of the booklet applied a range of scriptures, especially from the life of Christ, to the question of finding peace amid the turmoil of life. Until at least 1950 the Presbyterian publishers seem to have subsumed devotional literature into the more general categories established by published sermons and popular scriptural commentary.[11] A 1958 history of the northern Presbyterian's official publishing efforts highlighted biblical works—including Margaret Lamos's *Old Testament Bible Lessons for the Home,* J. Carter Swaim's *Right and Wrong Way to Use the Bible,* and Joy Davidman's exposition of the Ten Commandments *Smoke on the Mountain*—as the heart of its devotional publishing.[12]

Concentration on the Bible in devotional literature continued as an important note into the 1950s. Robert McAfee Brown's *The Bible Speaks to You,* one of Westminster Press's "50 all-time best-sellers," was published in 1955. It was a lively, engaging, and traditionally pious book that, while noting the Bible's importance for social reform and politics, still stressed the way that scripture conveyed the message of a transcendent God. As Brown described that being, "he's not a 'safe' or 'tame' God, securely lodged behind the bars of a distant heaven; he has the most annoying manner of showing up when we least want him; of confronting us in the strangest ways. And he usually turns out to be very different from the sort of God we would have invented for ourselves."[13] Similar themes and approaches inspired Joseph M. Gettys's *How to Study John,* which John Knox Press published in 1960. This book took as its utterly traditional aim the effort to introduce Christ to the seeking by study of the Fourth Gospel.

Along with a traditional concentration on the Bible, devotional literature into the early 1960s also often made considerable room for the voices of the Christian past. Popular devotional writing, by its very nature, has never been overly pedagogical in its use of history, but within the traditions of Roman Catholicism and the churches of the Magisterial Reformation, a considered respect for classic spiritual experience has always held a secure place. So it continued to be with the Presbyterians in the period after World War II. Owen M. Weatherly's *The Fulfillment of Life* from John Knox Press in 1959 called upon witnesses from the past to describe God's laws of truth, liberty, and kindness, and to show how these laws might be fulfilled by divine grace. Weatherly did quote George Washington, Al-fred North Whitehead, Robert Burns, and Dorothy Sayers to make some of his points, but he also had room for stalwarts of the Reformed traditions, including John Calvin, Martin Luther, James Henley Thornwell, Louis Berkhof, and Emil Brunner. In the same year John Knox Press published a book of readings entitled *In His Likeness,* on "the imitation of Christ through the centuries," edited by G. McLeod Bryan. This volume was eclectic, with selections from St. Francis, Erasmus, William Penn, and Dietrich Bonhoeffer, but prominent as well were readings from Reformed leaders like Calvin. A similar immersion in the acknowledged guides of Reformed spirituality could be found in J. K. S. Reid's *Our Life in Christ,* the 1960 Warfield Lectures at Princeton Seminary published by Westminster Press in 1963. Besides full attention to the Bible—especially Genesis, Matthew, John, and Romans—Reid also drew freely on the history of the church, with Calvin put to use only slightly less often than Karl Barth.

Even as late as the early 1960s, therefore, much of what had been traditional in Presbyterian devotional literature was still being served up by the denominational publishers. Piety rooted in the scriptures, attempts to make theology livable, free use of notable historical examples as the prime spiritual authorities—these were the marks of traditional Presbyterian devotion.

The apparent unity of devotional literature and its common focus on the scriptures until roughly 1960 are all the more striking in the light of the growing theological pluralism among American Presbyterians. As early as the 1920s the well-publicized theological struggles in the General Assembly were reflected in lists of spiritual reading materials provided by competing publishers. In April 1920, for example, the Presbyterian Board of Publication took out an advertisement in *The Presbyterian* to promote works by Shailer Mathews, Henry Churchill King, Henry Sloane Coffin, and Harry Emerson Fosdick. In April 1926, the Presbyterian Publishing Company was advertising in *Presbyterian Life* works of very different theological tendency by Francis L. Patton, Clarence Macartney, Abraham

Kuyper, J. Gresham Machen, and John D. Davis as "Publications of Outstanding Value and Significance."[14] In the 1930s and 1940s, it was widely held that the northern Presbyterians had embraced a more pluralistic theology than their southern counterparts. Yet despite growing theological diversity, Presbyterians continued to assume that the life of devotion grew best in the soil of scripture and could be cultivated with the traditional means of evangelical piety.

Signs of change marked the devotional literature of the late 1950s, and emerged with full force in the decade of the 1960s. Care must be taken in describing these changes, however, because they did not involve the wholesale replacement of one set of concepts with another. Rather, they involved the addition of a new language of spiritual life alongside of, and sometimes interwoven with, the traditional concepts of evangelical piety. John B. Coburn's *Twentieth-Century Spiritual Letters,* published by Westminster Press in 1958, was a harbinger. This book by the dean of the Episcopal Theological Seminary in Cambridge, Massachusetts, was "an introduction to contemporary prayer" that was more concerned with present possibilities than with past ecclesiastical resources. Coburn called his effort "an introduction to contemporary spirituality," one of the first times that a Presbyterian book put to use that generic term instead of more traditional words like "godliness" or "holiness."[15] The next year, Lewis S. Mudge, theological secretary of the World Presbyterian Alliance, published with Westminster Press a book on the need for world consciousness entitled *In His Service.* Mudge's exhortation, that his readers forsake a preoccupation with theology in order to find a truth that could be applied, amounted to a sign of dissatisfaction with devotional language rooted in traditional concepts. That same year Westminster Press published a volume by David Wesley Soper, professor of religion at Beloit College, which also reflected changed expectations. While the book's title *God Is Inescapable* sounded traditional, its emphasis on the way readers might find truth and purpose by better understanding their own consciousness was not.

"Modern Devotion"

The new orientation toward piety, hinted at in these works from the 1950s, came into its own in the next decade. With variations, it has remained a staple of Presbyterian devotional literature since then. This "modern devotion" was extraordinarily varied, for one of its key tenets was that every passage of life may promote human development and so augment piety. Thus, books on spirituality for the aged, the divorced, the bereaved, the homemaker, the young, and the affluent became a regular feature of the offerings from Westminster Press and John Knox Press. Examples included Erma Hallmark's *Here in This House* (John Knox Press, 1975), Louis Baer's *Let the Patient Decide* (Westminster Press, 1978), Miriam Nye's *But I Never Thought He'd Die* (Westminster Press, 1978), William Thompson's *Devotions for the Divorcing* (John Knox Press, 1985), and David Maitland's *Aging: A Time for New Learning* (John Knox Press, 1987). Richard Ray, the editor of John Knox Press during the 1970s, has well captured the purposes, but also the limitations, of the publishing strategy that led to such books. "Looking at what we did produce, I think that we thought we should direct devotional publications to specific uses. That is to say an upbeat, entirely contemporary idea of marketing made a significant contribution to the design of the books. . . . Instead of producing books which mined the richness of the Christocentric devotional tradition, our particular heritage looked to the function of the book to meet the strategic needs of readers in certain circumstances."[16]

As varied as devotional literature had become, it is still possible to make general statements about the new trend. First, authors of the new devotional literature were impatient with traditional theological foundations for piety, or rejected them entirely. Second, they were fascinated with the self.

In theological terms, the new devotional literature largely rejected a set of dichotomies that had provided the framework for traditional materials of Presbyterian devotion. For example, the holiness of all life came to replace the dichotomy between sacred and secular. In 1963, Joseph McLelland's *Living for Christ* from John Knox Press proposed "a radical and creative Christian approach" as an alternative to a "selfish, materialistic way of life."[17] The book took its cue from the first question of the Westminster Shorter Catechism, which the author held to have obliterated all distinctions between the sacred and the secular. God's love, according to McLelland, was applicable to all people in all situations. E. Glenn Hinson, in the 1974 Westminster Press book, *A Serious Call to a Contemplative Life-Style,* welcomed secularization, as defined by Harvey Cox's *Secular City,* since it broke down the artificial compartmentalization of life that had characterized many churches. The search for the sacred in all of life led Frederick Happold, in a 1975 John Knox Press book *The Journey Inwards,* to recommend Christian Yoga and Zen Buddhism as aids to "contemplative meditation by normal people."

Authors who found sacred-secular dichotomies obsolete were open to new ways of posing the relationship of God to the world. E. Glenn Hinson's *A Serious Call to a Contemplative Lifestyle,* for example, showed how native human instincts would carry us back to a Tillichian "ground of our being." And he felt that the process theologians— Charles Hartshorne, Norman Pittenger, and especially Pierre Teilhard de Chardin—pointed the way to a better spirituality. Moderns did suffer from a loss of transcendence, Hinson felt, but that loss could be supplied by art and poetry, dancing, and even drugs (but only for those of "great emotional maturity"), as well as through the more traditional means of prayer, fasting, and reading the Bible along with other devotional literature.[18]

A final dichotomy superseded in the newer devotional literature was sin and grace. Brian Grant's *From Sin to Wholeness,* published by Westminster Press in 1982, explored ways of counteracting the seven deadly sins. Traditionally pious remedies were effective, to be sure, but Grant felt that it was even more profitable to regard our problems as unfulfilled needs crying out for creative solutions than to define them simply as sin.

The language of "human need," which contributed to the different theological orientation, pointed to the second important characteristic of the new devotional material. A major premise of its exposition was the importance of self-realization, a premise expressed in numerous ways. In 1972, A. J. Ungersma showed his readers how the Divided Self, the Conflicted Self, the Isolated Self, and the Problematic Self could become the Complete Self. The next year Dennis Benson offered "the electric tools of electric love" as a means for becoming "authentically human as God in Jesus was and is."[19] William Jones provided *A Guide to Living Power*, published by John Knox Press in 1975, in which he urged readers to follow Jesus and Paul in recognizing that slavish knuckling under to the law was an obstacle to personal growth. Positive thinking and the right mental exercises were often enough to end physical disorders. "As your liberated Christian spirit begins to strengthen with these exercises [recommended in the book]," Jones wrote, "you will discover that because you do not think about headaches, insomnia, indigestion, ulcers, these will disappear."[20] And Wolfhart Pannenberg's *Christian Spirituality* bemoaned the "penitential mentality" of pietistic Protestantism that frustrated the creation of a unified "self-concept." As an antidote, Pannenberg thought that Buddhism could contribute positively to the Christian's search for an "authentic self."[21]

Within Presbyterian devotional literature from the early 1960s, in other words, readers found a new theological orientation and a new attitude toward the self. It goes almost without saying that, when expounding these convictions, devotional authors made little use of traditional authorities for whom older theological dichotomies framed the doorway to heaven and for whom fixation on the self looked like idolatry.

At the same time, the general situation for Presbyterian devotional literature was not entirely simple. For one thing, some of those who promoted the newer perceptions retained considerable elements of the old. For example, Suzanne de Dietrich's meditation on the Gospel of John (Westminster Press, 1969) employed the language of "listening and contemplating" that had become *de rigueur* in the new devotion, but also wrote of Christ and his work for humanity in terms that recalled traditional patterns. Westminster Press also published works by Paul Tournier, such as his *Reflections* in 1982, which similarly combined the modern vocabulary of the self with considerable traditional material.

In addition, Presbyterian publishers continued to provide devotional material similar in assumptions and execution to the standards of Warfield, Van Dyke, and Fosdick early in the century. Books using parts of the Bible, or readings from scripture, as an aid to prayer or contemplation remained a staple. William Barclay's seventeen-volume *Daily Study Bible—New Testament* from Westminster Press was an especially popular fund of such material, combining as it did thoughtful exegesis with warm devotion.[22] Books of shorter readings or meditations, in which biblical material featured more prominently than modern psychology, were also a regular part of annual lists.[23] The situation by the mid-1980s, in short, was one in which a traditional language of Protestant piety coexisted alongside the newer languages of self-fulfillment and divine immanence. A graphic illustration of the situation fostered by the contrasting conceptions is the list of "50 all-time best-sellers" provided by Westminster Press in its 1987 catalog. The list is strikingly diverse. Titles that could be categorized generally as "devotional" include both Paul A. Hauck's *Overcoming Depression* (1973), a book dominated by the thought of Albert Ellis and innocent of reference to Christ or the Bible, as well as Roberta Hestenes's *Using the Bible in Groups* (1985), which promotes scripture, the whole scripture, and nothing but scripture.

The confusion, or possibilities, depending upon one's

point of view, opened up by the conjunction of the two devotional languages is well illustrated in two ambitious series that Westminster published in the mid-1980s: Spirituality and the Christian Life and Potentials: Guides for Productive Living.

A few of the books in these series came close to embodying the new devotional emphases with little remainder. William Stringfellow's *Politics of Spirituality,* for example, argued that spirituality involved the whole person not just the soul. The conclusion Stringfellow drew from this premise was that the political realm should be a principal arena for the growth of piety. Or as he put it, "Politics describes the work of the Word of God in this world for redemption and the impact of that effect of the Word of God upon the fallen existence of this world, including the fallen life of human beings and that of the powers that be."[24] Other authors portrayed piety as issuing in a protest against nuclear arms or in affirmation of a simple life-style.[25] In these and other instances, the authors reiterated a leitmotif of the 1960s, that the spiritual was to be found *in* the world rather than in separation from it.

The language of self-fulfillment also loomed large in the two series. To Myron Madden, "the spiritual task . . . is the task of becoming and owning the self we are and rejecting the temptation to eliminate that part of our self that we don't like." Madden's volume, entitled *Claim Your Heritage,* took time to explore the resources provided in scripture for personal well-being. But his analysis of biblical passages had a distinctly contemporary ring. God, he concluded, "wants you to affirm his creation, beginning with yourself. Affirming yourself and choosing your self, is an act of the Spirit, the starting place of the New Order."[26] Edward E. Thornton's contribution to the Potentials series, *Being Transformed: An Inner Way of Spiritual Growth,* depicted spirituality in similar terms. Life's most important questions could not be answered by studying Greek and Hebrew; they were only obscured by what Thornton called the "tyrannical conscience formed in a Victorian, pietistic clan and church"; and they would not yield to "rational ways of knowing." Rather, meditation, silence, body awareness, measured breathing, and other techniques provided by the psychological sciences offered a way to find the true self and, thus, by this "inner way," to "experience the presence of God directly."[27] To Helen Barnette in *Your Child's Mind,* the first thing children needed in order to mature properly was to feel good about themselves. Other necessary ingredients for the mental growth of children included a sense of wonder, definite goals for living, clear moral standards, and an ability to connect causes and effects. Traditional injunctions to love Jesus, read the Bible, or even to consider one's guilt before God had no place in such a developmental scheme. While not as prominent in all of the books in the two series, the newer stress on self-awareness and self-fulfillment was evident in many of the volumes.

At the same time, however, as a balance to immanentist self-fulfillment, the Westminster series also comprehended arguments and advice that, while couched in contemporary language, forthrightly advocated traditional notions of devotion. Thus, Paul Holmer argued in *Making Christian Sense* that the basis for Christian morality lay not in the resources of the self but in the actions of a transcendent God over against humanity. The imputation of divine righteousness means, he suggested, that virtue is not required in order to please God. Morality, and, by implication, self-fulfillment, are good, but as means of getting along in the practical circumstances of life, rather than as means of ultimate justification. In a book entitled *The Strengths of a Christian,* Robert Roberts made something of the same distinction. Christian spirituality was different from other kinds of spirituality because of how God acted toward humanity in Jesus Christ. The ability to practice the virtues was a result of the Holy Spirit's life-bringing power. Again, in other volumes in the two series similar themes could be heard. And in many of the books, even in those most in synch with modern conceptions, the Bible held a central place. Sometimes more a diffuse inspiration or a simple source of quotation than an authority deferred

to automatically, scripture nonetheless remained prominent. This feature of recent writing suggests substantial
continuity with older devotional styles.

The most interesting books in the series were no doubt
those in which the two languages of devotion were inter-
mingled. Wayne Oates's contributions are perhaps the best
example of that fusion. His book *Your Right to Rest*
sounded the modern note of spiritual utilitarianism by
suggesting that the words of Jesus were the master guides
both "to the realization of your own potentials and to productive living in the nitty-gritty of your day's work." Yet
much of the exposition of the book—on the rhythms of
life, sleep, prayer, greed, and home—amounted to sustained meditations on biblical teaching, culminating in an
appeal to see the gospel, not as a burden to be achieved,
but as Christ's invitation to rest in his way of grace.[28] In a
similar fashion his book, *Convictions That Give You Confidence,* asked readers, who "have been intimidated by the
negative," to "decide now to draw on positive strengths."
But the bulk of the study was an effort to show, through
extensive employment of the scriptures, that Christian
convictions, which Oates expressed in quite traditional
terms, led up to the purpose of all life, which was, in
Oates's quotation of 2 Timothy 1:12, to "know *whom* I
believe."[29] Such exposition, of which the two series contained a great deal, showed the new and old devotional
forms mixed thoroughly with one another.

That such a mixture carries its own uncertainties, however, is attested by the range of authorities the authors
drew upon for their devotional purposes. As might be expected in series aimed at a wide readership, references to
movies, like *Chariots of Fire* and *E.T.,* were frequent. The
authors also put to use popular modern authors like Rabbi
Harold S. Kushner and Chuck Swindoll out of, one assumes, a similar desire to connect with a contemporary
audience. The use of more academic authorities was, however, as mixed as the devotional styles themselves. William Arnold, in an effort to describe "theologically . . .
what it means to be human," drew mostly on the psycholo-

gists Carl Jung, William Glasser, Erik Erikson, and Aaron Beck.[30] Richard Bell made more use of Christian tradition, but leaned to the Catholic and Orthodox: Alexander Schmemann, Simone Weil, and John of the Cross. A few of the writers cited figures from the Reformed tradition, but Wayne Oates was a rarity in his reference to Calvin.[31] What even a casual examination of quotations and authorities suggests is that Presbyterian devotional writing in the 1980s enjoyed or was cursed by (again depending upon standpoint) unusual pluralism and diversity.

Westminster's two series offer the most impressive examples of recent devotional writing sponsored by American Presbyterians. As found in the series, the range of that writing is very broad, and its orientations are multiform in the extreme. Many of the books testify to concentrated efforts at communicating Christian spirituality to contemporary lay people who lack grounding in even basic theology. Most of them also have very little use for the long history of Christian devotion. In a word, where Presbyterians once shared a language of devotion derived from traditional theological resources, they now possess a profusion of devotional constructs. Some are obvious descendants of patterns to be found earlier in the century. Others are as different from that earlier literature as night is from day.

Conclusions

Several conclusions are possible from even this preliminary survey of Presbyterian devotional writing in the twentieth century. A first is that devotional writing has a resonance all its own, whether traditional and saturated with scripture or modern and big with the self. At its best, as in some of the works of Robert McAfee Brown, the prose of Presbyterian devotion is sprightly and engaging. It is not too harsh to add, however, that a pall of the hortatory broods over much of Presbyterian devotional writing. Devotional writers set out with great sincerity to describe the liberations of divine grace, but all too easily—on behalf of what is traditional or in support of what is trendy—

they end by imposing the mandates of necessity. *Facere quod in se est,* they seem to say: Do what is within you—read the Bible, pray in this or that way, attend to Zen, see God everywhere, nurture yourself to the full—and you shall be saved. The most enduring devotional writing, from throughout the Christian centuries as well as from Presbyterians in the twentieth century, strengthens the bruised reed. The examples that pass most rapidly away—again throughout history and in the recent past—quench the smoldering flax.

Beyond such matters of form, it is altogether obvious that Presbyterian devotional materials have shared in the transit of the twentieth century. This literature is a faithful barometer of contemporary change. Have Presbyterian devotional writings recently taken the inward turn and become spiritual manuals of self-help? So, it must be said, has most devotional writing by other American Protestants.[32] James Smylie once perceptively described the situation of family worship among Presbyterians over the last century in terms of three crises: the crisis of the Sabbath and the secularization of time and space; the crisis of the family and the professionalization of religious services; and the crisis of faith and the trivialization of life.[33] The same crises have exerted every bit as much impact on Presbyterian devotional writing. Perhaps in the light of such considerations, the wonder is not that so much of this literature mimics the received wisdom of the age, but that any of it does not.

From a longer historical view, the presence of competing devotional languages among late-twentieth-century American Presbyterians seems to be repeating a persistent Protestant pattern. Early in the Reformation Thomas Müntzer railed at Luther's insistence on external authority as "Bible, Babel, bubble," and Luther responded by conceding he would not believe Müntzer if "he swallowed the Holy Ghost feathers and all." Little more than a century later Roger Williams, acting in the uncharacteristic role of cultural conservative, upbraided George Fox for supplanting the sure word of scripture in favor of the Quakers' vaporous Inner Light of Christ. In the nineteenth century, Edwards Amasa Park, Charles Hodge, and Horace Bushnell debated the question whether God is best known objectively or subjectively. And drowning out almost all other discussions within the Protestantism of the last century is the roar of Karl Barth's "nein!" to Friedrich Schleiermacher's belief that the human feeling of dependence charts the surest path to God.[34] So it has been no new thing for Protestants to debate the relative merits of devotion grounded in external revelation as opposed to devotion welling up from human resources within. From this angle, Presbyterians since the 1960s have merely joined a debate that began before the Reformation was a decade old.

From another angle, however, the contrast in devotional languages is more significant than simply another illustration of spiritual yin and yang. Something as profound as Reformed identity itself may be at stake in the dialogue between the traditional language of biblical and historical piety and the new language of self-expression and divine immanence. The range of questions worried by devotional writers is narrow. Who am I? Who is God? Who am I in relation to God? To be sure, infinite variation is possible when responding. But the general drift of answers to questions about how we come to know God and ourselves is as vital as anything could possibly be for the fate of a Christian church. The supreme importance of devotional orientation, however, is a matter hardly needing to be stressed among Presbyterians, who trace their genesis, at least in part, to a devotional writing by a young scholar introduced with the words, "Nearly all the wisdom we possess, that is to say, true and sound wisdom, consists of two parts: the knowledge of God and of ourselves."[35]

8

From Old to New Agendas: Presbyterians and Social Issues in the Twentieth Century

Benton Johnson

Anyone familiar with the recent history of the churches of the Protestant "mainline"[1] in the United States is aware that the national conventions and assemblies of these denominations have adopted positions on a wide variety of social issues that are quite different from the positions they previously held. On such issues as abortion, homosexuality, and civil disobedience, they have made pronouncements and adopted programs that would have been unthinkable just a few decades ago.

Many observers have claimed that in taking these stands the mainline denominations have abandoned a distinctively Christian witness and embraced the values and policy preferences of the secular left. Just recently, for example, Robert Booth Fowler wrote that the "activist leaders" of the mainline denominations "appear to parallel . . . the left wing of the Democratic party."[2] In the opinion of Wade Clark Roof and William McKinney, both astute sociological observers of mainline religion, "by the late 1950s the liberal religious faith and modern liberal culture were virtually indistinguishable."[3]

But despite widespread agreement that a change of perspective on social issues has occurred in mainline denominations, no systematic investigation of the subject has been made.[4] Have the policy-setting agencies of these great churches really turned their backs on their own traditions and adopted the agenda of social causes generated by the political left? If so, when did this process begin, what were its major sources, what responses has it evoked, how far-reaching have the changes been, and what implications do they have for the future of the church?

This essay is a first step toward answering these questions. It is based on my investigation of the positions on social issues adopted by the General Assemblies of the major Presbyterian denominations during the course of the twentieth century. These denominations are the Presbyterian Church in the United States of America (PCUSA), its immediate successor the United Presbyterian Church in the United States of America (UPCUSA),[5] the Presbyterian Church in the United States (PCUS), and the Presbyterian Church (U.S.A.) (PC (USA)), which was formed in 1983 by the reunion of the UPCUSA and the PCUS. I will occasionally refer to the first two denominations as the "northern" church, and to the third as the "southern" church.[6]

The General Assembly meets annually and is the highest legislative body in the Presbyterian system of government. Its voting members consist of lay and clerical commissioners elected for one-year terms by the lower governing bodies of the church. Most General Assembly pronouncements have their origin in an overture from a presbytery or the report and recommendations of a denominational agency. In almost all cases these overtures, reports, and other communications are reviewed by a standing committee of the Assembly itself, which makes recommendations that the Assembly debates, sometimes amends, and then votes on. On some occasions pronouncements originate in resolutions offered from the floor by individual commissioners. Acts of the General Assembly are binding only on the agencies and institutions under its direct control. They are meant to inform, but not bind, the consciences of individual members, including the clergy, and they leave much freedom of action to the lower governing bodies of the church.

Methods

In order to determine how far-reaching the shift of Presbyterian perspective may have been I have used a very broad definition of what constitutes a social issue. I have defined as "social" any pronouncement or action of a Presbyterian General Assembly concerning economic questions, matters of health, education, welfare, human rights, intergroup relations, church-state relations, and war and peace. I have also defined as social any pronouncement on the norms that Presbyterians, and sometimes others as well, should use in conducting their own lives, including their relationship to civil authority, their family relations, their reproductive, sexual, and recreational behavior, and their use of the Lord's Day.[7]

I have examined the *Minutes* of all the General Assemblies from 1926 through 1988 and, in certain instances, material from Supplements or Appendixes that bears on social issues. As my work progressed I decided to review the *Minutes* of a number of Assemblies held prior to 1926 in order to gain a fuller understanding of the development of Assembly thinking on particular issues. My conclusions concerning shifts in Presbyterian policy are based on reports, recommendations, resolutions, and responses to overtures, memorials, and communications that were adopted or approved by votes of the Assembly.

The question of whether and when General Assembly positions on social issues became more liberal is easy to answer because Assembly *Minutes* contain the full text of adopted reports and all other official actions. As a check on my judgment as to whether a given pronouncement on a social issue can be regarded as liberal, I have compared General Assembly pronouncements on social issues with a selection of articles and editorials from *The Nation* during the period covered by the research.[8] The question of whether secular political ideologies have directly influenced the positions adopted by General Assemblies cannot be answered without investigating whether each position was advocated by secular liberals before it was adopted by General Assemblies. Given the time and resources available for this research, it was not possible to investigate this matter systematically. Materials collected from *The Nation* and from a variety of secondary sources proved helpful, however, in interpreting the trend in General Assembly pronouncements and should be useful in guiding future research into the sources of this trend.

In reviewing General Assembly *Minutes* I have been on the alert for clues as to how changes of positions on social issues came about. It has been well documented that within the mainline churches themselves, theologians, staff members of denominational agencies, and many of the clergy hold views on a wide variety of issues that are less traditional than those of most of the laity.[9] It has also been claimed that shifts of position on social issues have been promoted by national leaders and their allies among the clergy, who exert a direct influence on the reports and recommendations that agencies present to national assemblies, thereby indirectly affecting the outcome of Assembly votes on key issues despite widespread opposition in the church as a whole.

General Assembly *Minutes* sometimes contain important clues about the range of opinion at Assemblies, the reaction of the church at large to Assembly pronouncements, and the general climate of opinion at the grass roots. For the most part they do not reveal the content of floor debates, of defeated amendments, or how many commissioners supported or opposed a given motion.[10] On the other hand, they always include a tally of votes on issues referred to the presbyteries. When one or more commissioners strongly object to an Assembly action their protests are usually recorded and on some occasions commissioners successfully request that minority reports and the exact outcome of close votes also be recorded. Overtures from the lower governing bodies of the church, all of which are printed in the *Minutes,* provide important insights into attitudes at the grass roots. For example, if a flood of overtures requests that the General Assembly act in a certain way it can be safely inferred that a strong body of opinion on the issue exists in the church as a whole. If the General Assembly rejects the overtures, it can be inferred that a strong body of contrary opinion also exists. On the other hand, if an act of the General Assembly evokes no overtures of protest to the following General Assembly, it can be inferred that the great majority of clergy and laity have no objection to it. I have carefully monitored Assembly *Minutes* for these and other signs of consensus and conflict as well as for evidence of the processes that have led to Assembly pronouncements.[11]

Then and Now: A Comparison

A comparison of General Assembly pronouncements on social issues made in the late 1920s with pronouncements made in 1988 leaves no doubt that a great change of emphasis and outlook has taken place. A change of *emphasis* is evident in the fact that in 1988 the sheer *number* of Assembly actions on social issues was vastly greater than it was in any year during the late 1920s. The amount of time and energy that Assemblies and their agencies devote to social issues has increased at a rate far faster than the rate at which the church has grown since 1926, and most of the increase took place after 1965, when church membership actually declined. In 1928 no standing committee of the General Assembly of either the northern or the southern church was charged exclusively with making recommendations on social questions. In 1988 there were several such committees as well as a number of special task forces. Social concerns are now of much greater importance to Presbyterian policymakers than they used to be.

A change of *outlook* is evident in the *kinds* of social issues considered important and the positions that Assemblies adopt regarding them. Only three social issues were deemed urgent enough to be pronounced on annually by the PCUSA in the late 1920s and early 1930s. Two of them involve topics that Presbyterians no longer consider important. One of these was temperance, a cause many Presbyterians had been promoting since the 1830s. In 1927, for example, the General Assembly declared its "unalterable opposition" to the repeal of the 18th Amendment and deplored "the lack of conscience on the part of many people, generally regarded as upright and worthy citizens, who, in their intimate social relations, use liquor as they please."[12]

The second issue of prime importance sixty years ago was Sabbath observance. Like temperance, the proper use of Sunday had been of vital interest to Presbyterians for generations. In 1931 the PCUSA, in a pronouncement typical of the times, congratulated "all members of the Senate and House of Representatives of Pennsylvania who have shown a readiness to resist efforts recently made by promoters to commercialize Sunday Baseball in this great Commonwealth," and it commended the Lord's Day Alliance "for the noble part it had in the defeat of the proposed legislation for a liberal Sabbath."[13]

The third issue on which PCUSA General Assemblies made regular deliverances six decades ago was world peace, a concern that dates from the turn of the century. It is the only issue considered urgent in the 1920s that is still regularly addressed by General Assemblies. Liberal Presbyterians of today would applaud the strong support that earlier Assemblies gave to arms limitation[14] and the rights of conscientious objectors,[15] but they would consider naive the Assemblies' faith in the Kellogg-Briand Pact[16] and they would look in vain for any connection between peacemaking and social justice.

Among the social issues on which PCUSA General Assemblies occasionally pronounced in the late 1920s and early 1930s were marriage and the family, divorce, national loyalty, race relations, and the content of motion pictures. In 1930, for example, the Assembly endorsed a program for observing the two hundredth anniversary of George Washington's birth "so that future generations of American citizens may be inspired to live according to the example and precepts of Washington's exalted life and character, and thus perpetuate the American Republic."[17] In 1932 the Assembly complained about the failure of the motion picture industry "to produce decent entertainment for the public."[18] As for marriage and family life, a lengthy report adopted in 1931 warned of a "sex stampede" and a "recrudescence of paganism with Hollywood blazing the way and Nevada prostituting its statehood and pandering to the weaknesses of human nature for thirty pieces of silver."[19] The "lamentable prevalence of divorce," the report added, produces a "general deterioration of society and the lowering of the moral tone of its individuals."[20] In the period just prior to the Great Depression, the pronouncements on peace, a few mild statements on American racial matters[21] and legislation allowing the ordination of women as elders[22] were the only actions of the PCUSA that were liberal in tone.

During the same period the southern church made fewer pronouncements than the PCUSA on social issues. The fact that it took no action at all on racial issues or the ordination of women indicates a climate of opinion even less liberal than that of the PCUSA. In general, however, southern Assemblies took positions that were similar in spirit, if not in exact content, to those of the northern church. They supported temperance, Sabbath observance, civil obedience, and world peace, and they worried about divorce.[23] There is, however, one striking difference between the social pronouncements of the PCUS and those of the PCUSA during the late 1920s and early 1930s. Whereas northern Assemblies did not hesitate to commend or criticize public officials by name, address communications to them, and make recommendations about specific laws and treaties, southern Assemblies were very reluctant to do so. They endorsed temperance, but they never referred to the 18th or 21st Amendments; they supported Sabbath observance, but they never mentioned Sunday laws and they were troubled by the political activities of the Lord's Day Alliance.[24]

The official reason for this aloofness from matters of state was part of the rationale for the very existence of the

PCUS as a separate denomination. In withdrawing from the PCUSA in 1861, southern Presbyterians claimed that by voting to support the Union cause the General Assembly had violated a section of the Westminster Confession of Faith that forbids church courts from "intermeddling" in civil affairs except in "cases extraordinary." In their view, the mission of the church is purely spiritual. Thereafter, with a few important exceptions, the southern church avoided intermeddling, and on several occasions in the 1920s and early 1930s it reaffirmed its "historical position" regarding the practice.[25]

During these years *The Nation* took positions on social issues that were rather different from those adopted by Presbyterian General Assemblies. It favored temperance and opposed the old-fashioned saloon, but by the late 1920s it had turned against prohibition, and just after Repeal it pronounced the 18th Amendment "the worst legislative mistake this country ever made."[26] *The Nation* strongly supported world peace, but it regarded the Kellogg-Briand Pact as a farce.[27] It opposed the "blue laws" of "entrenched religion" that forbade commercial amusements on Sunday[28] and condemned the "cruel, barbarous, theological, and antiquated divorce laws" of the times.[29] It disliked the movies, but for reasons rather different from those advanced by Presbyterian General Assemblies, and it opposed attempts to censor them.[30] Moreover, it addressed many issues that General Assemblies ignored, for example, birth control, labor questions of the 1920s, Wall Street speculation, the conservation of natural resources, publicly owned electric power plants, women's rights, and the U.S. occupation of Nicaragua. Sixty years ago *The Nation* and the Presbyterian General Assemblies were, by and large, not of one mind on social issues.

By 1988 the climate of Presbyterian General Assemblies had changed dramatically. The Assembly of that year had nothing to say about temperance, the control of alcoholic beverages, divorce, the duty of Sabbath observance, or the use of foul language in the entertainment media. It rejected "judgments that condemn all sexually explicit materials"[31] and defined as pornographic only those materials that eroticize "violence, power, humiliation, abuse, dominance, degradation, or mistreatment of any person."[32] It reaffirmed its 1986 declaration that "AIDS and ARC [AIDS Related Complex] should be viewed as an illness and not as punishment for behavior deemed immoral,"[33] took no action on an overture condemning "abortion for convenience as a means of birth control,"[34] and turned down a request that the denomination's Benefits Plan stop paying for abortions "without regard to the reason for them."[35]

In other actions, the 1988 General Assembly affirmed that individuals have a right to be excused from obeying laws that violate their conscience and urged that conscientious objector status be given to people who oppose particular wars.[36] It granted additional money to the National Sanctuary Defense Fund,[37] endorsed the Guatemalan bishops' paper on land reform,[38] and asked for "prompt passage of legislation providing Extended Voluntary Departure Status for affected groups of Central Americans, particularly Salvadorans and Guatemalans."[39] The Assembly expressed gratitude to the United Nations "for its pioneering and ongoing efforts to build a world community in which the rights of all are assured,"[40] asked Congress and the President to "provide the means for imposing immediate and comprehensive sanctions" against South Africa,[41] and voted to participate in the World Council of Churches' Ecumenical Decade on solidarity with women.[42] It took no action, however, on a complaint that the council, in its communications about world affairs, tends to condemn actions of the United States and to ignore those of Marxist dictatorships.[43]

In 1988, the value perspective embodied in General Assembly pronouncements was far closer to that of *The Nation* than was the case six decades earlier. The Presbyterian Church has indeed moved left in its position on social issues. There is, however, an important remaining barrier to a complete assimilation between the perspective of General Assemblies and that of secular liberals. Whenever the 1988 Assembly justified or explained its position on a social issue it did so in *theological* terms. *The Nation* never used such language. The agendas of the religious and the secular left may have become similar, but their official rationales remain distinct.

The Eclipse of the Old Agenda

The record clearly shows that over the past sixty years Presbyterianism's "old agenda" of social issues has been supplanted by a "new agenda." The old agenda included observing the Sabbath; abstaining from alcoholic beverages and such "worldly amusements" as dancing and card playing; upholding traditional norms governing gender roles, sexuality, reproduction, and family life; obeying the law and exercising moral superintendency over various aspects of public life. The new agenda has much in common with the agenda of the political left.

What do General Assembly *Minutes* reveal about when, how, and why the old agenda was set aside and the new agenda adopted? Was the process of change gradual and continuous or was it abrupt? To what extent did it involve conflict? What clues does the record provide about who within the church promoted the changes and why they did so?

In attempting to answer these questions I will begin by reporting what General Assembly *Minutes* show, and suggest, about the erosion of interest in old agenda issues. The record makes it clear that the erosion has proceeded steadily and without periods of reversal. It has not, however, affected all issues simultaneously, but only a few at a time. Changes A and B occurred before changes C and D, which in turn preceded changes E and F. The opposition to immodest female fashions and to such amusements as dancing and card playing faded away during and immediately after World War I. Throughout this period, however, General Assemblies were strongly committed to temperance and Sabbath observance, and the PCUSA supported legislation on both subjects. By 1940, however, there were unmistakable signs of a lagging interest in a strict Sunday.

Traditional rules concerning the remarriage of divorced persons were relaxed during the 1950s, and soon afterward General Assemblies endorsed birth control. By the mid-1960s the UPCUSA had formally renounced all attempts to write elements of its old agenda into law, and by 1970 both denominations had liberalized their position on capital punishment, the use of alcoholic beverages, and the ordination of women to the ministry. In the 1970s they supported abortion rights for women and accorded homosexual relationships a measure of legitimacy. By 1988 among the few old agenda positions that General Assemblies had not abandoned or liberalized in some way were the preference for sexual fidelity and heterosexual marriage, the ban on the ordination of avowed homosexuals, and the opposition to gambling.

A close reading of the record strongly suggests that the erosion of commitment to some of the old agenda positions was a genuinely popular process with deep roots in the life of the church as a whole. This is most clearly evident in the case of subjects which General Assemblies simply stopped addressing. A good example is the matter of immodesty and "worldly amusements." In 1914 the General Assembly of the PCUSA adopted a long report criticizing "the vulgar tendency of modern fashion" and lamenting the fact that "to-day many of our women are going to such extremes of dress as to shock even the least prudish, and to open American womanhood to the charge of complete forfeiture of modesty." The report went on to charge that "the dance, never perhaps what could be wished, has become the subject of indescribably vulgar jokes."[44] Less than fifteen years later, when both the dance and women's fashions were far more "vulgar" and "immodest" than they had been in 1914, no overtures were received, no study commissions were appointed, and no General Assembly pronouncements were made on these matters.[45] The whole issue of modesty and worldly amusements faded away with little or no discussion.[46]

The same thing can be said about family worship and family-centered piety in general. In the early years of the twentieth century the PCUS actively promoted family altars, family religious instruction, and a home environment in which Christian virtue was cultivated. In 1922 the General Assembly declared that "in God's plan the school of religion in the home antedated the Sunday School by 60 centuries."[47] The following year, in a long report, its Permanent Committee on the Sabbath and Family Religion announced that "the greatest menace which faces this nation today" is "the failure of the modern home to function according to the principles of the Word of God." "The morale of the average American home," it complained, "is in a state of jazz."[48] But the church was evidently becoming irritated by such jeremiads, for soon thereafter the Permanent Committee was abolished. In the early 1930s a new committee on Sabbath observance was established, but a concern for family spirituality and family virtue never reemerged as a major theme within either denomination. That subject, too, was simply dropped.

The interest in promoting Sabbath observance lasted a while longer. Once the very centerpiece of Presbyterian piety and the subject of innumerable strongly worded pronouncements adopted annually for many decades into the present century, the issue of Sabbath observance eventually disappeared without acrimony or debate. In all three cases it appears that the whole church changed its mind and its practice but was unwilling or unable to say why.[49]

It is probable that the same deep-rooted process that produced a more liberal position on dancing and Sabbath observance also produced a more liberal position on many of the old agenda items on which General Assemblies actually adopted new positions. The record contains numerous indicators of a churchwide process of liberalization on quite a few issues. In 1930, for example, the presbyteries of the PCUSA roundly rejected a proposal to permit women to be ordained as ministers, but a quarter of a century later they approved a similar measure by a lopsided majority.[50]

The history of General Assembly actions on the subject of birth control reveals a similar pattern. There was outrage in both denominations in 1931 when a study committee of the Federal Council of Churches recommended that parents consider using artificial methods of birth control. The PCUS was so incensed that it withdrew from the Council.[51] The PCUSA did not withdraw, but it asked the Council to "hold its peace on questions of delicacy and morality" and tersely announced that "the General Assembly disapproves ecclesiastical pronouncements on the subject of birth control."[52] Both denominations then held their own peace on the matter until 1960, when they adopted a joint statement approving of birth control.[53] No protests or dissents were recorded and no overtures of disapproval were subsequently received. As for the use of alcoholic beverages, in 1962 a few presbyteries voiced their unhappiness that the previous UPCUSA General Assembly had softened the denomination's time-honored stand against drinking, but no movement to reaffirm the stand emerged.[54]

It is impossible, given the limitations of this study, to identify conclusively the ultimate sources of the steady process of change that has eroded Presbyterians' support for their old agenda. A systematic examination of the theological motifs in General Assembly statements might provide evidence that one source of the change was a broad shift of theological orientation. As a sociologist, I suspect that another source lies in the fact that Presbyterians have been deeply involved at the very center of a society and culture that in the course of the twentieth century has become more urban, more individualistic and tolerant of diversity, more consumer-oriented, and better educated in secular subjects and modes of thought. Much of the old agenda involved restrictions and disciplines affecting the lives of church members themselves. When these became burdensome or embarrassing they were discarded and individuals became free to conduct their lives as they saw fit.

The Rise of the New Agenda

The rise of the new agenda within Presbyterianism not only involves the revision of attitudes on old issues such as drinking and the censorship of movies, it also involves adopting positions on many new social issues of an economic and political character with which General Assemblies did not concern themselves in earlier times.

The record shows that well before 1926 General Assemblies occasionally made pronouncements on certain political and economic issues that were liberal, or progressive, in the modern sense of those terms. It is not true that the liberal turn is of recent origin, for it actually originated in the social gospel movement that flourished in the years just before World War I.[55] It is also incorrect to assume that this movement simply imported a secular liberal orientation to social issues into the mainline churches. The social gospel had much in common with the Progressive movement in politics, but both emerged at virtually the same time and appear to have been a joint effort of religious and secular leaders, many of whom were lay Christians, to find solutions to the new social problems of the industrial order. In its earliest days the liberal voice within the church was not simply the religious expression of an already existing political culture.[56] Religious liberals did, however, create a community within the churches that forged close and permanent ties to the emerging political left.

In both branches of Presbyterianism the commitment to peace is the very oldest and the most consistently reaffirmed of all the new agenda items.[57] Moreover, a linking of issues of social justice with issues of world peace is evident as early as 1943, when both General Assemblies adopted an important document drawn up by a commission of the Federal Council of Churches that formed the basis of the subsequent position of the mainline Protestant churches on issues of the postwar world.[58] The PCUSA made its first statement on domestic economic issues in 1910, two decades after its first deliverance on world peace. The statement, though fairly general in content, was markedly progressive in tone. "The urgent secular questions of the day," it declared, "are the questions of wealth and poverty, of luxury and want, of capital and labor, of peace and war." It condemned the "immoderate exaltation of riches" and the pursuit of private gain "in disregard of the rights and the welfare of others," and called for safe industrial working conditions, a day of rest each week for workers, arbitration in industrial disputes, the reformation of criminal offenders, assistance to the needy, and the abolition of child labor.[59]

From 1921 until the onset of the Great Depression the social gospel advocates lost influence in the Presbyterian Church, and neither denomination pronounced again on economic issues. In 1931 the General Assembly of the PCUSA established a special committee on social and industrial relations,[60] which made its first report in 1932. This lengthy and strongly worded document was the first of several harsh critiques of the existing industrial system adopted by the PCUSA. "The present economic distress," the report declared, "is an indictment of our whole economic system," which is "now on probation" and whose "continued existence and justification must be found not in the wealth produced or the power gained, but in its contribution to social service and social justice." It is difficult to find any General Assembly pronouncements on domestic economic issues that are more "left-leaning" than these Depression-era deliverances.[61] The standing committee on social welfare, established in 1933, was the first of a continuing line of Assembly committees that have made annual reports recommending liberal positions and policies on economic issues.

The southern church was slower to pronounce on these topics. In 1933 the General Assembly adopted a highly traditional resolution attributing "our harsh experiences during the past years" to "moral laxity" and "unchristian thoughts, feelings and acts" and condemned "frantic efforts" to bring back "the same godless prosperity of the past decade."[62] But in 1934 it created the first of a continuing series of permanent committees whose work and general outlook would roughly parallel those of the northern church.[63]

The impetus for these early deliverances on economic

issues did not come from the broad rank and file of the church. The 1910 pronouncement was a response to a request from nine presbyteries in the industrial sections of New York and New Jersey,[64] and in 1931, only three presbyteries requested the study of Depression issues that led to the hard-hitting report adopted the following year.[65] Judging from the content of overtures in both denominations during the 1920s and 1930s, there was less popular concern with economic issues than with issues of temperance, Sabbath observance, peace, the content of movies, and the Federal Council's controversial recommendation on birth control. In 1933, at the very depth of the Depression, the northern General Assembly was deluged with overtures asking that its own costs be reduced, but it received none that addressed the national economic crisis.

Three Generations

The original impetus for committing the Presbyterian Church to liberal positions and policies on a host of new economic and social issues seems to have come from a small but strategically situated circle that was committed to the social gospel. One of their objectives was to maintain the influence of the church by engaging it in a campaign to alleviate the serious and unprecedented set of social problems that had arisen in the wake of industrialization, immigration, and urbanization. The 1910 pronouncement on commercial and industrial life observed that many who proposed remedies for modern social problems were in "open opposition to Christianity," believing that their "programme of exclusively external betterment" was "a sufficient substitute" for religion. Moral and religious ideas, the pronouncement continued, "have not kept pace with industrial and commercial progress."[66] In short, if the church was to prevail, it would have to address the most pressing problems of the times, and these problems required material as well as spiritual remedies.

It is probable that the original generation of social gospel advocates continued to support most of the church's old agenda,[67] but there is evidence that the second generation found the old agenda embarrassing. During the cultural upheavals of the 1920s the traditional ethos and program of American Protestantism were publicly ridiculed by secular writers such as H. L. Mencken and Sinclair Lewis. Once in a while *The Nation* joined the attack. In 1929, for example, it observed that matrimony "now trails along with church-going and Sabbath observance as a force in human life" and predicted that the sex standards of tomorrow will not be based on "some passé holiness."[68]

The Nation's sarcastic coverage of the 1932 General Assembly of the PCUSA revealed a perception of Protestant culture that had probably become quite common on the secular left and that must have been acutely embarrassing to liberals within the churches. The article focused entirely on addresses and pronouncements that affirmed the church's old agenda, for example, national prohibition and the censorship of motion pictures. "Stuffy clerics from all parts of the United States," it reported, "went on a moralistic rampage and put on a show which in its general self-righteous irrelevance reminds one of nothing so much as a political rally staged by the contented members of the G.O.P." If the leaders of the General Assembly, the article went on, "find it strange that those who are interested in human happiness and social well-being have lost faith in organized Christianity, we would like to suggest that they contemplate the history of modern Europe and ask themselves at what moment the church took the lead in any serious effort to establish a more equitable society."[69] *The Nation*'s report must have been particularly humiliating to Presbyterian progressives because it completely ignored the fact that the Assembly had also adopted a statement on economic issues that was fully as radical as anything *The Nation* had advocated. The only thing this organ of the left was ready to perceive in the Assembly's actions was the same old agenda themes that secularists had been ridiculing for a decade or more.

But a new era was about to begin. Reinhold Niebuhr, whose Depression-era writings profoundly influenced the second generation of Protestant social activists, published his first major book that same year. Although he was not entirely opposed to the old agenda, it held little interest for him. Niebuhr was preoccupied almost exclusively with issues of social justice and with the political struggle to attain it. His exposure and critique of the class-based character of mainline Protestantism inspired a new generation of religious leaders to define a genuine Christian witness almost exclusively as a struggle on behalf of the oppressed.[70] By sidetracking the old agenda, Niebuhr's generation of social activists began the process by which the social witness of Protestant liberals became indistinguishable from that of the secular left. The publishers of *The Nation* liked Niebuhr's brand of Christianity. Before the 1930s ended they had made him one of its contributing editors.

The third generation of politically oriented clergy, the generation Harvey Cox referred to as the "new breed,"[71] assumed positions of leadership in the mainline Protestant denominations during the 1960s. It was even more militant than its predecessors. Its militancy was in part inspired by the example set by the black religious leaders of the civil rights movement, the revolutionary struggles of third world peoples, and a horror of nuclear war. Moreover, the new breed was more openly antagonistic to traditional church culture than its predecessors had been and far more eager to take the initiative to abandon what remained of the church's old agenda and to commit the church to a wide variety of new programs. The new breed's perspective on popular piety was reflected in the many published attacks on the smugness and self-absorption of the American churches that began appearing in the late 1950s.[72]

The spirit of the new breed is reflected with great clarity in three successive reports to the General Assembly in the late 1960s by the board of directors of *Presbyterian Survey,* then the official magazine of the southern church. Defending *Survey's* new militancy on social issues, the directors proclaimed that "churches which are irrelevant will produce irrelevant magazines to report on irrelevancies."[73] The next year they proudly quoted a national news story calling *Survey* a "top-flight denominational magazine" that is no longer "filling its pages with bland little homilies and treacly short stories" but is writing instead about "pacifism, black power, poverty and 'death of God' theology." Although the new militancy had led many to cancel their subscriptions, the directors had no intention of shifting course to attract more readers. *Survey,* they explained, is "not published to provide Presbyterians escape or entertainment."[74] Two years later they asserted that "if churches protect their people from seeing the moral crisis, they do not deserve to survive . . . , nor will they."[75]

Some critics have alleged that in adopting this new militant posture, new breed leaders were simply trying to bring the churches into line with the drift of secular culture of the 1960s, which was decidedly to the left. But this charge ignores the long history of social progressivism among mainline Protestant leaders and fails to perceive the moral seriousness of most of the new breed. As Anne Motley Hallum has recently observed, it is a mistake to assume that in wanting to make the churches "relevant" to the modern age, the new breed was simply trying to be trendy. If that were the case, they would later have moved with the rest of the nation in a more conservative direction. In fact, however, as the nation moved right, key Presbyterian and other mainline church leaders kept firmly on their liberal course.[76] Like the editors of *Survey* in the late 1960s, these leaders remain unmoved by opposition, unintimidated by controversy, and unperturbed by membership loss. The seriousness of their moral convictions seems beyond dispute.

Promoting the New Agenda: From Harmony to Conflict

It is likely that the unabrasive style adopted by earlier generations of new agenda advocates was essential to their success. Though these advocates were initially a very small group within the church, it is noteworthy that the General

Assembly of the PCUSA adopted the 1910 pronouncement on economic issues unanimously and reaffirmed it
unanimously four years later.[77] It is also noteworthy that
the far more radical declaration of 1932 evoked no recorded dissent or overtures of protest to the following
General Assembly. The church at large did not request
these early deliverances, but neither did it oppose them. In
fact, there is little evidence of sharp or sustained controversy over social issues in the northern church until the
late 1960s. Yet from the depths of the Great Depression
onward, General Assemblies were allowing old agenda
items and postures to fall by the wayside and were adopting an increasing number of new agenda positions. A single illustration will suffice to show how much change had
already occurred by the mid-1940s. In the final year of
World War I, the Sabbath issue occupied seventeen and a
half pages of General Assembly *Minutes,* and issues of
world peace and postwar planning occupied only four.
Twenty-seven years later, in the final year of World War II,
sixteen pages dealt with the postwar world and only a few
lines dealt with the Sabbath.

The most likely explanation for the easy acceptance of
these earlier changes is that the denominational leaders
who worked for the adoption of a new agenda did not push
the church too hard on too many fronts at once and were
willing to back off in the face of strong opposition. The
economic pronouncement of 1910, for example, was calm
in tone and invoked such traditional themes as the duty of
stewardship, the danger of greed and materialism, and the
supremacy of spiritual values. In 1931, when the furor
erupted over the Federal Council's recommendations on
birth control, a special commission that had prepared similar recommendations to the General Assembly withdrew
them in order to preserve the peace of the church.[78] The
issue was not brought to the Assembly floor again until it
became clear that a general shift of opinion had occurred.
It is also likely that the anti-Communist statements[79] that
appeared in committee reports on social issues in the early
years of the cold war were inserted to forestall controver-

sies about the reports as a whole, which continued to be markedly liberal in tone.[80]

Prior to the 1960s, the strategy of new agenda advocates appears to have been to advance their program as steadily as they could, but to avoid the risk of precipitating a conservative reaction that might result in a permanent opposition movement that could command a majority of votes in the General Assembly. Although this strategy enabled the social progressives to achieve victories in an atmosphere of harmony, it did not create a substantial amount of support for liberal causes within the church at large. With the partial exception of a few programs relating to world peace, the earlier generations of new agenda advocates were no more successful than the new breed of the 1960s in producing the kind of mass enthusiasm that had given the temperance movement its victories.

The earlier generations of southern liberals also adopted a nonconfrontational style, but they were unable to prevent serious conflicts from erupting in the PCUS because traditionalists in that denomination were ever alert for any sign of a violation of the spirituality doctrine.[81] Consequently, when, in 1933, new agenda advocates first proposed that the southern church make pronouncements on a wide variety of social and economic issues, strong opposition immediately emerged.[82] From that date onward, acrimonious disputes concerning certain new agenda items were a periodic feature of southern church life.[83] By the 1940s a virtual two-party system had developed in the PCUS, with each party publishing an unofficial journal.[84] Despite conservative opposition, however, new agenda advocates won many important votes and by 1960 had succeeded in persuading General Assemblies to adopt policies on issues of race, economics, and world order that closely resembled those of the UPCUSA.[85] In that year the southern Assembly formally abandoned the spirituality doctrine.[86]

By 1970 sharp conflicts had broken out in the UPCUSA and the tumult in the PCUS had reached a crisis point. The social turmoil and cultural ferment in the nation at large probably contributed to the heightened conflict, but so did the militant strategy of the new breed or generation of social activists, who were beginning to assume positions of leadership in both denominations. One element of their strategy seems to have been to purge the church quickly of its remaining old agenda positions and commit it just as quickly to a greatly expanded set of new agenda programs. In 1970, for example, just five years after the northern General Assembly had reaffirmed its disapproval of pre-marital sex,[87] a study commission recommended that a more permissive standard be adopted. This recommendation created a storm of opposition. "No subject," its opponents contended, "is more certain to arouse indignation and to cause alienation in the sector of our membership that supports most sacrificially the program and mission of our church."[88] A similar uproar followed the revelation soon afterward that a denominational agency had donated $10,000 to the Angela Davis defense fund.[89]

By the early 1970s the UPCUSA had become as fully politicized as the southern church. This state of affairs has continued in the reunited church. National caucuses and special interest groups representing a variety of old and new agenda concerns have become a permanent feature of Presbyterian life as well as the life of most of the other mainline Protestant denominations. Robert Wuthnow has recently reported national survey findings showing that disagreements among religious liberals and conservatives in the nation at large are sharper and more numerous now than they were twenty years ago and that the very sharpest divisions concern social issues.[90]

Surveys conducted by the Presbyterian Panel show that lay Presbyterians hold more conservative views than the clergy on most social issues[91] and that a majority oppose many of the policies advocated by General Assemblies.[92] Yet the conservative caucuses and committees now operating within the Presbyterian Church have rarely been able to mobilize enough support to modify or defeat the liberal recommendations of General Assembly agencies and task forces, and they have not succeeded in placing many conservatives in key positions within the denomination. In the field of social issues, their only major successes in the past twenty years have been the defeat of proposals to liberalize sexual standards and to encourage civil disobedience.[93] One reason for their lack of success may be the fact that most lay Presbyterians simply do not know what stands General Assemblies have taken.[94] Perhaps another reason is that many conservatives who do know are unwilling to expend the time and effort required to become politically effective within the denomination. Moreover, a large number of the most militantly conservative have preferred to leave the denomination rather than to stay and fight. In the twelve months following June 1973, approximately 6 percent of the members of the PCUS left the church in this manner, inspired in part by a statement of twenty-four charges against the denomination that was drawn up by conservatives and sent to churches considered likely to secede.[95] A lesser secession of the same sort occurred in the UPCUSA between 1979 and 1981.[96]

Passive resistance to the liberal pronouncements and programs of the denominational agencies appears to have been far more common than active resistance. Since the mid-1960s, per capita financial contributions to General Assembly causes have declined. By 1970 the UPCUSA was facing financial hardship,[97] and by 1976 financial support for General Assembly agencies of the PCUS had fallen, in constant dollars, to "less than one-half the amount given ten years earlier."[98] Moreover, in recent years there have been no signs of increased giving to the various causes of the reunited church.[99]

Social Issues and Church Decline

It is difficult to predict the long-term results of the chronic battles between liberals and conservatives in the Presbyterian Church. New leaders must emerge in the 1990s to replace the large number who will be retiring in that decade, and perhaps this cohort will chart a course for the church that will redefine its mission in such a way as to reconcile those who are now at odds. In the meantime, in the midst of the current controversies a serious problem of institutional survival has developed that will limit the courses of action they can successfully pursue in the future. This is the problem of membership loss, a problem common to all the mainline Protestant churches. Since many in both of today's religious camps believe that virtually all the steep and continuing decline in membership since the mid-1960s is yet another form of resistance to the churches' leftward turn, it is important to assess the validity of this belief.

Religious conservatives argue that if the church is to grow again it must abandon its liberal social programs. An example of this viewpoint is contained in a 1988 overture to the General Assembly that interpreted the decline as a protest against the "purely 'political' " "statements, efforts, and emphases" of Assembly leaders. It urged the church to make evangelism its primary calling.[100] Many liberals agree with the premise, but not the conclusion, of this overture, for they seem to fear that a serious effort to reverse the decline would require compromising the social witness of the church. This fear probably underlay the remarks of Leon Howell, editor of *Christianity and Crisis,* to the 1989 annual dinner of the liberal Witherspoon Society, who complained that those who worry about church decline "betray a particularly American preoccupation with using numbers as a theologically dubious means of gauging who we are and what we are doing."[101]

But there is more than one reason why the churches are losing members. Secessions of noisy bands of disgruntled conservatives account for only a small fraction of the overall losses. The great bulk of the decline is much quieter, far more insidious, and probably has little if anything to do with positions that denominational assemblies have taken on social issues within the past twenty-five years. But if the decline is allowed to continue unchecked, within a few decades the mainline churches will be too small and too feeble in body and spirit to conduct an effective mission of any kind.

Although research has yet to discover the major causes of church decline, national surveys have identified its demographic dimensions. At the root of the problem is the fact that persons born after World War II and brought up in a mainline denomination have been much less inclined than those born before the war to affiliate with a church similar to the one in which they were reared. The Presbyterian and other mainline Protestant denominations are simply unable to attract a sufficient number of younger members to offset the ordinary losses incurred by the death of their older members.[102]

As for the causes of the decline, some research suggests that the loss was the result of a value shift in the direction of greater personal freedom and autonomy that originated outside the churches during the 1960s and affected middle-class white youth more strongly than other sectors of the population. Since the membership of the mainline denominations is predominantly white and middle class, the shift has hit those churches particularly hard.[103] That a liberalizing shift is in some way involved in the decline is suggested by the fact that most of the mainline churches' lost youth have not joined conservative churches and that their views on homosexuality, extramarital sex, abortion rights, and other "personal freedom" issues tend to be much more liberal than those of Presbyterian conservatives.[104] It seems clear that the churches' leftward turn is not the main reason why they are losing members.

Postscript: Toward a Third Agenda for Presbyterians

Although the leftward turn cannot explain the membership loss, I have believed for some time that factors internal to the life of the churches have contributed to it. My previous work on the subject has explored the possibility that the long-term depletion of theological resources and the relentless criticisms of popular religion by intellectuals during the 1950s and 1960s weakened the mainline churches and made them especially vulnerable to the value shift that occurred in the 1960s. To use a biological analogy, the churches' "immune system" was not strong enough to respond to the "virus" they encountered a quarter of a century ago.[105]

My review of General Assembly *Minutes* provides a glimpse of yet another internal factor that may have weakened the churches. I refer to the slow but steady abandonment of the distinctive spiritual practices and personal disciplines that were once a vital part of the churches' tradition. Consider, for example, the matter of Sabbath observance, a cause once considered crucial to the survival not only of the churches but of the nation as well. When Presbyterians were fully committed to keeping Sunday sacred, its observance was an act of personal and collective renewal that reminded them of their mission and helped rekindle their zeal to carry it out. Yet over the generations Sabbath observance and many other old disciplines vanished in a quiet process of change that eventually affected all segments of the church. Well before 1960, it would have been difficult to answer the question of what Presbyterians "did" that makes them different from other members of the white middle class.

In a rapidly changing, pluralistic, and competitive society such as ours, traditions of all sorts are subject to challenge and decay. Few organizations and communities can take their survival or the loyalty of their constituency for granted. If they are to remain strong and effective, their leaders must make a special effort to overcome the processes of devitalization that are constantly at work. It is not strange that in the course of the twentieth century these processes made such disciplines as Sabbath observance, family worship, and total abstinence seem burdensome and outmoded.

It seems likely that this long-term process of disengagement from the spiritual disciplines of church life has been spearheaded by a succession of younger cohorts, each better educated and more exposed to secular influences than their elders. An intriguing 1939 report concerning the decline of interest in Sabbath observance suggests that this may be the case. "We live in a time," the report observed, "when everything is being reconsidered. Nothing is accepted as correct because it is old. The general idea is that whatever is is probably wrong." Moreover, it is the youth who are most skeptical of tradition. Older people, "whose raising has been strict," have a ready answer to a question about Sabbath observance. "To the young," however, "whose surroundings are different the answer seems difficult."[106] One by one the disciplines ceased to rekindle commitment, became pointless and were discarded, until the time arrived when a new generation found churchgoing pointless as well.

It is noteworthy that over the years the institutional guardians of the churches themselves collaborated with the rank and file in allowing many of the old disciplines and spiritual practices to slip away without devising and promoting alternatives. By so doing they allowed one source of their own influence to slip away as well. Liberal leaders hoped to enlist the energies of the rank and file for a new agenda of social change, but they neglected to refuel the engines that produced these energies in the first place, which may help account for their inability to mobilize enthusiastic support for most of their programs. A 1970 overture to the southern General Assembly put their current problem concisely: The denominational leadership may indeed be "far ahead—even in the right direction—of its following," but to "relentlessly push for courses of action for which no widespread support exists" is a "sign of failure to lead, i.e., to win the understanding and support of its following."[107] Even if the leadership always prevailed in the General Assembly it would fail to make the church an effective force for social change.

To be true to its heritage the Presbyterian Church must continue to study and make pronouncements on social issues. Few would have it adopt a latter-day version of the spirituality doctrine. But in the interest of its own survival as a church in mission it needs to develop a third agenda aimed at revitalizing itself as a religious institution and to assign this task a very high priority in the critical period just ahead.[108]

In fashioning a third agenda it will not, of course, be possible simply to restore old standards of Sabbath observance or personal piety, but attention must once again be paid to nurturing the spiritual needs of individuals, to providing moral guidance in their intimate relations, to promoting peacemaking and celebration of diversity within the church itself, and to devising new and distinctive forms of spiritual practice that can generate energies for Christian service. No program of evangelism will succeed until compelling new messages and regimens have demonstrated their ability to help revitalize and reharmonize the life of the church.

I have no confidence that the Presbyterian or other mainline denominations will be willing or able to shift course. But unless they find ways to reverse the direction in which they are now headed their days of mission in the world will be numbered.

9

The Tie That No Longer Binds: The Origins of the Presbyterian Church in America

Rick Nutt

On December 4, 1973—112 years to the day after the founding of the Presbyterian Church in the Confederate States of America—the first General Assembly of the Presbyterian Church in America (PCA) was called to order at Briarwood Presbyterian Church in Birmingham, Alabama.[1] The formation of this new denomination within the Reformed tradition culminated over thirty years of dispute in the Presbyterian Church in the United States (the PCUS, or so-called southern Presbyterian church). It was ironic that a denomination which prided itself on its close-knit, even familial, nature should undergo division. This essay explores the forces that led a large number of conservatives to the conclusion that, in the words of the favored hymn, the ties that bound them to the PCUS were no longer strong enough to hold them within its fellowship.

This study begins with a brief history of the groups, events, and developments that precipitated the formation of the PCA, followed by an analysis of the forces which lay behind that story. The thesis argued is this: The people who gave rise to the PCA were fundamentalists of the type associated with the Princeton theology and J. Gresham Machen in the North earlier in the century. Arguing for the inerrancy of scripture and opposing theological innovation and higher critical biblical study, the Princeton theologians maintained a rigid Old School Presbyterianism in the face of changing attitudes in the Presbyterian Church in the United States of America. Machen, the last of that Princeton line, eventually left the seminary to found Westminster Seminary in Philadelphia and subsequently left the denomination to establish the Orthodox Presbyterian Church. The matrix of factors out of which this fundamentalism grew was twofold: a particular sociocultural situation and the people's theological stance.

The Continuing Church Movement

The Presbyterian Church U.S. underwent significant changes between the two world wars. The heir of Old School Presbyterianism in the South, the denomination had always maintained a social and theological conservatism. It held self-consciously to such traditional Calvinist doctrines as the infallibility of scripture, the absolute sovereignty of God, total depravity, justification by grace through faith—with an attendant high view of predestination, and *jure divino* Presbyterianism. The debate over slavery and the church's relation to that institution eventuated in the doctrine of the spirituality of the church. Formulated in order to sanction slavery and given its classic statement before the Civil War by James Henley Thornwell, that doctrine held that the sole mission of the church was to convert individuals that they might be saved and lead new lives. The reformation of society would take place through the exemplary behavior of those converted. Individual Christians could, and ought to, be politically and socially active in attempts to better society. The church, as the church, however, had the responsibility to see to its spiritual mission, which left no place for social or political activities. If the church became involved in social or political issues, it would either forsake or corrupt its higher calling of preaching the "pure" gospel. The PCUS took this doctrine to represent the ideal form of church-state separation. The doctrine of the spirituality of the church, then, tended to endorse the status quo and manifested a social conservatism correspondent to the denomination's aversion to theological innovation.

After World War I change made its way into the PCUS. Higher biblical criticism found adherents among seminary and college professors, as did the dialectical, or neo-orthodox, theology. Simultaneously the denomination began to reject the spirituality of the church in favor of a broader understanding of the mission of the church which involved a commitment to alleviating systemic evil (which in the South meant, above all, segregation). The 1934 General Assembly established a Committee on Moral and Social Welfare, a watershed for the development of a social mission in the PCUS. During these years there were periodic attempts to amend the Westminster Confession of Faith and to effect reunion with the (northern) Presbyterian Church U.S.A. (the United Presbyterian Church U.S.A. after the 1958 union with the United Presbyterian Church of North America), perceived by many in the PCUS to be doctrinally suspect.[2]

The opposition to this trend coalesced into a group that designated itself the Continuing Church Movement. That name is important because it has always been the contention of the movement that they were neither schismatic nor "troublers of Israel";[3] the conservatives argued that they continued the true line of the PCUS in their Old School beliefs. They argued that those who were changing the denomination were guilty of fostering division. This position provided no small psychological foundation for the debates ahead, especially those regarding ownership of church property. Most important to the Continuing Church Movement was the establishment, in 1942, of the *Southern Presbyterian Journal* (subsequently the *Presbyterian Journal*). The key means of communication for the movement, "it acquainted people with the issues, developed a network of conservatives, brought the story of the church's departure into the open, and told its constituents who the players in the struggle were. Without its ministry, there would have been no Continuing Presbyterian Church."[4]

Perhaps the best known of the Continuing Church leaders was the associate editor of the *Journal*, L. Nelson Bell. A longtime medical missionary to China and father-in-law of Billy Graham, Bell was devoted to Old School Calvinism and was central to the organization of fundamentalists in the PCUS. (Bell chose not to leave the PCUS, however.) Henry B. Dendy was first editor of the periodical, but more important was the second, the acerbic G. Aiken Taylor. Taylor was a loud and consistent voice for the Continuing Church Movement through his commentary on developments in the PCUS.

Leadership was also provided by Rev. Bill Hill, who left a twenty-nine-year pastorate at West End Presbyterian Church in Hopewell, Virginia, to become a full-time evangelist. In 1964 he established the Presbyterian Evangelistic Fellowship (PEF); the ministers who circulated with this body provided a network of information and organization for disgruntled Presbyterians. Furthermore, in 1970 the PEF formed the Executive Commission on Overseas Evangelism, a board designed to support mission work which had as its sole purpose evangelism apart from social action (that is, within the definition of the spirituality of the church). Ruling Elder Kenneth Keyes, a Florida real estate developer who had also developed a direct-mail marketing agency, founded the Concerned Presbyterians in 1964 to organize lay people, church sessions in particular, around the conservative agenda.

Rev. Donald Patterson (who followed Bill Hill at West End church and later served the wealthy First Presbyterian Church of Jackson, Mississippi) and Rev. Morton H. Smith (professor at Belhaven College and Reformed Theological Seminary, and, subsequently, Stated Clerk of the PCA General Assembly) were instrumental in the formation of the Presbyterian Churchmen United—a body parallel to the Concerned Presbyterians, but for clergy.

Finally, to preserve their point of view, the conservatives in 1964 founded Reformed Theological Institute (in

1966 it became a seminary) in Jackson, Mississippi. The independent school provided ministers to the PCUS who were favorable to the Continuing Church Movement; it was often these ministers who led congregations out of the PCUS in 1973 and years following. The conservatives organized so extensively (and it should be noted that these groups became highly political) because they perceived the situation in urgent terms. As early as 1942 Dendy suggested his understanding of developments in the PCUS as he wrote of the ability of Satan to make error appear as truth.

> Let *us* not be deceived, when he [Satan] thus speaks, for whether he comes as a man in the street; as a voice from the pew or even from the pulpit; yea, even though he may come in the guise of a learned college or university or even seminary professor, it is the voice of Satan and should be so recognized.[5]

Statements of the conservative position were usually expressed negatively, that is, they were written to show points of divergence from the official denominational position on particular issues.[6] Above all, during the 1950s and 1960s the Continuing Church people were enraged by denominational support for integration and the civil rights movement. Racism, embodied in Jim Crow laws, was still a powerful force in the South and the PCUS. Conservatives in the PCUS were constantly calling for an end to church participation in efforts to integrate society; like their Confederate forebears, their argument was put in terms of the spirituality of the church. Racism as a factor in the origin of the PCA is clear when one notes that the strength of the denomination was in Mississippi, Alabama, and South Carolina. Mississippi presbyteries repeatedly sent overtures to the General Assembly requesting withdrawal from the National Council of Churches; those overtures were occasioned by the role of the NCC in the civil rights movement.

Those who would form the PCA further opposed the introduction of higher biblical criticism and moderate Calvinist theology into church school literature and seminary instruction, efforts to modify the Westminster Confession of Faith and to write a new confession of faith, attempts to unite with non-Reformed bodies through the Consultation on Church Union, efforts to reunite with the United Presbyterian Church U.S.A. (UPCUSA) (doctrinally suspect and confessionally unsound since the adoption of the Confession of 1967), realignment of synods and establishment of union presbyteries with the UPCUSA (understood to be a ploy to divide conservative strength and give more power to those in General Assembly offices who favored social and theological change), denominational calls to end the war in Indochina, the ordination of women as elders and ministers, support for a woman's right to abortion, and the claim that local congregations did not own church property themselves but held it in trust for the denomination. For the Continuing Church Movement, all of these errors in the PCUS resulted from forsaking proper Reformed theology and an inerrant view of scripture. Reformed Theological Seminary, for instance, taught four positions it was argued the denominational seminaries had abandoned: inerrancy, strict subscription to the Westminster Confession of Faith, *jure divino* Presbyterianism, and the spirituality of the church.[7]

As a result of its labor the Continuing Church Movement grew in strength. In 1969 the Presbyterian Churchmen United drafted a Declaration of Commitment which outlined the four stances just delineated and called for ministers and sessions to register their support. Frank Smith reports that by 1970 over 600 ministers and 263 sessions had endorsed the document.[8] Convinced that no relief from their complaints and concerns would be forthcoming from either the denomination or seminaries, some people began to believe they must withdraw from a church that was theologically mistaken and endangering the salvation of its members. Matters came to a head early in 1973; the Steering Committee of the Continuing Church Movement met on February 15 and 16, 1973, and adopted a resolution to form a new denomination.[9]

That organizing General Assembly was, of course, an exciting time for the conservatives—convinced as they were that they now had the opportunity to institutionalize proper Reformed theology in the South. The General Assembly first issued a resolution of fellowship to all Presbyterian and Reformed bodies and then, in the fashion of the Presbyterian Church in the Confederate States of America in 1861, sent "A Message to All Churches of Jesus Christ Throughout the World from the General Assembly of the National Presbyterian Church." Declaring that reluctance and sadness marked their separation from the PCUS, the PCA nonetheless felt compelled by loyalty to Christ over against loyalty to a church which they felt had erred.

> A diluted theology, a gospel tending towards humanism, an unbiblical view of marriage and divorce, the ordination of women, financing of abortion on socio-economic grounds, and numerous other non-Biblical positions are all traceable to a different view of Scripture from that we hold and that which was held by the Southern Presbyterian forefathers.[10]

In contrast the PCA held that "the Bible is the very Word of God, so inspired in the whole and in all its parts, as in the original autographs, to be the inerrant Word of God."[11] The message to the churches then affirmed that the PCA would accept only the Westminster Confession of Faith (and the Larger and Shorter Catechisms) as their doctrinal standards, and declared further their belief that the church is a spiritual body and therefore has a spiritual mission.[12] With such a view to propagating their beliefs and bringing increasing numbers to faith in God through Jesus Christ, the Presbyterian Church in America was born.

The PCA still holds to the theory of biblical inerrancy and fundamentalist theology. The denomination has grown and prospered in the seventeen years since its birth, founding new congregations and becoming a national church. Union with the Reformed Presbyterian Church, Evangelical Synod, has given the PCA strength in Eastern Ohio and Pennsylvania.

Fundamentalist Reaction to Postwar Social Change

How is one to explain the origin of this new denomination and the series of events that brought it to pass? The Continuing Church Movement is best understood as an heir of the fundamentalism which had been so prominent in the North earlier in the century. George Marsden's well-known definition of fundamentalism is "militantly anti-modernist Protestant evangelicalism." His definition identifies two elements in fundamentalism: a reaction to socio-economic change in the twentieth-century United States and a commitment to nineteenth-century evangelical theology. Fundamentalism became a virtually invisible subculture in the 1930s, but emerged again in the 1940s with the founding of the National Association of Evangelicals, the rise of Billy Graham, the founding of Fuller Theological Seminary, and, later, *Christianity Today.* Certainly this new fundamentalism, which called itself evangelicalism, was not a simple duplication of its previous forms; it was, however, designed to present and preserve fundamentalism as a reasonable, educated, and respectable form of Christianity in the tradition of the Princeton theology. Accompanying this point of view was a strong reaction to the secularization of society.[13]

The southern Christian sense of security in society and its guiding belief system underwent a crisis after World War II, which mirrored the situation confronting the churches in the North earlier in the century. In the North rapid urbanization, growing pluralism, and secularization of society loosened the hold of the "Protestant establishment" on the values and habits of people. Biblical criticism and modernist theology seemed of a piece with those developments. In the South the civil rights movement served notice that segregation and racism could no longer be assumed as the order of things. Jim Crow laws were challenged on every front from drinking fountains to the voting booth. The conflict in Indochina precipitated an intensely acrimonious debate within the nation regarding our self-identity and mission in the world. Thus, domestically and internationally the nation's belief in itself as a nation that fostered freedom and equality was thrown into question.

The Presbyterian church in the South, which had endorsed the status quo and was overwhelmingly conservative in blessing the morals and beliefs of the people, experienced this crisis as earlier fundamentalists in the North and Northeast had been forced to do before and immediately after World War I. Furthermore, the issues that concerned the Continuing Church Movement seemed evidence to conservatives that Christianity, which should have been a fortress against such turmoil and crises of social belief systems, was in danger of succumbing to secularizing forces to the point of complete distortion of the gospel. (Of course, fundamentalism had made an impact in the South before World War II. But the South remained relatively free of this general crisis in self-understanding until after the war because secularization and biblical criticism were not yet significant factors in the South; early fundamentalism was primarily a movement in the North.)

Marsden himself suggests this situation in southern society and its churches. "In the South the debates were in most cases short-lived, because dissent was simply not tolerated," he writes. "As early as the first half of the nineteenth century, advanced theological views had usually been associated with advanced social views and abolition. . . . This theological conservatism . . . created in Southern religion many characteristics that resembled later fundamentalism."[14] Samuel Hill observes that Southerners at the turn of the century believed that their churches were, in contrast to the North, maintaining orthodoxy against the inroads of biblical criticism and evolutionary thought.[15] Of the experience of southern Christianity in the postwar world, Hill argues:

> Until the 1960's, it has been part and parcel of the region's cultural horizon, indistinguishable in its personality from the other facets of southern life. . . .
>
>   In finding itself embroiled in crisis, the southern church mirrors the general regional situation in the 1960's.

Change—dramatic, basic, overarching change—is today's ranking fact. Everywhere old moorings are breaking loose, deeply entrenched attitudes are being shaken, traditional patterns of social life are gradually giving away and being replaced by new.[16]

That these sociocultural forces lay behind the Continuing Church Movement is clear. An analysis of the composition of the PCA at the time of its first General Assembly reveals that its strength lay in three states: Mississippi, Alabama, and South Carolina (of 260 churches in the denomination, 171 were in those three states, as were 108 of 196 ministers—with correspondent percentages in membership).[17] The first two states were, perhaps, the most deeply enmeshed in racism and southern folkways and most profoundly affected by change, as evidenced by the violent reactions to the civil rights movement there.[18]

Even more telling are those moments when the Continuing Church people themselves expressed their reaction to changes within society and the church. Bell, in the inaugural issue of the *Southern Presbyterian Journal,* declared that civilization tottered in a precarious state (he wrote in the midst of World War II), due in part to the church. The church had abandoned its purpose of preaching salvation in Jesus Christ, and in so doing had forsaken belief in the Bible as the Word of God. The desperate situation of the world was, at its root, spiritual; therefore, wrote Bell, "[the church] is to blame to the extent to which it has stepped out of its spiritual role, to meddle, as the Church, in political and economic matters and affairs of State."[19] A similar connection between diluted faith and the deterioration of society was made again thirty years later.

These attacks [on Christian faith] are evidenced by the downgrading of the Bible, the substitution of humanism for theism; the substitution of universalism for the necessity of Christ in salvation; the secularization and corrupting of worship; the substitution of situational for Bible ethics; a contempt for New Testament evangelism; the support of radical social activism; the glorification of civil disobedience; a surrender of the temples of God to extortioners by invitation [a reference

to the Black Manifesto movement]; advocating that Marxism
be heard from pulpits; the centralization of power and re-
moval of authority belonging to local church officers.[20]

These feelings became manifest with respect to specific
issues. Morton Smith, in his chronicle of General Assembly decisions to illustrate the decline of the PCUS, argued
that the 1954 report "The Church and Segregation" based
neither its analysis of the racial situation in the South nor
its exhortations for desegregation on any biblical command. It could not, for no such mandate existed. The
church in the South a century before had not condemned
slavery because it was a social institution outside the realm
of the church's mission. Had the Bible condemned slavery
the church could have acted, but it did not—indeed, the
Bible sanctioned it. So it was with segregation. "The fact
is," wrote Smith, "that God segregated Israel from the
Canaanites. It is debatable as to whether the Church
should get into the matter of trying to change that particular cultural pattern, and branding one form of culture sinful as opposed to another."[21]

A layman spoke to the other great issue of the age, the
Vietnam war. Those who opposed the war, he believed,
were disenchanted with the United States and had an "affinity" for communism. But they failed to realize that the
United States was a free and virtuous nation, hoping only
to stop the spread of an atheistic system throughout the
world. "Our side does not seek material gain," asserted
the writer, "but it is the side of Christianity."[22] That was
the very issue at stake in the debate concerning continued
involvement in the war, the Continuing Church people believed. That these fundamentalist Presbyterians felt traditional values and beliefs to be of paramount importance
and traditional understandings of the nation and society to
be virtually equated with true Christianity emerges in this
vitriolic passage.

> Oh, we are up to *here* with God-denying socialism, commu-
> nism, secularism, atheism, humanism, materialism, rational-
> ism—you name it—in the Church.

> We are up to *here* with youth-oriented magazines that condone illicit sex, the illegal use of narcotics, violent political revolution, and just about anything else that's unholy and profane. . . .
>
> We are up to *here* with conferences wherein God is blasphemed and holy worship is prostituted with profanity and carnal orgies of secularism.
>
> We are up to *here* with the devil's religion.[23]

Robert Wuthnow's study of religion in the United States since World War II proves helpful to our understanding of the PCA, and makes clear that the sociological factors for withdrawal were also at work in society at large.[24] Most pertinent for this study is his assertion that the civil rights movement led to a difference of opinion between liberals and conservatives regarding how to pursue change in society and the deeper theological question of the emphasis of the gospel (social transformation or personal salvation).[25] Attendant to this are two opposing civil religious understandings of the role of the United States in the world, brought into sharp focus by the war in Indochina. These divisions take place within and across denominations, leading to special interest groups that attempt to gain political influence within churches and in society.[26] Certainly this division became evident in the PCA-PCUS separation.

A constant lament within southern Presbyterian fundamentalism was that the leadership of the denomination and its seminaries had been captured by liberals who were taking the PCUS in a direction it should not go and turning a deaf ear to the voice of those in the pew and pulpit removed from the centers of power. Insofar as there were some who did seek change in the denomination's understanding of social mission and theology and sought to implement that change, that charge has merit. Further, some leaders wanted to see those changes occur more rapidly than did others, and may have appeared insensitive or unresponsive to the grass roots. Even when action was taken by a General Assembly or other body composed of ministers and lay people, the fundamentalists charged that it was the result of liberal political machinations. As Wuthnow observed,

> It seemed to many observers of American religion that the national hierarchies of the major denominations, for good or bad, were becoming increasingly powerful entities unto themselves. There was, in fact, some evidence that people were becoming alienated from the powerbrokers who operated these bureaucracies, and that the bureaucrats were set on taking their denominations on courses quite different from the ones favored at the grass roots.[27]

There was, then, a twist on the oft-cited clergy-laity division in the form of a General Assembly–congregation split. The PCUS, of which people thought in familial terms and as a place of refuge, now seemed to fundamentalists cut loose from traditional moorings and adrift. In the midst of profound upheavals in society and a crisis of established attitudes and beliefs, fundamentalist Presbyterians in the South reacted with a call to tradition.

Preserving Old School Calvinism

Southern Presbyterian fundamentalism was more than a reaction to sociocultural factors in the post-war South. If it is true that social forces in part determined the fundamentalist position, it is also true that those who brought the PCA into being were just what they held themselves to be: conservative Presbyterians who clung to the Calvinism of the past. More than just antimodernists, they were self-consciously Old School Presbyterians.

Morton Smith's *Studies in Southern Presbyterian Theology* was governed by the intent to show that southern Presbyterianism had never wavered from the strict Calvinism of the Westminster Confession and the Catechisms. He argued that the famous Adopting Act of 1729, which required ministers to subscribe to Westminster but allowed freedom of conscience in nonessential points, grew out of a debate over the place of experience in religion and was not understood to allow divergence from the creed in any but the most minor points.[28] The Adopting Act required strict subscription to the confession and catechisms.

Close adherence to Westminster was important to the fundamentalists in the PCUS because it taught the plenary inspiration of scripture and the doctrine of election. The former doctrine was necessary because at times human reason cannot harmonize or make reasonable all the ideas presented in the Bible, and the only hope for faith in that dilemma is to submit to the authority of God's will. Election, which involved that distinctive Presbyterian belief in double predestination, brought into tension the affirmations that God is sovereign and loving—and, therefore, acceptance of the teaching rests on accepting the full authority of God's Word in which it is taught.[29]

At issue was the understanding of the place of revelation and reason in Christian faith. For fundamentalists revelation must always take precedence over reason when the two seem to stand in opposition. Modern biblical scholarship, argues the fundamentalist, reverses that order. Biblical criticism built on hermeneutical theories which, in some manner, precluded the possibility of the supernatural at work within the natural, thus subjecting the revelation of God's will to dictates of reason for validation.

This supernatural authority of the Bible, to which one must submit even reason (and it should be noted that the Reformed tradition held reason and the power of the intellect in high esteem) carried over to the creeds—in particular, the Westminster Confession of Faith and Larger and Shorter Catechisms which comprised the standards of the PCUS and PCA. It was true that the confession was written by humans and in language that modern believers might update; the confession did not, however, grow out of human conviction or construction, the PCA taught. No true confession grows out of the historical situation in which it was written—it is an expounding of the system of doctrine presented in scripture.[30] The confession itself is absolutely true and even revelational in character.

This means that the Calvinistic Standards are of such directly Scriptural nature, that accordingly for one to deviate from strict subscription in any such point, is to reject the Scripture pertinent to that point! Therefore for one to stretch the acceptance of the system to cover so serious defection as denying the foundation-stone of the Confession itself, viz., an inspired and therefore infallible Bible, gives appearance of making language meaningless.[31]

As has been shown in Morton Smith's work, this authority of scripture and creed allows one to accept the teachings of the church—especially election—even though their meaning may be hidden in the power and majesty of God.

This conservative theology contained similarities to the Princeton branch of fundamentalism, most notably with regard to supernaturalism and a "high" view of scripture. More important, there were direct ties to Princeton as the southern fundamentalists turned to Charles Hodge and J. Gresham Machen and appropriated their work as a means to formulate a response to the spread of theological change in the South.[32] They were forced to look to their northern neighbors to locate a history of such a response. None had ever developed in the South; none had been needed. Protestantism in the United States, including the South, had long taught that the Bible was the inspired Word of God; in the absence of any direct challenge to that belief during the nineteenth century no theological basis for it had been forthcoming.[33] The Princeton theologians, especially Hodge, delineated just such a foundation as biblical criticism made its way into the nation from Germany. Biblical criticism did not become enough of a factor in the South to warrant a defense until just before World War II, by which time fundamentalists had recourse to Hodge and Machen.

The Princeton theology was distinguished by its commitment to Scottish Common Sense Realism, brought to the school by John Witherspoon. Scottish Realism, in turn, built on the scientific methodology of Francis Bacon. Baconian science argued that one begins with given observations (or, in religion, with given truth claims) and inductively moves toward appropriate conclusions. One does not formulate first a general working hypothesis and test to prove it; one moves from the particular to the general. As this method was appropriated in Scottish Common Sense Philosophy at Princeton, it was argued by Archibald Alexander that the theological task is to compile the assertions found in the Bible and from them to build a systematic theology. To speculate about the nature of God on the basis of philosophy and human religious experience and then measure the teaching of scripture against those subjective criteria, argued the Princetonians, put the theological cart before the horse. It also placed human reason over revelation. An honest and objective approach to both science and theology, however, would support biblically revealed truth; reason and revelation, both from God, were not ultimately contradictory.[34] Marsden points to Machen's position that liberalism was unscientific and unchristian. Christianity deals in facts; liberalism grows out of the relativities of subjective human experience. One did not properly speak of conservative and liberal Christianity, but of Christianity and liberalism—two distinct religions.[35] This scientific stress on scriptural fact was signaled by the shift from the word "infallible" to "inerrant" in describing the Bible's authority. The latter became popular among fundamentalists to affirm the reliability and accuracy of the Bible; it carried a more precise sense than the former, which was broader in scope and had previously predominated.

Such reasonable, objective, and knowable religious truth was the same for every age—it is fixed. This is seen in the Old School's strict subscription to Westminster. Hodge eventually resorted to the language of scholasticism to define Christianity. Christian religion is not essentially a saving experience of the risen Christ or some like characterization of faith.

> Religion is the reception of certain doctrines as true, and a state of heart and course of action in accordance with those doctrines. The Apostles propounded a certain system of doctrines. . . . The Bible everywhere assumes that without truth there can be no holiness; that all conscious exercises

of spiritual life are in view of truth objectively revealed in
the Scriptures. And hence the importance everywhere attributed to knowledge, to truth, to sound doctrine, in the
Word of God.[36]

Leading Presbyterian ministers in the South were prod-
ucts of Scottish Realist thought, and often of Princeton
itself. Morton Smith is aware of the connection, for he
notes that a "point of special significance for us in our
study of Southern Presbyterian theology is to realize its
close tie to what was later called 'Princeton theology.' "[37]
John Holt Rice, the teacher who gave life to Union Theological Seminary in Virginia, argued that the theologian's
task was to identify the facts of scripture and arrange them
scientifically in order that the whole truth of the Bible
could be known.[38] The connection is not surprising; after
all, the first of the seminary's theologians, Archibald Alexander, was an Old School Virginian and the South's strong
Old School stance lent support to Princeton. The Princeton influence is further seen in this: the southern Presbyterian theologians whom Smith studied speak often of
plenary verbal inspiration and the Bible's infallibility.
Only later in the nineteenth century do they begin to use
the word "inerrant," and then generally in reference to the
arguments of Hodge or Benjamin Warfield. The first such
reference is by John Lafayette Girardeau, of Columbia
Theological Seminary from 1876 to 1895; Smith quotes
Girardeau: "What is the source from which we derive information upon this subject? I adopt the answer of Dr.
Charles Hodge in this question, 'The nature of inspiration
is to be learnt from the Scriptures.' "[39]

The Princeton connection still obtained in the Continuing Church Movement. A number of ministers in PCA had
studied in the North. Morton Smith had studied one year
at Westminster Seminary in Philadelphia. John Reed
Miller, minister at First Presbyterian Church in Jackson,
Mississippi, at the time of the division, had come south. In
the minutes of the organizing assembly the PCA recommended a list of books to the officers of PCA congregations. On the list were the works of Machen, Francis

Schaeffer (who had roots in Carl McIntire's Bible Presbyterian Church, and therefore no direct tie to Princeton), Hodge, and others.

Southern Presbyterian fundamentalists joined the National Presbyterian and Reformed Fellowship, which provided contact with northern fundamentalists of the Orthodox Presbyterian Church, United Presbyterian Church of North America, and others. Eventually, in 1983, the PCA received the predominantly northern Reformed Presbyterian Church, Evangelical Synod (RPCES), into its membership. Mark Noll further identifies Reformed Theological Seminary, Covenant Theological Seminary (in St. Louis, Missouri, and since union with the RPCES the PCA's denominational seminary), Westminster Theological Seminary (founded by Machen), and Faith Seminary in Philadelphia, all with close ties to the PCA, as carrying on the Princeton tradition.[40] A 1970 piece by Joe Morecraft reiterated the Princeton theology in modern form. Delineating Calvinism as distinct from Barthian neo-orthodoxy, Morecraft argues the former understands the Bible to be rational and clear concerning what we can know of God. Conversely, in neo-orthodoxy,

> truth, upon which a person's life can be based is not reasonable, not systematic, contradictory, paradoxical, non-communicable, irrational, subjective, momentary and nebulous. "Talk-about-God" can never be sure or absolute. . . . We can never really know God because He is so different from us. Therefore, we can never be sure about what God has to say to us, if anything at all.[41]

With this absolute certainty that theology grows out of God's revelation and systematizes eternal truth, one finds a tendency to bifurcate (for instance, Machen's argument in *Christianity and Liberalism* that they are two religions). One either holds truth or falsehood; there is little, if any, middle ground between the two. "We have not been arguing over different approaches to the Gospel," G. Aiken Taylor declared, "but over the difference between the Gospel and no Gospel."[42] Morecraft, in the article cited, argued a similar point.[43] In concert with this outlook it was common to characterize the Soviet Union as atheistic and to aver there could be no mixing of Marxism and Christianity.[44]

The PCA, then, grew out of the attempt of conservative southern Presbyterians to preserve Old School Calvinism. The people embarked on that program in reaction to the increasing influence of modern biblical criticism and a broadening understanding of theology and mission in both seminaries and the General Assembly offices. In its theology and in its reaction to that change the PCA represented one branch of postwar fundamentalism in the South. The northern Presbyterian fundamentalism of an earlier period informed that movement and the PCA drew much of its thought from its Princeton cousins. And, as Machen and his followers had decided as they withdrew from the church in the North, the members of the PCA became convinced that the true gospel was little observed in the PCUS. They believed the blessed ties that bound them to the old church were gone; thus, a new church was born.

Paradoxical Ties Binding "Cousins"

What does the withdrawal of the PCA say about the post–World War II PCUS? It suggests that the denomination reflected changes which seem present in old-line denominations generally. First, the PCUS did change significantly: it became much more socially and politically active and less stringent in its approach to the Bible and theology—what fundamentalists meant when they used the word "liberal." Second, the denomination grew into the 1960s. This required an expansion of programs and personnel, with an attendant increase in bureaucracy. That process necessarily made many feel less connected to denominational offices and feel a decrease in the traditionally intimate nature of the PCUS.

Above all, the PCUS manifested the secularization of religion which Wuthnow cites as a major component to understanding postwar religion in the United States.[45]

Noting surveys that have explored why people become members of churches, Wuthnow observes the answers reflect reasons of a secular nature: the church offers opportunity for social action, it provides a support group, it has a good program of charitable work, and it offers social interaction and fellowship. Those needs can be met by any number of other organizations. Too often the role of religion in society became to legitimate God as a psychological healer or supporter of causes; it appeared the church failed to maintain a vision of its unique message in society and allowed its agenda to be determined by secular concerns.[46] Thus developed the proliferation of special interest groups in the churches (and they were legion in the PCUS) which meant the churches, "instead of simply being aggregations of people who come together to worship, are likely to reflect other divisions in the wider society."[47]

The loss of membership in old-line churches aside from conservative withdrawals may be the result of people not seeing or realizing the difference between this form of Christianity and secular institutions that attempt to do the same things. Studies indicate that old-line churches are losing members not to conservative congregations but to the ranks of the unchurched.[48] To the extent that the denomination failed to convey to others that it embarked on this type of mission as a response to an understanding of God's call and will for the world, there was merit to the fundamentalist charge that the denomination had become a political and social action agency—although it was also true that the PCUS was applying the gospel to social and political issues in prophetic and exciting ways that challenged long-standing injustices.

There are two ironies in the PCUS-PCA developments. The first is that the change sought in theology and mission for the PCUS offered a prophetic element missing in a denomination believed to have been "culturally captive." The identification of the PCUS with Southern culture has been noted; the reformers saw themselves moving the church away from a situation in which theology, biblical study, and mission were determined by social mores and the status quo (note Morton Smith's biblical defense of segregation, for example). The gospel needed to be applied to society in a prophetic way which made clear that the church was not of the world (that is, secular) but bore a gospel that was responsive to the world. As stated, many have perceived that the world instead held too much sway over the church's mission. The denomination, intending to battle secular control of the church, itself became secularized in a different way.

On the other hand, the PCA is secularized as well. Wuthnow declares that conservative Christians are organized around special interest groups concerned for such issues as abortion, strong defense, and "pro-family" legislation. That is, conservative Christianity has become political as well. While claiming to maintain the pure gospel, the PCA sought to preserve the Southern status quo and traditional attitudes on sociopolitical questions.

The Presbyterian Church in America charged the Presbyterian Church in the United States with adopting a secular agenda; unconsciously, it has done the same. Perhaps there is this paradoxical tie that even now binds these "cousins" together.

Notes

Series Foreword

1. Arthur M. Schlesinger, Sr., "A Critical Period in American Religion, 1875–1900," first appeared in the *Massachusetts Historical Society Proceedings* 64 (1930–32) and is reprinted in John M. Mulder and John F. Wilson, eds., *Religion in American History: Interpretive Essays* (Englewood Cliffs, N.J.: Prentice-Hall, 1978), pp. 302–317.

2. Robert T. Handy, "The American Religious Depression, 1925–1935," *Church History* 29 (1960): 3–16, reprinted in Mulder and Wilson, *Religion in American History,* pp. 431–444; Handy, *A Christian America: Protestant Hopes and Historical Realities,* 2nd ed. (New York: Oxford University Press, 1984), pp. 159–184.

3. Sydney E. Ahlstrom, "The Radical Turn in Theology and Ethics: Why It Occurred in the 1960s," *Annals of the American Academy of Political and Social Science* 387 (1970): 1–13, reprinted in Mulder and Wilson, *Religion in American History,* pp. 445–456; Ahlstrom, "The Traumatic Years: American Religion and Culture in the 1960s and 1970s," *Theology Today* 26 (1980): 504–522; Ahlstrom, *A Religious History of the American People* (New Haven, Conn.: Yale University Press, 1972), pp. 1079–1096.

4. Wade Clark Roof and William McKinney, *American Mainline Religion: Its Changing Shape and Future* (New Brunswick,

N.J.: Rutgers University Press, 1987); Robert Wuthnow, *The Restructuring of American Religion: Society and Faith Since World War II* (Princeton, N.J.: Princeton University Press, 1988).

5. John V. Taylor, *The Primal Vision: Christian Presence Amid African Religion* (Philadelphia: Fortress Press, 1964), chapter 13, "The Practice of Presence," pp. 196–205.

Introduction

1. American religious historians traditionally include among the mainstream Protestant denominations the Presbyterian Church (U.S.A.), the American Baptist Churches, the Disciples of Christ, the Protestant Episcopal Church, the United Church of Christ, the United Methodist Church, and their denominational antecedents.

2. Lefferts A. Loetscher, *The Broadening Church: A Study of Theological Issues in the Presbyterian Church Since 1869* (Philadelphia: University of Pennsylvania Press, 1954) p. 135.

3. Robert Wuthnow, *The Restructuring of American Religion: Society and Faith Since World War II* (Princeton, N.J.: Princeton University Press, 1988), pp. 71–99.

4. John H. Leith, *The Reformed Imperative: What the Church Has to Say That No One Else Can Say* (Philadelphia: Westminster Press, 1988), p. 21.

5. R. Laurence Moore, "Secularization: Religion and the Social Sciences," in *Between the Times: The Travail of the Protestant Establishment in America, 1900–1960,* ed. William R. Hutchison (New York: Cambridge University Press, 1989), pp. 233–252.

6. Wuthnow, *Restructuring,* pp. 132–172.

1: Pluralism and Policy in Presbyterian Views of Scripture

1. Lefferts A. Loetscher, *The Broadening Church: A Study of Theological Issues in the Presbyterian Church Since 1869* (Philadelphia: University of Pennsylvania Press, 1954). An extensive discussion of the Princeton view of scripture is found in Jack B. Rogers and Donald K. McKim, *The Authority and Interpretation of the Bible: An Historical Approach* (San Francisco: Harper & Row, 1979), chs. 5 and 6. For parallels to the Old Princeton approach in the South see Ernest Trice Thompson, *Presbyterians in the South,* vol. 3: *1890–1972* (Richmond: John Knox Press, 1973), ch. 20, and Morton Howison Smith, *Studies in Southern*

Presbyterian Theology (Amsterdam: Jacob Van Campen, 1962), Introduction and chs. 4 and 5.

2. Loetscher, *Broadening Church,* pp. 133–134.

3. Ibid., p. 135.

4. See Karl Barth, *Church Dogmatics,* trans. G. W. Bromiley (Edinburgh: T. & T. Clark, 1956), I/2, pp. 508, 457. Cf. Rogers and McKim, *Authority and Interpretation of the Bible,* pp. 406–426, and Donald K. McKim, *What Christians Believe About the Bible* (Nashville: Thomas Nelson Publishers, 1985), ch. 6. On the reception of neo-orthodoxy in America see Dennis N. Voskuil, "America Encounters Karl Barth, 1919–1939," *Fides et Historia* 12 (1980): 61–74, and "American Protestant Neo-Orthodoxy and Its Search for Realism (1925–1939)," *Ultimate Reality and Meaning* 8 (1985): 277–287. On Barth's influence on theologians trained in this era see Donald K. McKim, ed., *How Karl Barth Changed My Mind* (Grand Rapids: Wm. B. Eerdmans Publishing Co., 1986).

5. James C. Goodloe IV, "Kenneth J. Foreman, Sr.—A Candle on the Glacier," *Journal of Presbyterian History* 57 (Winter 1979): 469.

6. Thompson, *Presbyterians in the South,* 3:493–494. On Dabney see Douglas Lloyd Kelly, "Robert Lewis Dabney," in *Reformed Theology in America,* ed. David F. Wells (Grand Rapids: Wm. B. Eerdmans Publishing Co., 1985), pp. 208–231.

7. Thompson, *Presbyterians in the South,* 3:496–498.

8. "A Brief Statement of Belief" (Richmond: Board of Christian Education, PCUS, 1962), p. 2. The membership of the Ad Interim Committee to Prepare a Brief Statement of Belief included: Charles L. King, Chair, Felix B. Gear, Vice Chair, John H. Leith, Secretary, Wade H. Boggs, Jr., Mary L. Boney, Kenneth J. Foreman, Roland M. Frye, Warner L. Hall, T. B. Jackson, Ashby Johnson, Laurence F. Kinney, James G. Leyburn, J. R. McCain, Harry M. Moffett, Jr., David L. Stitt.

9. *Journal of Presbyterian History* 59 (Summer 1981) presented a series of articles that attempted to update the study begun in Loetscher's *Broadening Church.* See especially W. Eugene March, " 'Biblical Theology,' Authority and the Presbyterians," pp. 113–129, and Jack B. Rogers, "Biblical Authority and Confessional Change," pp. 131–156.

10. "A Brief Statement of Belief," p. 6.

11. *The Confessional Statement of the United Presbyterian Church of North America* (Pittsburgh: Board of Christian Educa-

tion of the United Presbyterian Church of North America, 1951). For background on the preparation, debate, and acceptance of this confessional statement see Wallace N. Jamison, *The United Presbyterian Story: A Centennial Study, 1858–1958* (Pittsburgh: Geneva Press, 1958), pp. 136–143.

12. *Confessional Statement of UPCNA,* p. 9.

13. Jamison, *United Presbyterian Story,* pp. 128, 137–139. At the one seminary of the denomination, Pittsburgh-Xenia, a similar attitude of conservative profession but flexible practice prevailed during the 1950s. The professor of church history, John H. Gerstner, a graduate of Westminster Seminary, authored a *Bible Inerrancy Primer* and was a strong advocate for the Old Princeton theology. Addison H. Leitch, professor of systematic theology and president from 1955 to 1959, represented a more moderate viewpoint. His inaugural address, however, was devoted to a defense of the authority of the Bible as verbally inspired. See John H. Gerstner, *A Bible Inerrancy Primer* (Grand Rapids: Baker Book House, 1965), pp. 63–65; and *Theological Conflict: The Inaugural Address of Seminary President Addison H. Leitch, October 27, 1955* (Pittsburgh-Xenia Theological Seminary), p. 13: "Our own church confession states, 'inspired *in language* as in thought.' " See Addison H. Leitch, *Beginnings in Theology* (Pittsburgh: Geneva Press, 1957), chapter 2, "The Bible: The Word of God."

14. For background see *Report of the Special Committee on a Brief Statement of Faith to the 177th General Assembly, The United Presbyterian Church in the United States of America, May 1965* (Philadelphia: Office of the General Assembly, 1965), pp. 9–13. Over the next four years eleven more members, including one woman, were added to the original nine men. Several members retired or resigned, including the former president of the UPCNA seminary, Pittsburgh-Xenia, Addison H. Leitch, who privately complained of the dominance of Princeton Seminary neo-orthodox theologians on the committee. Members of the committee are recorded in Rogers, "Confessional Change," pp. 153–154, nn. 27–29.

15. *Report,* p. 11.

16. For a broader perspective of the sources that informed the Confession of 1967, see Arnold B. Come, "The Occasion and Contribution of the Confession of 1967," *Journal of Presbyterian History* 61 (Spring 1983): 18, 25–26; and Arnold B. Come, "The Confession of 1967: Its Place in Twentieth-Century Theology," *Princeton Seminary Bulletin* 9 (July 1988): 19–20.

17. Edward A. Dowey, Jr., "A Critique of the Report on Biblical Authority and Interpretation Written to Follow That of Arnold B. Come" (unpublished paper presented to a Standing Committee of the General Assembly, June 23, 1982). Dowey concluded: "One would not guess from this Report that the Confession of 1967 was and is the only full scale confessional achievement in any Reformed church in the world that shows the church both responding to and triumphing over the attacks on Scripture that were suffered for nearly two hundred years. . . . The fundamental shift from the Westminster Confession's inspiration doctrine to Calvin, Luther's and Barth's revelation doctrine is not even noticed."

18. *Report,* p. 29.

19. *The Constitution of the Presbyterian Church (U.S.A.),* Part I: *Book of Confessions* (New York and Atlanta: The Office of the General Assembly, 1983), 9.27; further citations in the text. For a study of the backgrounds and issues involved with the issue of scripture in the Confession of 1967, see Rogers, "Confessional Change," pp. 131–156.

20. Edward A. Dowey, Jr., *A Commentary on the Confession of 1967 and An Introduction to "The Book of Confessions"* (Philadelphia: Westminster Press, 1968), pp. 98–103.

21. "Lay Committee Advertisements Assail Proposed Confession," *Presbyterian Life* (Feb. 1, 1967): 23, quotes the advertisement.

22. See Jack B. Rogers, "The Search for System: American Theology in the 1980s," *Theology, News and Notes* (Pasadena, Calif.: Published for the Fuller Theological Seminary Alumni, December 1981), 5–6; Thor Hall, "Does Systematic Theology Have a Future?" *Christian Century* (March 17, 1976): 253–256; Deane Williams Ferm, *Contemporary American Theologies: A Critical Survey* (New York: Seabury Press, 1981), pp. 19–20.

23. See Bernard Murchland, ed., *The Meaning of the Death of God* (New York: Vintage Books, 1967).

24. Thompson, *Presbyterians in the South,* 3:503.

25. "How It Started," *Presbyterian Journal* (Jan. 7, 1970): 10–11; Morton H. Smith, *How Is the Gold Become Dim,* 2nd ed. (Jackson, Miss.: The Steering Committee for a Continuing Presbyterian Church, 1973), p. 26: "For example women elders, endorsement of abortion, rejection of capital punishment, and many other such actions of recent Assemblies are decried by the Bible believer, just because they are contrary to the Bible, and

not for some politico-social attitude as some would claim"; "The Time Is at Hand," *Presbyterian Journal* (Dec. 20, 1972): 19; "Committee Votes to Scrap Plan of Union," *Presbyterian Journal* (Feb. 21, 1973): 4; "The Time Has Come for Love," *Presbyterian Journal* (March 7, 1973): 12; Paul G. Settle, "God's Investment for Revival," *Presbyterian Journal* (May 14, 1975): 7–8.

26. *The Proposed Book of Confessions of the Presbyterian Church in the United States, Together with Related Documents* (Atlanta: General Assembly of the Presbyterian Church in the United States, 1976), p. 240.

27. "Out of the Blue, A Vote," *Christianity Today* (Feb. 18, 1977): 52.

28. Jack Rogers, "The Kenyon Case," in *Women and Men in Ministry,* ed. Roberta Hestenes (Pasadena, Calif.: Fuller Theological Seminary, 1985), p. 148.

29. Rogers, "Kenyon," pp. 148–149; Kenyon's father had been a pastor in the former United Presbyterian Church of North America. When Wynn Kenyon went to Pittsburgh Seminary he became part of a group of students who felt especially loyal to Professor John H. Gerstner, one of the few remaining faculty members from the former Pittsburgh-Xenia Seminary. Among their shared convictions was the belief that the Bible "clearly teaches women should be subordinate ('silent') in the official teaching and ruling ministry of the Christian church." During the controversy over Kenyon's ordination he shared with Gerstner and several others in authoring a booklet entitled *Ordination and Subordination,* which contended that the real issue was biblical authority. Kenyon and others thus held that the UPCUSA was in error in ordaining women. However, they felt free to remain in the church while scrupling against this point since it was, in their judgment, a nonessential matter. See Rogers, "Kenyon," p. 148.

30. Rogers, "Kenyon," p. 150.

31. Ibid.

32. "The Church and Homosexuality," *Blue Book I, 190th General Assembly (1978) of The United Presbyterian Church in the United States of America, San Diego, California, May 16–24, 1978,* pp. D-1–D-201.

33. Ibid., pp. D-57–D-100.

34. For more detailed descriptions of these models see McKim, *What Christians Believe About the Bible.*

35. *Minutes of the General Assembly of the United Presbyterian*

Church in the United States of America, Part I: *Journal* (New York: Office of the General Assembly, 1976), p. 584. See Rogers and McKim, *Authority and Interpretation of the Bible,* p. 455, n. 244. On scripture in liberation theology see McKim, *What Christians Believe About the Bible,* ch. 11. Cf. Robert McAfee Brown, *Theology in a New Key: Responding to Liberation Themes* (1978); *Unexpected News: Reading the Bible with Third World Eyes* (1984); *Saying Yes and Saying No: On Rendering to God and Caesar* (1986); *Spirituality and Liberation: Overcoming the Great Fallacy* (1988). All were published by Westminster Press in Philadelphia.

36. For an overview of the philosophy of Albert North Whitehead which forms a foundation for process theology, see Jack B. Rogers and Forrest Baird, *Introduction to Philosophy: A Case Method Approach* (San Francisco: Harper & Row, 1981), "The Case of Whitehead," pp. 183–192.

37. On scripture in process theology see McKim, *What Christians Believe About the Bible,* ch. 9. For an approach by a Presbyterian, see Benjamin A. Reist, "Dogmatics in Process," *Pacific Theological Review* 19 (Spring 1986): 4–21.

38. "Report of the Committee on Pluralism in the Church to the 190th General Assembly (1978) of The United Presbyterian Church in the United States of America," *Minutes,* 1978, Part I, p. 293.

39. See *Presbyterian Use and Understanding of Scripture,* a Position Statement of the General Assembly, Presbyterian Church (U.S.A.) (New York and Atlanta: Office of the General Assembly, 1983), n.p.

40. "Taking a Stand on Scripture," advertisement in *Christianity Today* (Dec. 30, 1977): 25.

41. See James Montgomery Boice, ed., *The Foundation of Biblical Authority* (Grand Rapids: Zondervan Publishing House, 1978); and for the papers given at the 1978 "summit" see Norman Geisler, ed., *Inerrancy* (Grand Rapids: Zondervan Publishing House, 1979). Events of the early 1980s suggested that the warning of the UPCUSA Pluralism Committee was prophetic. By 1981, some sixty congregations had separated from the UPCUSA, most of them claiming that their differences with the denomination rooted in a differing understanding of the nature and function of the Bible. Many of these congregations affiliated with the newly formed Evangelical Presbyterian Church. Some went elsewhere, including the Tenth Presbyterian Church in Phil-

adelphia, pastored by James M. Boice. It joined the Reformed Presbyterian Church, Evangelical Synod, which by merger a few years later became part of the Presbyterian Church in America, the 1973 split off the PCUS.

42. *Biblical Authority and Interpretation,* a Resource Document, received by the 194th General Assembly, June 1982, The United Presbyterian Church in the United States of America (New York: Advisory Council on Discipleship and Worship, 1982), p. 4

43. Ibid., p. 5.

44. Ibid., p. 3.

45. Ibid., p. 5.

46. Ibid.

47. Ibid., p. 6.

48. Ibid., p. 7–10.

49. Ibid., pp. 13–15.

50. Both the UPCUSA and the PCUS were originally scheduled to report in 1980. The UP General Assembly gave its task force a third year and the task force later asked for and received an extension until 1982. The PCUS group presented a 100-page report to the Council on Theology and Culture in 1980. Disagreements within the Council over the report caused it to languish for two years. Then the task was turned over to an individual, Professor D. Cameron Murchison, Jr., of Union Seminary in Virginia, who developed a report that was presented to and adopted by the PCUS Assembly just prior to the reunion in 1983.

51. "Approaches to the Bible: An Analysis of the PCUS Paper on 'Understanding and Use of Holy Scripture' in Relation to the United Presbyterian Paper on the Same Subject," *Presbyterian Outlook* (May 16, 1983): 6.

52. Ibid., p. 7: "It is evident from a study of the two documents that our two churches go into reunion with a common understanding of the authority and interpretation of the Bible. The differences in approach are interesting, however, as an illustration of the different ways our two churches have dealt with a common subject. The PCUS assumes a uniformity and consensus in faith which the UPC cannot accept so readily, given its diversity. The PCUS tends to be affirmative, the UPC dialectic. The melding of these two approaches will affect the theological dialogue of the years ahead."

53. See "Adventure and Hope: Christians and the Crisis in

Central America," Report to the 195th General Assembly of the Presbyterian Church (U.S.A.), 1983, pp. 17ff.

54. See "Christian Faith and Economic Justice," Presbyterian Church (U.S.A.) (New York and Atlanta: Office of the General Assembly, 1984), p. 2. Two paragraphs with biblical citations support this implication.

55. "The Confessional Nature of the Church" (New York: Advisory Council on Discipleship and Worship of the Presbyterian Church (U.S.A.), 1986), 29.153.

56. *Biblical Authority and Interpretation,* pp. 15–16.

57. *Minutes of the General Assembly of the Presbyterian Church (U.S.A.),* Part I: *Journal* (New York and Atlanta: Office of the General Assembly, 1987), pp. 428–429 (28.151; 154; 160; 181).

58. Cynthia Campbell, "Theologies Written from Feminist Perspectives: An Introductory Study," Commended to the Church for Study by the 199th General Assembly (1987) (New York: Office of the General Assembly, PC(USA), 1987).

59. Ibid., p. 22.

60. Ibid., pp. 53–54. Implications of these conclusions are also drawn on pp. 54–56. Cf. Letty M. Russell, *Human Liberation in a Feminist Perspective—A Theology* (1974); ed., *The Liberating Word* (1976); *The Future of Partnership* (1979); *Growth in Partnership* (1981); *Becoming Human* (1982); ed., *Feminine Interpretation of the Bible* (1985); *Household of Freedom: Authority in Feminist Theology* (1987). All were published by Westminster Press in Philadelphia.

61. *Is Christ Divided? Report of the Task Force on Theological Pluralism Within the Presbyterian Community of Faith* (Louisville, Ky.: Office of the General Assembly, PC(USA), 1988).

62. Ibid., p. 5.

63. Ibid., p. 6.

64. Ibid., p. 51.

65. *Articles of Agreement Between the Presbyterian Church in the United States and the United Presbyterian Church in the United States of America to Form the Presbyterian Church (U.S.A.)* (New York and Atlanta: Office of the General Assembly, n.d.), Article 3.2.

66. *Initial Draft of a Proposed Brief Statement of Reformed Faith for Response by the Church* (Louisville, Ky.: Office of the General Assembly, PC(USA), 1988), lines 45–47.

67. *A Brief Statement of Faith, Presbyterian Church (U.S.A.),* A Proposal to the 201st General Assembly (1989) from the Special

Committee on a Brief Statement of the Reformed Faith (Louisville, Ky.: Office of the General Assembly, 1989), lines 48–50.

68. *A Brief Statement of Faith,* submitted to the 202nd General Assembly of the Presbyterian Church (U.S.A.) (Louisville, Ky.: Office of the General Assembly, 1990), lines 59–61.

69. Robert Wuthnow, *The Restructuring of American Religion: Society and Faith Since World War II* (Princeton, N.J.: Princeton University Press, 1988), p. 164: "The period from about 1973 through the mid-1980s was a time . . . of deepening division between religious liberals and religious conservatives"; and p. 219: "The division between religious liberals and conservatives is one that *cuts across* denominational lines." Wuthnow's data in this instance are on Baptists, Lutherans, Methodists, and Catholics.

70. The bell-shaped curve which was exhibited in Presbyterians' views of scripture suggests that nearly half of Presbyterians are ensconced firmly in an often uncomfortable and ambiguous middle position. Rarely more than 15 percent of persons are found on the far right and usually less than 10 percent are on the far left. The Panel Survey on scripture done in the early 1980s shows that at worst, some 37 percent were right of the middle and 15 percent were left of center.

71. Indeed Wade Clark Roof and William McKinney, *American Mainline Religion: Its Changing Shape and Future* (New Brunswick, N.J.: Rutgers University Press, 1987), pp. 5ff., dwell on "the collapse of the middle." William Joseph Weston, "The Emergence of the Idea of Religious Pluralism with the Presbyterian Church U.S.A. 1896–1940" (Ph.D. diss., Yale University, 1988), suggests that the middle group always has the majority of votes but rarely has had as articulate a voice as those on the extremes.

72. See, for example, Wuthnow, *Restructuring,* p. 216; Roof and McKinney, *American Mainline Religion,* p. 79.

73. Wuthnow, *Restructuring,* ch. 6.

74. Ibid., p. 131.

75. Ibid., pp. 119–120.

76. Roof and McKinney, *American Mainline Religion,* ch. 6, "Mainline Morality."

2: Redefining Confessionalism

1. See, for example, Lefferts A. Loetscher, *The Broadening Church: A Study of Theological Issues in the Presbyterian Church*

Since 1869 (Philadelphia: University of Pennsylvania Press, 1954), esp. pp. 125–136; and Ernest Trice Thompson, *Presbyterians in the South,* 3 vols. (Richmond: John Knox Press, 1963–73), 3:302–339.

2. The United Presbyterian Church of North America, which merged with the Presbyterian Church in the U.S.A. in 1958, carried out a significant creedal revision immediately prior to the period covered by this essay. After more than forty years of discussion about the possibility of making piecemeal amendments to the Westminster Confession, the UP Church adopted a wholesale revision in 1925. Condensing and rearranging Westminster, the new Confessional Statement omitted certain doctrines that were no longer widely held, for example, hyper-Calvinist views of the atonement and election. The Confessional Statement was warmly evangelical and irenic in tone. See Wallace N. Jamison, *The United Presbyterian Story, 1858–1958* (Pittsburgh: Geneva Press, 1958), pp. 133–143.

The common use of "southern" and "northern" to denote the two major denominations of American Presbyterianism prior to 1983 merits brief comment. The Presbyterian Church in the U.S. was a regional church, limited to the states of the old southern Confederacy and to immediately adjacent border states. The PCUSA (later UPCUSA), while having its major areas of strength outside the South, did have a southern constituency, much of it composed of Black Presbyterians.

3. See, for example, Dennis N. Voskuil, "Neo-Orthodoxy," in *Encyclopedia of the American Religious Experience,* 3 vols., ed. Charles H. Lippy and Peter W. Williams (New York: Charles Scribner's Sons, 1988), 2:1147–1157; Deane William Ferm, *Contemporary American Theologians: A Critical Survey* (New York: Seabury Press, 1981), pp. 1–20; William R. Hutchinson, *The Modernist Impulse in American Protestantism* (Cambridge, Mass.: Harvard University Press, 1976), pp. 288–311; and Sydney E. Ahlstrom, "Continental Influence on American Christian Thought Since World War I," *Church History* 27 (September 1958): 256–272.

4. Elmer G. Homrighausen, "Calm After Storm," *Christian Century* 56 (April 12, 1939), 477–479; John W. Hart, "Princeton Theological Seminary: The Reorganization of 1929," *Journal of Presbyterian History* 58 (Summer 1980): 124–180; Stanton R. Wilson, "Studies in the Life and Work of an Ecumenical Churchman (Studies of John A. Mackay)" (Th.M. thesis, Princeton

Theological Seminary, 1958); Hugh T. Kerr, "John A. Mackay: An Appreciation," in *The Ecumenical Era in Church and Society: A Symposium in Honor of John A. Mackay,* ed. Edward Jurji (New York: Macmillan Co., 1959), pp. 1–17.

5. W. Eugene March, " 'Biblical Theology,' Authority and the Presbyterians," *Journal of Presbyterian History* 59 (Summer 1981): 113–130; Brevard S. Childs, *Biblical Theology in Crisis* (Philadelphia: Westminster Press, 1970); James D. Smart, *The Past, Present, and Future of Biblical Theology* (Philadelphia: Westminster Press, 1979); Floyd V. Filson, *One Lord, One Faith* (Philadelphia: Westminster Press, 1943); G. Ernest Wright, *The God Who Acts: Biblical Theology as Recital* (London: SCM Press, 1952).

6. William B. Kennedy, "Neo-Orthodoxy Goes to Sunday School: The Christian Faith and Life Curriculum," *Journal of Presbyterian History* 58 (Winter 1980): 326–370. Robert McAfee Brown, *The Bible Speaks to You* (Philadelphia: Westminster Press, 1955), pp. 97–99, illustrated the tactic of acknowledging contemporary biblical scholarship while reasserting traditional themes. In his discussion of the resurrection, Brown noted that the various biblical accounts did not tally in every respect. He made no effort to force these discrepancies into an artificial harmony but rather emphasized that all the writers, whatever their minor disparities, agreed on the fundamental truth: Jesus is risen. For more on the philosophy undergirding the *Christian Faith and Life* curriculum, see James D. Smart, *The Teaching Ministry of the Church* (Philadelphia: Westminster Press, 1954).

7. William R. Miller, ed., *Contemporary American Protestant Thought, 1900–1970* (Indianapolis: Bobbs-Merrill Co., 1973), p. lxvi; Sydney E. Ahlstrom, *A Religious History of the American People* (New Haven, Conn.: Yale University Press, 1972), pp. 949–963; James W. Hoffman, "Reinhold Niebuhr, Protestant Prophet," *Presbyterian Life* 2 (July 9, 1947): 6–7, 29.

8. Ahlstrom, *Religious History,* p. 947. As early as 1957, Ahlstrom was already among the few recognizing that the "usefulness of the term neo-orthodoxy has waned. Whatever value it may have had in the 1930s or early 1940s to designate a then existing movement has faded away." See Sydney E. Ahlstrom, "Neo-Orthodoxy Demythologized," *Christian Century* 74 (May 22, 1957): 649–651.

9. Arnold B. Come, "The Occasion and Contribution of the Confession of 1967," *Journal of Presbyterian History* 61 (Spring

1983): 13–32; Edward A. Dowey, Jr., *A Commentary on the Confession of 1967 and An Introduction to "The Book of Confessions"* (Philadelphia: Westminster Press, 1968). The other documents in the *Book of Confessions* were the Nicene Creed, the Apostles' Creed, the Scots Confession, the Heidelberg Catechism, the Second Helvetic Confession, the Westminster Confession of Faith, the Shorter Catechism, and the Theological Declaration of Barmen. See *The Constitution of The United Presbyterian Church in the United States of America,* Part I: *Book of Confessions,* 2nd ed. (Philadelphia: Office of the General Assembly of the UPCUSA, 1970).

10. *Book of Confessions,* 9.07; 9.27; 9.30; 9.29. For further treatment of the issue of scripture in C-67, see Jack B. Rogers, "Biblical Authority and Confessional Change," *Journal of Presbyterian History* 59 (Summer 1981): 131–157.

11. *Book of Confessions,* 9.09; 9.05; 9.01.

12. Ibid., 9.31, also 9.34-9.40 and 9.49-9.52.

13. Ibid., 9.44-9.47.

14. Ibid., 9.43; Come, "The Occasion and Contribution of the Confession of 1967," p. 21; Dowey, *Commentary on the Confession of 1967,* pp. 34–37.

15. *A Digest of the Acts and Proceedings of the General Assembly of the Presbyterian Church in the United States, 1861–1965* (Atlanta: Office of the General Assembly, 1966), pp. 26–35; Thompson, *Presbyterians in the South,* 2:414–441.

16. Thompson, *Presbyterians in the South,* 3:486–503; James C. Goodloe IV, "Kenneth J. Foreman, Sr.—A Candle on the Glacier," *Journal of Presbyterian History* 57 (Winter 1979): 467–484; March, " 'Biblical Theology,' Authority and the Presbyterians, " pp. 113–130; Rachel O. Henderlite, "We Can't Go Home Again," *Austin Seminary Bulletin* 82 (April 1967): 7–32. For another example of the new attitude see the widely popular Egbert Watson Smith, *The Creed of Presbyterians,* rev. ed. (Richmond: John Knox Press, 1941).

17. *The Confession of Faith of the Presbyterian Church in the United States* (Richmond: Board of Christian Education, 1965), pp. 331–336. Prior to the adoption of "A Brief Statement of Belief," the PCUS had adopted a modest revision of the Westminster Confession. Added to the Standards in 1942 were two chapters—one on the Holy Spirit and the other on the gospel. The import of these changes was to mitigate the double predestinarianism of Westminster by affirming that "God declares his

love for the world and his desire that all men should be saved."
The new chapter on the gospel ended with a strong assertion of
Christians' obligation to help make that universal purpose a reality by supporting missionary enterprise. These changes did not,
of course, represent the most advanced thought in the seminaries, for the new chapters were the identical texts the northern
church had appended to the Confession in 1903. See *Digest,* p. 3;
also *The Confession of Faith of the Presbyterian Church in the
United States,* pp. 61–68. Compare *The Book of Confessions,*
6.168–6.175.

18. *The Proposed Book of Confessions of the Presbyterian
Church in the United States* (Atlanta: Presbyterian Church in the
United States, 1976) was similar to the *Book of Confessions* of the
UPCUSA, but it omitted the Confession of 1967 as well as the
Second Helvetic Confession and added the Geneva Catechism,
the Westminster Larger Catechism, and A Declaration of Faith.
See also *Minutes of the One Hundred Seventeenth General Assem-
bly of the Presbyterian Church in the United States,* Part I: *Journal*
(Atlanta: General Assembly of the Presbyterian Church in the
United States, 1977), pp. 167–168.

19. *The Proposed Book of Confessions,* esp. p. 217.

20. Ibid., p. 161.

21. Ibid., pp. 166–168.

22. Robert Wuthnow, *The Restructuring of American Religion:
Society and Faith Since World War II* (Princeton, N.J.: Princeton
University Press, 1988), pp. 57–61; "Social Teachings of the
Presbyterian Church," content ed. Dieter T. Hessel and author
James D. Beumler, *Church and Society* 75 (November–Decem-
ber 1984); Dale T. Irvin, "Social Witness Policies—An Historical
Overview," *Journal of Presbyterian History* 57 (Fall 1979): 353–
403; "A Letter to Presbyterians," in *The Presbyterian Enterprise:
Sources of American Presbyterian History,* ed. Maurice W. Arm-
strong, Lefferts A. Loetscher, and Charles A. Anderson (Philadel-
phia: Westminster Press, 1956), pp. 317–320; R. Douglas
Brackenridge, *Eugene Carson Blake: Prophet with Portfolio* (New
York: Seabury Press, 1978), pp. 92–105; *Book of Confessions,*
9.43.

23. Sydney E. Ahlstrom, "The Radical Turn in Theology and
Ethics: Why It Occurred in the 1960's," *Annals of the American
Academy of Political and Social Science* 387 (January 1970): 1–
13; Wuthnow, *Restructuring,* pp. 241–267; Wade Clark Roof and
William McKinney, *American Mainline Religion: Its Changing*

Shape and Future (New Brunswick, N.J.: Rutgers University Press, 1987), p. 34.

24. *Presbyterian Outlook* 148 (June 6, 1966): 3–4; ibid. 149 (Jan. 9, 1967): 3–4; ibid. 149 (Jan. 23, 1967): 2; ibid. 149 (May 29, 1967): 6; ibid. 149 (June 5, 1967): 4, 6; E. V. Toy, Jr., "The National Lay Committee and the National Council of Churches: A Case Study of Protestants in Conflict," *American Quarterly* 21 (Summer 1969): 190–209; *Minutes of the 116th General Assembly of the Presbyterian Church in the United States,* Part I: *Journal* (Atlanta: General Assembly of the Presbyterian Church in the United States, 1976), p. 107; *Presbyterian Outlook* 158 (Sept. 20, 1976): 5–7; ibid. 158 (Nov. 8, 1976): 5–7; ibid. 159 (Jan. 31, 1977): 5. See also Rogers, "Biblical Authority and Confessional Change," pp. 142–149.

25. *Minutes of the Two Hundredth General Assembly (1988) of the Presbyterian Church (U.S.A.)* (hereafter cited as GA, PC(USA)), Part I: *Journal* (Louisville, Ky.: Office of the General Assembly, 1988), p. 848. For a sample of the proliferating theologies which replaced the dominant "middle" position once held by neo-orthodoxy, see Deane William Ferm, *Contemporary American Theologies II: A Book of Readings* (New York: Seabury Press, 1982). This "collapse of the middle," as Wade Clark Roof and William McKinney call it, was, of course, not merely a theological phenomenon, but a wider cultural one as well. See Roof and McKinney, *American Mainline Religion,* pp. 25–39.

26. *Minutes of the General Assembly of The United Presbyterian Church in the United States of America,* Part I: *Journal,* 7th series, vol. 9 (New York: Office of the General Assembly, 1975), pp. 254–258.

27. GA, PC(USA), 1988, pp. 1119–1143; Wuthnow, *Restructuring,* pp. 100–132. For an example of efforts to assure representation of various groups, see *The Plan for Reunion,* final ed. (New York and Atlanta: Joint Committee on Presbyterian Union, 1981), pp. 21–23.

28. *Minutes of the General Assembly of the UPCUSA,* vol. 12 (1978), pp. 290–293.

29. Ibid., vol. 16 (1982), pp. 316–335.

30. *Initial Draft of a Proposed Brief Statement of Reformed Faith for Response by the Church* (Louisville, Ky.: Office of the General Assembly of the Presbyterian Church (U.S.A.), 1988). For an analysis of the final version of the Brief Statement, see

James H. Moorhead, "Presbyterians Confess Their Faith Anew," *The Christian Century* 107 (July 11–18, 1990): 676–680.

31. Ibid., lines 45–47. The commentator was a discussant of the proposed statement at the meeting of Orange Presbytery, Presbyterian Church (U.S.A.), July 26, 1988.

32. See Loetscher, *The Broadening Church,* pp. 1–8; Leonard J. Trinterud, *The Forming of an American Tradition: A Re-examination of Colonial Presbyterianism* (Philadelphia: Westminster Press, 1949).

33. For recent efforts to assess this diversity and its meaning for the confessional identity of the church, see the report on the confessional nature of the church in GA, PC(USA), 1986, pp. 516–527; and the report "Is Christ Divided?" in GA, PC(USA), 1988, pp. 826–852.

3: Changes in the Authority, Method, and Message of UPCUSA Preaching

1. *Teaching with Authority? The Changing Place of Mainstream Protestantism in American Culture,* prepared for The Council on Theological Education, Presbyterian Church (U.S.A.), Nov. 5, 1986, p. 4.

2. Dieter T. Hessel, "Contours of the Quest for Political Relevance in Social Teachings of the (United) Presbyterian Church in the U.S.A., 1936–1964" (Th.D. diss., San Francisco Theological Seminary, 1966). Part I notes this preoccupation before 1936 when the Presbyterian Church instituted a small Department of Social Education and Action.

3. Henry van Dyke, "Salt," in *Masterpieces of Modern Oratory,* ed. Edwin DuBois Shurter (Boston: Ginn & Co., 1906), p. 325; Charles N. Davidson, Jr., "George Arthur Buttrick: Christocentric Preacher and Pacifist," *Journal of Presbyterian History* 53 (Summer 1975): 143–160; Morley Francis Hodder, "Social Concerns in the Preaching of Henry Sloane Coffin" (Th.D. diss., Boston University School of Theology, 1963); George H. Nash III, "Charles Stelzle: Social Gospel Pioneer," *Journal of Presbyterian History* 50 (Fall 1972), 206–228; and Betty Jane Brandon, "Alexander Jeffrey McKelway: Statesman of a New Order" (Ph.D. diss., University of North Carolina at Chapel Hill, 1969).

4. Another notable Presbyterian pulpit from which both the social gospel and liberal theology were preached was at First

Presbyterian Church in New York City by (ex-Baptist) Harry Emerson Fosdick. Other influential mainstream pulpits of the social gospel were Methodist pulpits held by preachers such as Merton S. Rice, William L. Stidger, Edwin H. Hughes, and G. Bromley Oxnam.

5. George M. Marsden, *Fundamentalism and American Culture: The Shaping of Twentieth-Century Evangelicalism 1870–1925* (New York: Oxford University Press, 1980), pp. 171–173.

6. John E. Lankford, "The Impact of the New Era Movement on the Presbyterian Church in the United States of America, 1918–1925," *Journal of Presbyterian History* 52 (December 1962): 219. Lankford notes that "the death of Dr. J. Wilbur Chapman in December of 1918 deprived the NEM of its director of spiritual resources: and as a consequence of this . . . spiritual values were not stressed to any great degree."

7. L. T. Newland, "The Biederwolf Meetings in Korea," *Presbyterian Survey* (April 1924): 287. Newland gives expression to the same kind of evangelistic optimism observed by Robert T. Handy, *A Christian America: Protestant Hopes and Historical Realities* (New York: Oxford University Press, 1971), p. 117.

8. "Macbride [sic], Francis Scott," *Standard Encyclopedia of the Alcohol Problem,* ed. Ernest Hurst Cherrington (American Issue Publishing Co., 1928), p. 1621; James H. Timberlake, *Prohibition and the Progressive Movement 1900–1920* (Cambridge, Mass.: Harvard University Press, 1963), p. 28.

9. Wyndham B. Blanton, *The Making of a Downtown Church: The History of Second Presbyterian Church, Richmond, Virginia, 1845–1945* (Richmond: John Knox Press, n.d.), p. 325.

10. *The Story of Our Church* (Richmond: Presbyterian Committee of Publication, 1932), p. 110.

11. Mrs. Aleathea T. Cobbs, "A Preacher of Yesterday," *Presbyterian Survey* (July 1924): 494.

12. Arthur S. Hoyt, "The Modern Pulpit," *Biblical World* 47 (1916): 228.

13. Ibid., p. 229.

14. Ibid.

15. Ibid., p. 226.

16. Robert T. Handy, "The American Religious Depression, 1925–1935," in *Religion in American History: Interpretive Essays,* ed. John M. Mulder and John F. Wilson (Englewood Cliffs, N.J.: Prentice-Hall, 1978), pp. 431–444.

17. Fred B. Craddock, *As One Without Authority* (Nashville: Abingdon Press, 1971), p. 14.

18. Elwyn Allen Smith, *The Presbyterian Ministry in American Culture: A Study in Changing Concepts, 1700–1900* (Philadelphia: Westminster Press, 1962), p. 246.

19. Ibid., p. 249.

20. Elmer G. Homrighausen, "Can the Protestant Sermon Survive?" *Christian Century* 49 (1932), p. 114.

21. Gerald Kennedy, "Seventy-five Years of American Preaching," *Christendom* 7 (1942), 214.

22. Ibid.

23. Dwight E. Stevenson, "Trends in Contemporary Preaching," *College of the Bible Quarterly* (July 1950): 17.

24. Hoyt, "Modern Pulpit," p. 246.

25. Homrighausen, "Can the Protestant Sermon Survive?" p. 114.

26. Sydney E. Ahlstrom, *A Religious History of the American People,* 2 vols. (New York: Image Books, 1975), 2:458. Ahlstrom also speaks of the postwar Liturgical Renewal Movement which had as one specific proposal "invigorating the preaching office" in mainstream churches (p. 457).

27. Robert Wuthnow, *The Restructuring of American Religion: Society and Faith Since World War II* (Princeton, N.J.: Princeton University Press, 1988), p. 27.

28. An increase in the publication of sermons by Presbyterians and in other mainstream denominations during the 1950s seems to indicate this new climate. A similar increase can be noted in the late 1970s and 1980s.

29. Wuthnow, *Restructuring,* p. 32.

30. For examples of such sermons by Presbyterians see Harrison Ray Anderson, "The Witness of the Church" in Harrison Ray Anderson, *God's Way: Messages for Our Time* (Old Tappan, N.J.: Fleming H. Revell Co., 1955), p. 52; John A. Redhead, "Can You Recommend Your Religion," in *Notable Sermons from Protestant Pulpits,* ed. Charles L. Wallis (New York: Abingdon Press, 1958), p. 123; Donald Macleod, "Waiting for the Sunrise," in ibid., p. 159. For a more critical use of this kind of selective history, see George M. Docherty, "One Nation Under God," in his *One Way of Living* (New York: Harper & Brothers, 1958), p. 158.

31. Wuthnow, *Restructuring,* p. 32.

32. Harry Levinson, "The Trouble with Sermons," *Journal of Pastoral Care* 22 (June 1968): 66.

33. Eric Waterhouse, *Psychology and Pastoral Work* (London: University of London Press, 1939), p. 184.

34. M. Furgeson, "Preaching and the Personality of the Preacher," *Pastoral Psychology* 10 (October 1959), 9–14.

35. David Belgum, "Preaching and the Stresses of Life," *Lutheran Quarterly* 20 (1967): 355.

36. R. M. Pearson, "Preaching and the Understanding of the Congregation" *Pastoral Psychology* 10 (March 1959): 37–46. See also Edgar Jackson, *How to Preach to People's Needs* (New York: Abingdon Press, 1956).

37. In the late 1960s and on through the mid-1970s most homiletical texts felt compelled in their introductions to address this apathy and suspicion. For a bibliography of such texts, see Clyde Fant, *Preaching for Today* (New York: Harper & Row, 1975), pp. 1–12.

38. Frederick Buechner, *Telling the Truth: The Gospel as Tragedy, Comedy and Fairytale* (New York: Harper & Row, 1977); Don M. Wardlaw, ed., *Preaching Biblically: Creating Sermons in the Shape of Scripture* (Philadelphia: Westminster Press, 1983); David Buttrick, *Homiletic: Moves and Structures* (Philadelphia: Fortress Press, 1987); and Craddock, *As One Without Authority,* (n. 17 above).

39. J. Randall Nichols, *The Restoring Word: Preaching as Pastoral Communication* (New York: Harper & Row, 1987), and William H. Willimon, *Integrative Preaching* (Nashville: Abingdon Press, 1981).

40. Donald Macleod, *The Problem of Preaching* (Philadelphia: Fortress Press, 1987).

41. Andrew Blackwood added such a component to the middler course in the 1930s and Macleod reinstituted the model in the 1970s. Students would read model sermons and discuss them in class. Such courses also appeared at Union Seminary in Virginia in the 1930s and at Dubuque in 1925.

42. *Union Theological Seminary Catalogue, 1929–1930* (Richmond, 1929), p. 73. Special thanks to Dr. William Harris, archivist at Princeton Theological Seminary, for permitting me unlimited access to back catalogs of Presbyterian seminaries during June 1988.

43. *Princeton Theological Seminary Catalogue, 1930; Union Theological Seminary Catalogue, 1929–1930;* and *Princeton Theological Seminary Catalogue, 1940.*

44. Edwin C. Dargan and Ralph G. Turnbull, *A History of*

Preaching, 3 vols. (Grand Rapids: Baker Book House, 1974), 3:178.

45. A. Duane Litfin, "The Five Most-Used Homiletics Texts," *Christianity Today* 10 (August 1973), 14.

46. Walter Wink, *The Bible in Human Transformation: Toward a New Paradigm for Biblical Study* (Philadelphia: Fortress Press, 1973), pp. 1–18; Ernest Best, *From Text to Sermon: Responsible Use of the New Testament in Preaching* (Atlanta: John Knox Press, 1978). Demythologizing methods such as those of Rudolf Bultmann seemed to have had little effect in overcoming these interpretive problems. Most preachers at that time seemed to see his methods as too radical. See Rudolf Bultmann, *Theology of the New Testament,* vol. 1 (New York: Charles Scribner's Sons, 1951).

47. "Preaching and Recycling," *Princeton Seminary Bulletin* (July 1972): 4.

48. See also by Reuel Howe, "Overcoming the Barriers to Communication," *Pastoral Psychology* 14 (1963): 26, and "Rediscovery of Dialogue in Preaching," *Pastoral Psychology* 12 (1961): 10. Another significant author was Clyde H. Reid, "Preaching and the Nature of Communication," *Pastoral Psychology* 14 (1963): 40, and "Toward a Theology of Communication," *Religious Education* 69 (1974): 355. See also William D. Thompson and Gordon C. Bennett, *Dialogue Preaching: The Shared Sermon* (Valley Forge, Pa.: Judson Press, 1969).

49. "Preaching and Recycling," p. 3.

50. J. Randall Nichols, "What Is the Matter with the Teaching of Preaching?" *Anglican Theological Review* 62 (1980): 224–225.

51. David Buttrick, "Interpretation and Preaching," *Interpretation* 35 (January 1981): 57.

52. Wink, *Bible in Human Transformation.*

53. Brevard Childs, *Introduction to the Old Testament as Scripture* (Philadelphia: Fortress Press, 1979), and James A. Sanders, *From Sacred Story to Sacred Text* (Philadelphia: Fortress Press, 1987).

54. David Buttrick, *Homiletic: Moves and Structures* (n. 38 above). Although discussions at the Academy of Homiletics center on this subject from time to time, David Buttrick is the first to clearly address this issue in a book. It is certain that homileticians rarely write books on the theoretical issues that prompt their "methods." Their reactions to theological and philosophical movements and developments are seldom documented. This is probably because preachers need and ask for

methods not reasons. This state of affairs may change with the introduction of more Ph.D.-trained homileticians into the work force and a potential new interest in the writing of "homiletical theology." See David Buttrick, *Preaching Jesus Christ* (Philadelphia: Fortress Press, 1988), p. 69.

55. Richard Lischer, "The Limits of Story," *Interpretation* 38 (January 1984): 26–38.

56. See J. Randall Nichols, *Restoring Word.* Nichols has implemented a more empirical model at Princeton Theological Seminary in the D.Min. program. He is aware of the pedagogical problems involved in implementing a training program of this type at the Master of Divinity level. See especially "What Is the Matter with the Teaching of Preaching?"

57. There are now programs at Princeton Theological Seminary, Drew University, Emory University, Vanderbilt University, and Southern Baptist Theological Seminary.

58. The Academy of Homiletics was founded by Presbyterian professor of homiletics Donald Macleod of Princeton Theological Seminary.

59. Kennedy, "Seventy-five Years," p. 221 (n. 21 above).

60. Charles E. Quirk, "Origins of the Auburn Affirmation," *Journal of Presbyterian History* 53 (Summer 1975): 120–141.

61. William P. Merrill, "The True Protestantism," in *Best Sermons 1924,* ed. Joseph Fort Newton (New York: Harcourt, Brace & Co., 1924), p. 327. For a more modernist example note Robert Russell Wicks, "The Habit of Living on Other People" in *What Can Students Believe?* ed. Elmore McNeill McKee (New York: Richard R. Smith, 1931), p. 103.

62. Henry Sloane Coffin, "The Practical Aims of Liberal Evangelicalism," *New York Times,* May 19, 1915, p. 8.

63. Paraphrased from John C. Bennett, "After Liberalism—What?" *Christian Century* 50 (Nov. 8, 1933): 1403.

64. "Keeping the Prophet Alive" by Arthur Lee Odell, pastor of Westminster Presbyterian Church, Detroit, 1926, in *Preachers and Preaching in Detroit,* ed. Ralph Milton Pierce (New York: Fleming H. Revell Co., 1926), 168.

65. Paraphrased from Linn Creighton, "Reconciliation in American Protestant Preaching, 1910–1960" (Th.D. diss., Princeton Theological Seminary, 1972). See also William R. Hutchison, *The Modernist Impulse in American Protestantism* (Cambridge, Mass.: Harvard University Press, 1976).

66. Odell, "Keeping the Prophet Alive," pp. 167–168.

67. Quoted from a sermon by Lyman Abbott in Kennedy, "Seventy-five Years," p. 217.

68. From a sermon by George Brewer, pastor of Grosse Pointe Presbyterian Church, Detroit, 1926, in Pierce, *Preachers and Preaching in Detroit,* p. 48. Other examples of social gospel messages by Presbyterian preachers include "The Religious Sanction of the Social Gospel" (1932), by Rev. J. V. Moldenhawer of the First Presbyterian Church, New York City, and "The Duty of the Church in an Industrial Crisis," by Edmund B. Chaffee, in *Contemporary Religious Thinking: Seventeen Sermons on the Church's Responsibilities in the Period Just Ahead,* ed. Robert W. Searle and Frederick A. Bowers (New York: Falcon Press, 1933), pp. 137 and 33.

69. Mark Allison Matthews, "The Virgin Birth of Jesus," in *The American Pulpit,* ed. Charles Clayton Morrison (Chicago: Christian Century Press, 1925), p. 218.

70. Quirk, "Origins of the Auburn Affirmation," p. 122.

71. Lefferts A. Loetscher, *The Broadening Church* (Philadelphia: University of Pennsylvania Press, 1954), p. 91.

72. Quoted in Ernest Trice Thompson, *Presbyterians in the South* (Richmond: John Knox Press, 1973), 2:359. Sermons in this volume are representative of this kind of preaching. Look at the majority of northern Presbyterian sermons in the *Best Sermons* series during the 1920s. For the southern Presbyterian church, look also at Charles Haddon Nabers, ed., *The Southern Presbyterian Pulpit* (New York: Fleming H. Revell Co., 1928).

73. Guy Emery Shipler, ed., *Sermons of Goodwill* (New York: Association Press, 1948), p. 60.

74. Ibid. These are all titles in this collection of sermons.

75. *Best Sermons, 1962, Protestant Edition,* ed. G. Paul Butler (Princeton, N.J.: D. Van Nostrand Co., 1962), p. 257.

76. *Best Sermons, 1964, Protestant Edition,* ed. G. Paul Butler (Princeton, N.J.: D. Van Nostrand Co., 1964), p. 44.

77. William Sloane Coffin, *The Courage to Love* (San Francisco: Harper & Row, 1982), p. 13.

78. Justo L. González and Catherine G. González, *Liberation Preaching: The Pulpit and the Oppressed* (Nashville: Abingdon Press, 1980), and Robert McAfee Brown, *Theology in a New Key* (Philadelphia: Westminster Press, 1978).

79. This observation is based upon my own experience and conversations with colleagues. In the classroom and in the parish, these themes have become more noticeable. For examples of such

sermons see Winston A. G. Lawson's sermon "You Had to Leave Egypt," Joan M. Martin's sermon "We Can't Win for Losin' . . . or Can We?" and Robert McAfee Brown's sermon "Freedom and Political Responsibility" in *Proclaiming the Acceptable Year: Sermons from the Perspective of Liberation Theology,* ed. Justo González (Valley Forge, Pa.: Judson Press, 1982).

80. Reinhold Niebuhr, *The Nature and Destiny of Man,* 2 vols. (New York: Charles Scribner's Sons, 1951), 2:160.

81. Early in the century this worldview included a mixture of Deweyan pragmatism, Darwinism, and empiricism. See Richard Harvey Brown, "Rhetoric and the Science of History: The Debate Between Evolutionism and Empiricism as a Conflict of Metaphors," *Quarterly Journal of Speech* 72 (May 1986): 148–161, and John Angus Campbell, "Scientific Revolution and the Grammar of Culture: The Case of Darwin's Origin," *Quarterly Journal of Speech* 72 (November 1986): 351–376. Robert Wuthnow, noting the technologization of science after World War II, updates this worldview, calling it broadly "secular rationality" (*Restructuring,* p. 302), or more narrowly "technical rationality," or the "ethos of scientific technology" (*Restructuring,* p. 316). More recently, James Hopewell, in his book *Congregation: Stories and Structures* (Philadelphia: Fortress Press, 1987), notes this prevailing "empirical" worldview in the mainstream (United Methodist) churches in the South that he studied.

82. *Teaching with Authority?* p. 5 (n. 1 above).

83. Nathan Reingold, "History of Science Today, 1: Uniformity as Hidden Diversity: History of Science in the United States, 1920–1940," *British Journal for the History of Science* 19 (1986): 243.

84. Wuthnow, *Restructuring,* p. 300.

85. Sabapathy Kulandran, *The Message and the Silence of the American Pulpit* (Boston: Pilgrim Press, 1949), pp. 43 and 49.

86. Stevenson, "Trends," 16 (n. 23 above).

87. See William P. Merrill, "Can I Believe in God?" in *If I Had Only One Sermon to Preach,* ed. Charles Stelzle (New York: Harper & Brothers, 1927), pp. 37–45, and Harry Emerson Fosdick, "Belief in Christ," in *Best Sermons 1924,* ed. Joseph Fort Newton, pp. 81–100.

88. See Stevenson, "Trends," and Stelzle, *One Sermon.*

89. Benton Johnson, "Taking Stock: Reflections on the End of Another Era," *Journal for the Scientific Study of Religion* 21 (1982): 192.

90. Ibid.

91. Ibid., pp. 194–195.

92. William Howard Kadel, "Contemporary Preaching in the Presbyterian Church U.S. and the Presbyterian Church U.S.A. in Light of the Preaching of History" (Th.D. diss., Union Theological Seminary in Virginia, 1951), p. 1304.

93. Ibid., p. 1307.

94. H. Grady Davis introduced this function for preaching in 1958 in his book *Design for Preaching* (Philadelphia: Fortress Press, 1958), which was the most widely used textbook in Presbyterian seminary classrooms until the mid-1970s. Popular homiletical texts like Edgar Jackson's *How to Preach to People's Needs* (n. 36 above) contained chapters such as "Preaching to the Guilt Laden," "Preaching to the Fearful," "Preaching to Those Bothered by Alcohol," and "Preaching to the Insecure." This trend continues. See, for instance, the Preaching About . . . series recently introduced by the Westminster Press—especially Elizabeth Achtemeier's *Preaching About Family Relationships* (Philadelphia: Westminster Press, 1987). Sermon titles such as "Creative Insecurity," "Power Over All Your Difficulties," and "Overcoming Emotional Depression" were more likely during this period. See these and other titles in *The Twentieth-Century Pulpit: Sermons by Thirty-seven Pulpit Masters,* ed. James W. Cox (Nashville: Abingdon Press, 1978), and *Pastoral Preaching,* ed. Charles Kemp (St. Louis: Bethany Press, 1963).

95. Johnson, "Taking Stock," p. 193.

96. This is borne out by recent continuing education seminars I have conducted in which a theological "thematic idea inventory" was used by several participants. See J. Randall Nichols, *Building the Word* (San Francisco: Harper & Row, 1980), p. 135. These inventories failed to indicate a coherent theological perspective on the part of these participants. Indeed, it was discovered that, in some cases, there were inconsistencies and even counteracting theological messages at work from one sermon to the next.

97. Again, this is an observation based upon my experiences in teaching seminary students and continuing education classes. It is also based on conversations with colleagues at Louisville Presbyterian Theological Seminary and at the Academy of Homiletics.

98. Continuing education event "Preaching That Communicates," Spring 1988, Louisville Presbyterian Theological Seminary.

99. James H. Moorhead, "Between Progress and Apocalypse: A Reassessment of Millennialism in American Religious Thought, 1800–1880," *Journal of American History* 71 (1984).

4: Themes in Southern Presbyterian Preaching

1. Samuel S. Hill, ed., *Religion in the Southern States: A Historical Study* (Macon, Ga.: Mercer University Press, 1983), p. 1.

2. See Charles Reagan Wilson, *Baptized in Blood: The Religion of the Lost Cause, 1865–1920* (Athens, Ga.: University of Georgia Press, 1980), p. 1.

3. James Lewis MacLeod maintains that the Presbyterian Church "has been the traditional blue stocking church of the South. . . . The social history of the South, whatever its defects, might have been much the worse without the Presbyterian emphasis on character and literacy." From James Lewis MacLeod, *The Presbyterian Tradition in the South* (Oakwood, Ga.: Economy Printing–Educational Enterprises, 1978), p. 100. See also Wilson, *Baptized in Blood,* p. 2, for comment on the Presbyterian Church's influence due to the education of its clergy and social prominence of its members.

4. In this random sampling of sermons, the most frequently quoted piece of literature was Francis Thompson's poem "The Hound of Heaven." It was referred to across the century as a metaphor for God's pursuit of human faithfulness.

5. T. Watson Street, *The Story of Southern Presbyterians* (Richmond: John Knox Press, 1960), p. 94.

6. Harris E. Kirk, "The Presbyterian Mind," *Christian Observer* 117 (May 22, 1929): 5.

7. James I. Vance, *Worship God!* (New York: Fleming H. Revell Co., 1932), p. 8.

8. George L. Bitzer, "The Changeless Gospel in a Changing World," *Union Seminary Review* 42 (July 1931): 411–412.

9. Vance, *Worship God!* p. 148.

10. See "Religion in Two Worlds" in Harris E. Kirk, *One Generation to Another* (New York: Fleming H. Revell Co., 1924).

11. See "The Education of Moses" series in ibid.

12. Thomas W. Currie, "Humanity's Birthright," in *The Southern Presbyterian Pulpit,* ed. Charles Haddon Nabers (New York: Fleming H. Revell Co., 1928), p. 59.

13. Ibid.

14. Kirk, *One Generation to Another,* p. 73.

15. Ibid., p. 26.

16. Robert F. Campbell, "God and Man Finding Rest," in *Great Southern Preaching,* ed. Charles M. Crowe (New York: Macmillan Co., 1926), p. 7.

17. J. A. McClure, "The New Message of Jesus," in Nabers, *Southern Presbyterian Pulpit,* p. 211.

18. J. S. Lyons, "A Christmas Sermon," in Nabers, *Southern Presbyterian Pulpit,* p. 193.

19. Vance, *Worship God!* pp. 146, 151.

20. Robert F. Campbell, "God and Man Finding Rest," p. 12.

21. T. Watson Street maintains that evolution produced the greatest controversy the southern Presbyterian church had known up to that time, or since. See Street, *Story of Southern Presbyterians,* p. 95.

22. Vance, *Worship God!* p. 153.

23. J. Wayne Flynt, " 'Feeding the Hungry and Ministering to the Brokenhearted': The Presbyterian Church in the United States and the Social Gospel, 1900–1920," in *Religion in the South,* ed. Charles Reagan Wilson (Jackson, Miss.: University Press of Mississippi, 1985), p. 87. See the discussion in the endnotes to this article (pp. 82–137) concerning the differing views of scholars on the role of the social gospel in the PCUS.

24. James Henley Thornwell, *The Collected Writings of James Henley Thornwell,* Vol. 4: Ecclesiastical (Edinburgh: Banner of Truth Trust, 1974: first published 1875), p. 246.

25. Walter L. Lingle, "A Soul-Winning Church," in Nabers, *Southern Presbyterian Pulpit,* p. 174.

26. J. V. Johnson, "Ends," in Nabers, ibid., p. 145.

27. D. Clay Lilly, "Christianity Full-Grown," in Nabers, ibid., p. 174.

28. Kirk, *One Generation to Another,* p. 67.

29. Bitzer, "Changeless Gospel," p. 418.

30. See discussion in ibid., pp. 417–418.

31. Harris E. Kirk, "The Soul's Arabia," in Nabers, *Southern Presbyterian Pulpit,* p. 154.

32. See these and other sermons in Nabers, ibid.

33. Vance, *Worship God!* p. 110.

34. Street, *Story of Southern Presbyterians,* p. 110.

35. Teunis E. Gouwens, *Keep Your Faith* (New York: Fleming H. Revell Co., 1943), p. 86.

36. J. Kenton Parker, "Living Wisely in a War-torn World," *Southern Presbyterian Journal* 2 (October 1943): 9.

37. Gouwens, *Keep Your Faith,* p. 33.

38. Ibid., p. 43.

39. Samuel McP. Glasgow, "Thanksgiving and Tears," *Southern Presbyterian Journal* 1 (November 1942): 16.

40. Edgar A. Woods, "The Righteous Nation Which Keepeth Faith," *Southern Presbyterian Journal* 1 (June 1942): 14.

41. Ansley C. Moore, "The Hands of God," in *Best Sermons* (1946 Edition), ed. G. Paul Butler (New York: Harper & Brothers, 1946), p. 146.

42. Robert A. Lapsley, Jr., "Why Not Try God?" *Southern Presbyterian Journal* 1 (July 1942): 8.

43. Benjamin L. Rose, "A Call to Humility," *Southern Presbyterian Journal* 2 (June 1943): 9.

44. J. Kelly Unger, "The Great Delusion," *Southern Presbyterian Journal* 4 (August 1945): 8.

45. Ibid.

46. John Allan MacLean, *The Most Unforgettable Character I've Ever Met* (Richmond: John Knox Press, 1945), p. 35.

47. J. Blanton Belk, *Our Fighting Faith* (Richmond: John Knox Press, 1944), p. 71.

48. Ibid., p. 18.

49. See "Patriotism Plus," in MacLean, *Most Unforgettable Character.*

50. Belk, *Our Fighting Faith,* p. 74.

51. L. A. Gebb, "Blackouts Old and Modern or 'Broken Vessels,' " *Southern Presbyterian Journal* 1 (February 1943): 21.

52. Joseph B. Overmyer, "Spiritual Re-Armament," *Southern Presbyterian Journal* 2 (July 1943): 7.

53. MacLean, *Most Unforgettable Character,* p. 174.

54. Donald W. Richardson, "The Church Today—Its Need," *Southern Presbyterian Journal* 3 (July 1944): 9.

55. J. Kenton Parker, "Faithful Preaching," *Southern Presbyterian Journal* 4 (June 1945): 8.

56. Overmyer, "Spiritual Re-Armament," p. 9.

57. Belk, *Our Fighting Faith,* p. 21.

58. See Samuel McP. Glasgow, "A.W.O.L.," *Southern Presbyterian Journal* 3 (May 1944): 10–12.

59. Gouwens, *Keep Your Faith,* p. 11.

60. Hill, *Religion in the Southern States,* p. 419.

61. Ernest Trice Thompson, *Presbyterians in the South,* vol. 3: *1890–1972* (Richmond: John Knox Press, 1973), p. 9.

62. Ernest Trice Thompson, *Today's Church, Tomorrow's World* (Richmond: John Knox Press, 1960), p. 64.

63. R. Wilbur Cousar, "Preaching to Men of the Twentieth Century," *Southern Presbyterian Journal* 4 (Nov. 1, 1945): 8.

64. See William M. Elliott, Jr., *Lift High That Banner!* (Richmond: John Knox Press, 1950).

65. Massey Mott Heltzel, *The Invincible Christ* (Nashville: Abingdon Press, 1957), pp. 29–30.

66. Elliott, *Lift High That Banner!* p. 20.

67. Ernest Lee Stoffel, *The Strong Comfort of God* (Richmond: John Knox Press, 1958), p. 105.

68. Russell Cartwright Stroup, "The Two Tentmakers," in *Best Sermons* (1951–1952 Edition), ed. G. Paul Butler (New York: Macmillan Co., 1952), p. 55.

69. Stoffel, *Strong Comfort of God,* p. 17.

70. Ibid., pp. 109, 111–112.

71. Cousar, "Preaching," p. 9.

72. Ernest Trice Thompson makes the point that prior to 1940, PCUS theological students were trained in one system of theology only: old-line Calvinism. But "since 1940 they have been made increasingly aware of the wider spectrum of theological thought." See Thompson, *Presbyterians in the South,* 3:494.

73. Ibid.

74. Heltzel, *Invincible Christ,* p. 5.

75. Ibid., pp. 60–61.

76. Walter Dale Langtry, "Star Over Bethlehem," in Butler, *Best Sermons* (1951–1952 Edition), p. 60.

77. Ibid.

78. Heltzel, *Invincible Christ,* p. 35.

79. Elliott, *Lift High That Banner!* p. 62.

80. Street, *Story of Southern Presbyterians,* p. 114.

81. As recorded in ibid., pp. 114–115.

82. William Crowe, Jr., "Our Church and the Negro in the South," *Union Seminary Review* 4 (April 1940): 248–263.

83. Paul Tudor Jones, *Raising the God Question: Sermons by Paul Tudor Jones* (Louisville, Ky.: Louisville Presbyterian Theological Seminary, 1987), p. 8.

84. Stoffel, *Strong Comfort of God,* pp. 65–66.

85. William Howard Kadel, "Contemporary Preaching in the Presbyterian Church U.S. and the Presbyterian Church U.S.A. in Light of the Preaching of History" (Th.D. diss., Union Theological Seminary in Virginia, 1951), pp. 1470–1471.

86. Jones, *Raising the God Question,* p. 8.

87. Thompson, *Presbyterians in the South,* 3:9.

88. Street, *Story of Southern Presbyterians,* p. 124.

89. Jones, *Raising the God Question,* p. 48.

90. Thompson, *Presbyterians in the South,* 3:408.

91. Ibid., p. 410.

92. Frank H. Caldwell, "An Unfulfilled Doxology," *Christian Observer* 155 (June 14, 1967): 4.

93. "A Brief Statement of Belief," from *The Constitution of the Presbyterian Church (U.S.A.),* Part I: *Book of Confessions* (New York: The Office of the General Assembly, 1983), p. xvi.

94. John A. Redhead, *Guidance from Men of God* (Nashville: Abingdon Press, 1965), p. 16.

95. Jones, *Raising the God Question,* p. 46.

96. James O. Speed, *The Apostles' Creed: Fresh Water from an Ancient Spring* (Atlanta: Cherokee Publishing Co., 1988), p. 208.

97. John A. Redhead, *Finding Meaning in the Beatitudes* (Nashville: Abingdon Press, 1968), p. 20.

98. Jones, *Raising the God Question,* pp. 22, 57.

99. Speed, *The Apostles' Creed,* p. 212.

100. Jones, *Raising the God Question,* p. 22.

101. Kadel, "Contemporary Preaching," p. 1478. See also Gordon Clinard, "Changing Emphases in American Preaching," *Southwestern Journal of Theology* 2 (April 1962): 79–91, for a discussion of the changing role of the clergy in response to the needs of society and how these have brought about new emphases in preaching.

102. See Patrick J. Mahaffey, "Self-fulfillment and Culture Crisis: America's Search for Soul in the 1960s and 1970s" in *Liberal Protestantism: Realities and Possibilities,* ed. Robert S. Michaelsen and Wade Clark Roof (New York: Pilgrim Press, 1986), pp. 129ff.

103. Vance Barron, *Sermons for the Celebration of the Christian Year* (Nashville: Abingdon Press, 1977), p. 17.

104. Elias S. Hardge, Jr., "What a Way to Live," in *Black Preaching: Select Sermons in the Presbyterian Tradition,* ed. Robert T. Newbold, Jr. (Philadelphia: Geneva Press, 1977), p. 127.

105. Walter Rowe Courtenay, "The Church in the Twentieth Century," *Christian Observer* 158 (June 17, 1970), 4.

106. Holmes Rolston, *The Apostle Peter Speaks to Us Today* (Atlanta: John Knox Press, 1977), p. 82.

107. Jones, *Raising the God Question,* p. 18.

108. Diane Tennis, "Suffering," in *Spinning a Sacred Yarn: Women Speak from the Pulpit* (New York: Pilgrim Press, 1982), p. 206.

109. James E. Andrews, "God Is Going to Win," in *The Fortieth Anniversary of the Protestant Hour* (Atlanta: Office of Media Communications, Presbyterian Church (U.S.A.), 1985), p. 53.

110. Courtenay, "The Church in the Twentieth Century," p. 4.

111. Ibid.

112. Caldwell, "An Unfulfilled Doxology," p. 4.

113. Kenneth K. Bailey, *Southern White Protestantism in the Twentieth Century* (New York: Harper & Row, 1964), p. 166.

114. Barbara Campbell, "Beyond Ourselves," in Newbold, *Black Preaching,* p. 48.

115. Jones, *Raising the God Question,* p. 21.

116. Caldwell, "An Unfulfilled Doxology," p. 4.

117. See Samuel S. Hill, Jr., *Southern Churches in Crisis* (New York: Holt, Rinehart & Winston, 1967), p. 206.

118. Courtenay, "The Church in the Twentieth Century," p. 4.

119. Caldwell, "An Unfulfilled Doxology," p. 4.

120. Speed, *The Apostles' Creed,* p. 183.

121. Ernest Trice Thompson, *Changing Emphases in American Preaching* (Philadelphia: Westminster Press, 1943), p. 1.

122. Samuel S. Hill, Jr., et al., *Religion and the Solid South* (Nashville: Abingdon Press, 1972), p. 20.

123. Samuel S. Hill, ed., *Varieties of Southern Religious Experience* (Baton Rouge, La.: Louisiana State University Press, 1988), p. 226.

5: Challenging the Ethos

1. Charles W. Baird, *The Presbyterian Liturgies: Historical Sketches* (Grand Rapids: Baker Book House, 1957). The first edition was anonymous, entitled *Eutaxia, or the Presbyterian Liturgies: Historical Sketches* (New York: M. W. Dodd, 1855).

2. This story is told very well by Julius Melton, *Presbyterian Worship in America: Changing Patterns Since 1787* (Richmond: John Knox Press, 1967), pp. 75–110.

3. R. Sidney Pinch, "The First Church Service Society," *Reformed Liturgics* 1 (Spring 1964): 24.

4. *Minutes of the General Assembly of the Presbyterian Church in the U.S.A.* (hereafter cited as GA, PCUSA), 1903, pp. 113, 169.

5. Hugh T. Kerr, Sr., "The Story of the Book of Common Worship," *Journal of the Presbyterian Historical Society* 29 (December 1951): 208; GA, PCUSA, 1905, pp. 165–177; *The Book of*

Common Worship (Philadelphia: Presbyterian Board of Publication, 1906).

6. "Resolved, 2. That in the preparation of these volumes of services the Committee be instructed to draw from the Holy Scriptures and the usage of the Reformed Churches, to avoid those forms which savor of ritualism; to embody sound doctrine in the language of orderly devotion, and to keep ever in mind the end of Presbyterian worship, which is that all the people shall join in the service of God as He is revealed in Jesus Christ" (GA, PCUSA, 1903, p. 113).

7. Directory for the Worship of God, reprinted in *Psalms and Hymns Adapted to Social, Private, and Public Worship in the Presbyterian Church* (Philadelphia: Presbyterian Board of Publication, 1843).

8. *The Book of Common Worship,* 1906, p. viii. The Treasury of Prayers in this book are drawn from the *Book of Common Prayer,* 1549 and 1552; the *Book of Common Order,* 1556 and 1874; Calvin's "Forme of Prayers," 1542; and the *Presbyterian Book of Common Prayer,* 1864. Through these service books, a number of medieval prayers are used from such Sacramentaries as the Gelasian, Gregorian, Mozarabic, Leonine, Coptic, and Gallican. Other prayers were of contemporary composition. See David Rodney Bluhm, *Trends of Worship Reflected in the Three Editions of The Book of Common Worship of the Presbyterian Church in the United States of America* (Ph.D. diss., University of Pittsburgh, 1956; Ann Arbor, Mich.: University Microfilms International, 1988, 0019614), p. 174.

9. GA, PCUSA, 1928, p. 56. The book appeared dated for reasons that were articulated in the committee's report to the 1931 Assembly: "In revising the original book, we have had three aims. First, to give fuller expression to the deep and growing desire of the disciples of Christ today for Christian unity, world-peace, social justice and brotherhood. Second, to meet the wish of our young people for more beauty, joy, and spiritual reality in the forms of common worship, so that the whole congregation can take part in praise and prayer. . . . Third, to emphasize the purely voluntary character of the book, by increasing the possibilities of choice in the different forms of service, and by urging the cultivation of the free spirit of prayer" (GA, PCUSA, 1931, p. 69).

10. GA, PCUSA, 1931, p. 68.

11. Bluhm, *Trends of Worship,* p. 76.

12. Melton, *Presbyterian Worship,* p. 138.

13. George Miles Gibson, "The Revival of the Church Year," *McCormick Quarterly* 17 (May 1964): 33.

14. Von Ogden Vogt, *Modern Worship* (New Haven, Conn.: Yale University Press, 1927), p. 115.

15. *A Book of Worship for Free Churches:* Prepared under the Direction of The General Council of the Congregational Christian Churches in the United States (New York: Oxford University Press, 1948), p. 2.

16. *The Book of Worship for Church and Home: With Orders for the Administration of the Sacraments and Other Rites and Ceremonies According to the Use of The Methodist Church* (For Voluntary and Optional Use) (Nashville: Methodist Publishing House, 1944), 2.

17. James Hastings Nichols, "The Liturgical Tradition of the Reformed Churches," *Theology Today* 11 (July 1954): 223.

18. *Book of Common Order of the Church of Scotland:* By Authority of the General Assembly (London, Glasgow, Melbourne: Oxford University Press, 1940).

19. GA, PCUSA, 1941, pp. 196–197, 460. Members named to the committee were Rev. Park Hays Miller, Rev. William Chalmers Covert, Rev. J. Shackelford Dauerty, Rev. Eliot Porter, and Rev. Hugh T. Kerr, Sr.

20. *The Book of Common Worship:* Approved by the General Assembly of the Presbyterian Church in the United States of America (Philadelphia: Published for the Office of the General Assembly by the Publication Division of the Board of Christian Education of the Presbyterian Church in the United States of America, 1946).

21. In a letter to David Bluhm, J. Shackelford Dauerty wrote: "While the Committee was at work, the Protestant Episcopal Church and ours were exploring possibilities of union. To further that union (in the succession of Charles W. Shields' 'Presbyterian Book of Common Prayer') I prepared the Order for Holy Communion according to the Reformed or Presbyterian Standards but in much of the diction of the Book of Common Prayer." See Bluhm, *Trends of Worship,* pp. 83, 84. Dr. Dauerty was also a member of the Committee on Camp and Church Activities of the Wartime Service Commission of the Presbyterian Church in the U.S.A., which drew up the *Book of Worship and Devotion for the Armed Forces,* 1943. J. Allen Cabaniss remarks: "One will observe that this little book is a definite stage in the transition from

the 1931 revision of the Book of Common Worship to that of 1946" (J. Allen Cabaniss, "A Critical Review of The Book of Common Worship (1946)," *Journal of the Presbyterian Historical Society* 26 (June 1948): 90).

22. Harry Ernest Winter, *Catholic, Evangelical, and Reformed: The Lord's Supper in The (United) Presbyterian Church USA, 1945–1970* (Ph.D. diss., University of Pennsylvania, 1976; Ann Arbor, Mich.: University Microfilms International, 1976, 7710235).

23. GA, PCUSA, 1941, pp. 196–197.

24. Winter, *Catholic, Evangelical, and Reformed,* p. 253.

25. Winter defines "catholicity" among Presbyterians in terms of believing in the principle of continuity in time and universality in space, holding to an "incarnational" principle, concern for the visible church, use of the material to signify and evoke the spiritual, use of this physical world to lead to the world beyond, and an interest in church unity. Winter also points out that Dauerty was a graduate of the Philadelphia Divinity School, an Episcopal institution (ibid., p. 4).

26. "Knox favored the Apostles' Creed, but the Scottish General Assembly approved the Nicene Creed in 1566 and 1638, and it has appeared in the *Book of Common Order* since 1884" (Bluhm, *Trends of Worship,* p. 59).

27. *Minutes of the General Assembly of the Presbyterian Church in the United States* (hereafter cited as GA, PCUS), 1946, p. 75.

28. Eugene Carson Blake, letter to J. Hoytt Boles, May 14, 1954, Presbyterian Historical Society, Philadelphia (file on Directory for Worship).

29. GA, PCUSA, 1955, p. 84; GA, PCUSA, 1956, p. 244.

30. *Minutes of the General Assembly of the United Presbyterian Church of North America,* 1957, p. 919; GA, PCUS, 1957, p. 71.

31. George S. Hendry, Memorandum, September 25, 1959, MS, Presbyterian Historical Society, Philadelphia (file on Directory for Worship).

32. Ibid.

33. Ibid.

34. *Minutes of the General Assembly of The United Presbyterian Church in the United States of America* (hereafter cited as GA, UPCUSA), 1961, p. 52.

35. GA, PCUS, 1963, p. 113.

36. Directory for the Worship of God, in *The Constitution of The United Presbyterian Church in the United States of America,*

Part II: *Book of Order* (New York: Office of the General Assembly, 1967), VI, 1.

37. Ibid., VI, 3.

38. Lewis A. Briner, letter to Dr. William A. Morrison, November 2, 1963, Presbyterian Historical Society, Philadelphia (file on *Service for the Lord's Day and Lectionary for the Christian Year*).

39. Winter, *Catholic, Evangelical, and Reformed,* p. 4.

40. Hugh T. Kerr, Sr., "The Book of Common Worship," *Journal of the Presbyterian Historical Society* 30 (March 1952): 38. Henry Ernest Winter also credits Floyd Doud Shafer for leading the way in publicizing Karl Barth's discovery of worship, primarily through Shafer's book reviews in *Sanctus: The Newsletter of The Church Service Society (U.S.A.),* n.p.

41. *Service for the Lord's Day and Lectionary for the Christian Year* (Philadelphia: Westminster Press, 1964), p. 20.

42. Winter, *Catholic, Evangelical, and Reformed,* p. 218.

43. The papers presented were grouped under four major topics: "The Universal Church in God's Design," "The Church's Witness to God's Design," "The Church and the Disorder of Society," and "The Church and International Disorder" (Bluhm, *Trends of Worship,* p. 98).

44. Minutes of the Joint Committee on Worship, October 27–28, 1964, MS, Presbyterian Historical Society, Philadelphia (file on Joint Committee on Worship).

45. *Service for the Lord's Day,* p. 20.

46. Ibid.

47. Ibid., p. 22.

48. The "Explanatory Notes" stated that the Words of Institution might be used either within or before the Prayer of Consecration. The Reformed tradition had been wary of using the Words of Institution within the Prayer of Consecration for fear that they would be misunderstood as a formula for invoking a transubstantiation.

49. James Hastings Nichols, "The Liturgical Tradition," p. 224.

50. Howard G. Hageman, "Reformed Worship: Yesterday and Today," *Theology Today* 18 (April 1961): 32–33.

51. Presbyterian Historical Society, Philadelphia, MS (file on *Service for the Lord's Day*).

52. Minutes of the Joint Committee on Worship, October 27–28, 1964, MS, Presbyterian Historical Society, Philadelphia (file on *Service for the Lord's Day*). The chief criticisms reported to

the committee by James Appleby were that the 1964 SLD was too high church and too formal; too long—three lessons are too many; too complicated and difficult to follow; and the rubrics were not always clear. Another frequent complaint was that there was no provision in the lectionary for the use of psalms.

53. James Hastings Nichols, "Is the New 'Service' Reformed?," *Theology Today* 21 (October 1964): 362–363.

54. Ibid., pp. 365–366. This is not the only evidence that certain kinds of liturgical reform run the risk of being accused of effeminacy. In fact, this is a common method of dismissing the whole issue.

55. William D. Maxwell, "A Critique of the Proposed Liturgy," *Reformed Liturgics* 1 (Fall 1964): 11.

56. George E. Sweazey, "On the New 'Service for the Lord's Day,' " *Monday Morning* 29 (April 20, 1964): 5. Other criticisms appeared in this magazine. Of particular note is a series of charges and rebuttals beginning with a letter from the Session of the First Presbyterian Church of Ottawa, Illinois, which accused the committee of having presented "a high church ritualistic worship form with every Sunday Communion strongly emphasized. . . . This format is possibly due to the concern for merger with the Episcopal and eventually the Roman Catholic Church. . . . We also note that in churches with ritualistic worship patterns there is often a lack of vitality in the membership, attendance is low, and participants eventually lose their awareness of the relationship of worship to life" ("An Open Letter to Presbyterian Sessions" from the Session of the First Presbyterian Church, Ottawa, Illinois, Dale L. Heaton, Moderator, *Monday Morning* 29, April 20, 1964, 9).

57. Sweazey, "On the New 'Service,' " p. 18.

58. *The Book of Common Worship: Provisional Services and Lectionary for the Christian Year* (Philadelphia: Westminster Press, 1966).

59. *The Worshipbook—Services* (Philadelphia: Westminster Press, 1970). The same services were published in a single volume with hymns as *The Worshipbook—Services and Hymns* (Philadelphia: Westminster Press, 1972).

60. *Worshipbook—Services,* p. 9.

61. Ibid., p. 6.

62. Ibid., p. 7.

63. Horace T. Allen, Jr., *Hints on How to Use The Worshipbook* (N.p.: Office of Worship and Music, n.d.).

64. Howard G. Hageman, "Old and New in the Worshipbook," *Theology Today* 31 (October 1974): 207.

65. *Worshipbook—Services,* p. 6.

66. Hageman, "Old and New," p. 213. Winter also quotes James McCord with respect to the problem of secularism and language. " 'The goal toward which both scientist and philosopher are working is a state in which there will be no more mystery.' In a world such as ours, where mystery is denied, then there is a correlative denial of the possibility of revelation, holiness, prayer, and repentance" (James I. McCord, "Worship in the Reformed Churches," *Reformed World* 32, 1973, 242).

67. David G. Buttrick, "Renewal of Worship—A Source of Unity?," in *Ecumenism: The Spirit and Worship,* ed. Leonard J. Swidler (Louvain: Editions E. Nauwelaerts and Pittsburgh: Duquesne University Press, 1967), p. 233.

68. Ibid., p. 233.

69. Ibid., p. 220.

70. J. Randall Nichols, "Worship as Anti-Structure: The Contribution of Victor Turner," *Theology Today* 41 (January 1985): 407.

71. "Worshipbook to Be Published This Year," *Presbyterian Life,* June 15, 1970, p. 42.

72. Is twentieth-century "modernism" (cf. Karl Barth) a cooled form of revivalism? "And then when the revivalistic fire cooled, little was left of the pattern of worship save a moralistic sermon with a few sentimental embellishments fore and aft" (James Hastings Nichols, "Liturgical Tradition," p. 215; n. 17 above).

73. GA, UPCUSA, 1970, p. 632.

74. GA, UPCUSA, 1978, p. 28.

75. GA, PCUS, 1980, p. 125.

76. Directory for the Service of God, in *The Constitution of the Presbyterian Church (U.S.A.),* Part II: *Book of Order* (New York and Atlanta: Published by the Office of the General Assembly, 1983).

77. Directory for Worship, in *The Constitution of the Presbyterian Church (U.S.A.),* Part II: *Book of Order* (Louisville, Ky.: Published by the Office of the General Assembly, 1989).

78. Ibid., W-1.2002; W-1.2006; W-1.3012; W-1.3024; W-1.3034; W-1.4002; W-1.4005; W-2.1005; W-2.2002; W-2.2008; W-2.3013; W-2.4007; W-2.4009; W-3.3506; W-3.5402; W-5.4002.

79. *The Service for the Lord's Day: The Worship of God,* Sup-

plemental Liturgical Resource 1, Prepared by the Joint Office of Worship (Philadelphia: Westminster Press, 1984). The history of this project and a sophisticated commentary on the eucharistic prayers in SLR 1 can be found in Arlo D. Duba, "Presbyterian Eucharistic Prayers," in *New Eucharistic Prayers: An Ecumenical Study of Their Development and Structure,* ed. Frank C. Senn (Mahwah, N.J.: Paulist Press, 1987), pp. 96–120.

80. *Holy Baptism and Services for the Renewal of Baptism: The Worship of God,* Supplemental Liturgical Resource 2, Prepared by the Joint Office of Worship (Philadelphia: Westminster Press, 1985).

81. *Christian Marriage: The Worship of God,* Supplemental Liturgical Resource 3, Prepared by the Joint Office of Worship (Philadelphia: Westminster Press, 1986).

82. *The Funeral: A Service of Witness to the Resurrection: The Worship of God,* Supplemental Liturgical Resource 4, Prepared by the Joint Office of Worship (Philadelphia: Westminster Press, 1986); *Daily Prayer: The Worship of God,* Supplemental Liturgical Resource 5, Prepared by the Joint Office of Worship (Philadelphia: Westminster Press, 1987).

6: Hymnody

1. Louis Fitzgerald Benson, *The English Hymn: Its Development and Use* (Philadelphia: Presbyterian Board of Publication, 1915; repr. Richmond: John Knox Press, 1962), p. 27. Dr. Benson states that the first edition of the Psalter (1542) included metrical versions of the Lord's Prayer and the Creed, as well as the Ten Commandments and the Nunc Dimittis. The 1562 version dropped the Lord's Prayer and the Creed but added two metrical prayers for grace at meals.

2. *The Constitution of The Presbyterian Church in the United States of America* (Philadelphia: Board of Christian Eduction, 1954), p. 340. Much of the material for this study is based on James Rawlings Sydnor, "Presbyterian Hymnbooks in the United States," *American Presbyterians* 68 (Spring 1990): 1–13. I am indebted to Dr. Sydnor for sharing this article with me prior to its publication as well as for his wise counsel in the preparation of this essay.

3. James Hastings Nichols, *Corporate Worship in the Reformed Tradition* (Philadelphia: Westminster Press, 1968), pp. 166–169.

4. Sandra S. Sizer, *Gospel Hymns and Social Religion* (Phila-

delphia: Temple University Press, 1978), p. 20. Dr. Sizer's book is a detailed study of sociological factors in the creation of gospel hymnody, of its language, its forms and implications.

5. Benson, *The English Hymn,* p. 555.

6. Ibid.

7. Henry Wilder Foote, *Three Centuries of American Hymnody* (Cambridge, Mass.: Harvard University Press, 1940), p. 284.

8. Benson, *The English Hymn,* p. 555.

9. Erik Routley, *The Church and Music* (London: Gerald Duckworth & Co., 1950), p. 187.

10. Ira D. Sankey et al., *Gospel Hymns Nos. 1 to 6 Complete,* unabridged republication of the "Excelsior Edition" published originally in 1895, in *Earlier American Music,* ed. H. Wiley Hitchcock (New York: Da Capo Press, 1972), "Introduction," n.p.

11. *Minutes of the General Assembly of the Presbyterian Church in the United States,* 1910, p. 36.

12. James Rawlings Sydnor, "Hymns of the Social Gospel," Paper presented at the annual meeting of the Hymn Society of America, April 1979.

13. John Michael Spencer, "Hymns of the Social Awakening: Walter Rauschenbusch and Social Gospel Hymnody," *The Hymn,* April 1989, p. 21. The literature on the topic of hymnody and the social gospel is sparse. Much of Dr. Spencer's material is gleaned from manuscripts by Rauschenbusch.

14. Louis Fitzgerald Benson, *The Hymnody of the Christian Church* (Philadelphia: Westminster Press, 1927), pp. 220–224.

15. Information about musical errors in this book was related to the author by Dr. James R. Sydnor.

16. *Handbook to the Hymnal,* Presbyterian Church U.S.A., 1933, ed. William Chalmers Covert and Calvin W. Laufer (Philadelphia: Presbyterian Board of Christian Education, 1935), p. 19.

17. *Minutes of the General Assembly of the Presbyterian Church in the United States,* 1950, p. 33.

18. James F. White, "Public Worship in Protestantism," in *Altered Landscapes: Christianity in America, 1935–1985,* ed. David W. Lotz with Donald W. Shriver, Jr., and John F. Wilson (Grand Rapids: Wm. B. Eerdmans Publishing Co., 1989), p. 113.

19. Church music throughout America, and particularly in Presbyterianism, has been aided immeasurably by two institutions: the School of Sacred Music of Union Theological Seminary (1928–1973) and the Westminster Choir College (1926–). The

founders of the school in New York, Drs. Clarence and Helen
Dickinson and Dr. Henry Sloane Coffin were Presbyterian as
were Drs. John Finley and Rhea Williamson, who began the
Westminster Choir College at Westminster Presbyterian Church
in Dayton, Ohio.

7: The Language(s) of Zion

In the preparation of this essay, Darryl Hart canvassed devotional literature at the Presbyterian Historical Society in Philadelphia, the library of Princeton Theological Seminary, and the
library of Union Theological Seminary in Virginia. From Mr.
Hart's notes and bibliographies, as well as from his own reading
in this literature, Mark Noll wrote the essay. Facts of publication
not given in the Notes appear in the following list.

Devotional Works Consulted:

All Westminster Press books were published in Philadelphia; all
John Knox Press books before 1974 were published in Richmond; afterward, in Atlanta.

Arnold, William V. *The Power of Your Perceptions.* Potentials:
Guides for Productive Living. Westminster Press, 1984.

Baer, Louis Shattuck. *Let the Patient Decide: A Doctor's Advice to
Older Persons.* Westminster Press, 1978.

Barclay, William. *Daily Study Bible—New Testament.* 17 vols.
Westminster Press, 1958ff. (rev. ed., 1975f.).

————. *Men and Affairs.* Westminster Press, 1978.

Barnette, Helen P. *Your Child's Mind: Making the Most of Public
Schools.* Potentials: Guides for Productive Living. Westminster
Press, 1984.

Barnette, Henlee. *Your Freedom to Be Whole.* Potentials: Guides
for Productive Living. Westminster Press, 1984.

Bell, Richard H. *Sensing the Spirit.* Spirituality and the Christian
Life. Westminster Press, 1984.

Benson, Dennis C. *Electric Love.* John Knox Press, 1973.

The Book of Common Worship. Philadelphia: Presbyterian Board
of Publication and Sabbath-School Work, 1915 (orig. 1906).

The Book of Common Worship. Philadelphia: Board of Christian
Education of the Presbyterian Church in the United States of
America, 1946.

Borchert, Gerald L., and Andrew D. Lester, eds. *Spiritual Dimen-*

sions of Pastoral Care: Witness to the Ministry of Wayne E. Oates.* Westminster Press, 1985.

Brown, Robert McAfee. *The Bible Speaks to You.* Westminster Press, 1955.

Bryan, G. McLeod, ed. *In His Likeness: Forty Selections on the Imitation of Christ Through the Centuries.* John Knox Press, 1959.

Calian, Carnegie Samuel. *For All Your Seasons: Biblical Direction Through Life's Passages.* John Knox Press, 1979.

Campbell, Donald James. *If I Believe.* Westminster Press, 1959.

Coburn, John B. *Twentieth-Century Spiritual Letters: An Introduction to Contemporary Prayer.* Westminster Press, 1957.

Dietrich, Suzanne de. *And He Is Lifted Up: Meditations on the Gospel of John.* Westminster Press, 1969.

Duncan, Denis. *Victorious Living.* Westminster Press, 1982.

———. *The Way of Love.* Westminster Press, 1982.

Eastman, Addison J. *A Handful of Pearls: The Epistle of James.* Westminster Press, 1978.

Fosdick, Harry Emerson. *The Meaning of Prayer.* New York: Association Press, 1915.

George, Denise. *The Christian as a Consumer.* Potentials: Guides for Productive Living. Westminster Press, 1984.

Gettys, Joseph M. *How to Study John.* John Knox Press, 1960.

Grant, Brian W. *From Sin to Wholeness.* Westminster Press, 1982.

Great Peace Have They. New York: Board of National Missions, Presbyterian Church U.S.A., 1942.

Hallmark, Erma. *Here in This House.* John Knox Press, 1975.

Happold, Frederick C. *The Journey Inwards: A Simple Introduction to the Practice of Contemplative Meditation by Normal People.* John Knox Press, 1975.

Harkness, Georgia. *Disciplines of the Christian Life.* John Knox Press, 1967.

Hauck, Paul A. *Overcoming Depression.* Westminster Press, 1973.

Hestenes, Roberta. *Using the Bible in Groups.* Westminster Press, 1985.

Hinson, E. Glenn. *A Serious Call to a Contemplative Life-Style.* Westminster Press, 1974.

Holmer, Paul L. *Making Christian Sense.* Spirituality and the Christian Life. Westminster Press, 1984.

Johnson, Ben Campbell. *To Pray God's Will.* Westminster Press, 1987.
———. *To Will God's Will.* Westminster Press, 1987.
Jones, William M. *A Guide to Living Power.* John Knox Press, 1975.
Kuist, Howard Tillman. *How to Enjoy the Bible.* John Knox Press, 1939.
McCabe, Joseph E. *Handel's Messiah: A Devotional Commentary.* Westminster Press, 1978.
McLelland, Joseph C. *Living for Christ.* John Knox Press, 1963.
Mace, David R. *Whom God Hath Joined.* Westminster Press, 1953 (rev. 1973).
Madden, Myron C. *Claim Your Heritage.* Potentials: Guides for Productive Living. Westminster Press, 1984.
Maertens, Marlene. *God for All Seasons.* Westminster Press, 1969.
Maitland, David J. *Aging: A Time for New Learning.* John Knox Press, 1987.
Meiburg, Albert L. *Sound Body/Sound Mind.* Potentials: Guides for Productive Living. Westminster Press, 1984.
Mudge, Lewis S. *In His Service: The Servant Lord and His Servant People.* Westminster Press, 1959.
Nielsen, H. A. *The Bible—As If for the First Time.* Spirituality and the Christian Life. Westminster Press, 1984.
Nye, Miriam Baker. *But I Never Thought He'd Die: Practical Help for Widows.* Westminster Press, 1978.
Oates, Wayne E. *Convictions That Give You Confidence.* Potentials: Guides for Productive Living. Westminster Press, 1984.
———. *Your Right to Rest.* Potentials: Guides for Productive Living. Westminster Press, 1984.
Pannenberg, Wolfhart. *Christian Spirituality.* Westminster Press, 1983.
Rassieur, Charles L. *Christian Renewal: Living Beyond Burnout.* Potentials: Guides for Productive Living. Westminster Press, 1984.
Reid, J. K. S. *Our Life in Christ.* Westminster Press, 1963.
Roberts, Robert C. *The Strengths of a Christian.* Spirituality and the Christian Life. Westminster Press, 1984.
Saliers, Don E. *Worship and Spirituality.* Spirituality and the Christian Life. Westminster Press, 1984.
Shepherd, J. Barrie. *Praying the Psalms: Daily Meditations on Cherished Psalms.* Westminster Press, 1987.

Soper, David Wesley. *God Is Inescapable.* Westminster Press, 1959.

Stringfellow, William. *The Politics of Spirituality.* Spirituality and the Christian Life. Westminster Press, 1984.

Thompson, William E. *Devotions for the Divorcing.* John Knox Press, 1985.

Thornton, Edward E. *Being Transformed: An Inner Way of Spiritual Growth.* Potentials: Guides for Productive Living. Westminster Press, 1984.

Tournier, Paul. *Reflections.* Westminster Press, 1982.

Turnbull, M. Ryerson. *Studying the Book of Exodus.* Richmond: Presbyterian Committee of Publication, 1925.

Ungersma, Aaron J. *Escape from Phoniness.* Westminster Press, 1969.

Van Tatenhove, Frederick C. *Ambition: Friend or Enemy?* Potentials: Guides for Productive Living. Westminster Press, 1984.

Warfield, Benjamin B. "The Religious Life of Theological Students," in *Selected Shorter Writings of Benjamin B. Warfield,* Vol. I, ed. John E. Meeter. Phillipsburg, N.J.: Presbyterian & Reformed Publishing Co., 1970 (orig. 1911).

Weatherly, Owen M. *The Fulfillment of Life.* John Knox Press, 1959.

1. A complete list of the devotional works consulted for this essay is found above. Full bibliographical information can be found in that list for works that are only mentioned in passing or whose contents are summarized without direct quotation.

2. The potential diversity of devotional writings is well illustrated by two recent (and lengthy) series of books from Paulist Press, "The Classics of Western Spirituality" and "Sources of American Spirituality."

3. It should be kept in mind that books published by John Knox Press and Westminster Press do not represent official Presbyterian positions. Rather, these presses have been sponsored by the Presbyterians as a general service to the church as a whole. At the same time, books published by Westminster Press and John Knox Press that deal with spirituality, prayer, worship, or the development of religious and personal maturity give us a good preliminary reading on devotional currents within the denomination.

4. Benjamin B. Warfield, "The Religious Life of Theological

Students" (1911), in *Selected Shorter Writings,* ed. John E. Meeter, pp. 422, 424–425.

5. John Patton, "The New Language of Pastoral Counseling," in *Spiritual Dimensions of Pastoral Care: Witness to the Ministry of Wayne E. Oates,* ed. Gerald L. Borchert and Andrew D. Lester, pp. 73, 75, 76, 80, 84, 85, 86.

6. *The Book of Common Worship,* 1915 (orig. 1906), pp. iv–v.

7. On the book's nearly universal popularity, see Robert Moats Miller, *Harry Emerson Fosdick: Preacher, Pastor, Prophet* (New York: Oxford University Press, 1985), pp. 67–71.

8. Wayne E. Oates, "The Power of Spiritual Language in Self-understanding," in *Spiritual Dimensions of Pastoral Care,* ed. Borchert and Lester, pp. 58, 68.

9. M. Ryerson Turnbull, *Studying the Book of Exodus,* p. 7.

10. Howard Tillman Kuist, *How to Enjoy the Bible,* pp. 1–15.

11. For general confirmation of this observation for southern Presbyterian ministers, see Harold S. Prince, *A Presbyterian Bibliography: The Published Writings of Ministers Who Served in the Presbyterian Church in the United States During Its First Hundred Years* (Metuchen, N.J.: Scarecrow Press, 1983).

12. Anna Jane Mayer, "The Making of Many Books: A History of the Publishing House of the P.C.U.S.A." (M.L.S. thesis, Drexel Institute of Technology, 1958), p. 65.

13. Robert McAfee Brown, *The Bible Speaks to You,* p. 7.

14. *The Presbyterian,* April 20, 1920, p. 27; *Presbyterian Life,* April 15, 1926, p. 31.

15. John B. Coburn, *Twentieth-Century Spiritual Letters: An Introduction to Contemporary Prayer;* quotations are the subtitle and the heading of the book's second half.

16. Personal letter, Richard A. Ray to John M. Mulder, April 12, 1989.

17. Joseph C. McLelland, *Living for Christ,* dust jacket.

18. E. Glenn Hinson, *A Serious Call to a Contemplative Life-Style,* pp. 31, 38, 102–103.

19. Dennis C. Benson, *Electric Love,* p. 18.

20. William M. Jones, *A Guide to Living Power,* p. 8.

21. Wolfhart Pannenberg, *Christian Spirituality,* pp. 29–30, ch. 5.

22. See also in the list above the works by Calian, Eastman, McCabe, and Shepherd.

23. See in the list above the book by Maertens and the two books by Johnson.

24. William Stringfellow, *The Politics of Spirituality,* p. 26.

25. Respectively, Charles L. Rassieur, *Christian Renewal: Living Beyond Burnout,* p. 106; Denise George, *The Christian as a Consumer.*

26. Myron C. Madden, *Claim Your Heritage,* pp. 14, 110.

27. Edward E. Thornton, *Being Transformed: An Inner Way of Spiritual Growth,* pp. 23, 47.

28. Wayne E. Oates, *Your Right to Rest,* p. 10.

29. Wayne E. Oates, *Convictions That Give You Confidence,* pp. 22, 28.

30. William V. Arnold, *The Power of Your Perceptions,* p. 18.

31. Oates, *Convictions That Give You Confidence,* p. 66.

32. For a similar situation among the subjects of James Davison Hunter's investigations, see his *American Evangelicalism: Conservative Religion and the Quandary of Modernity* (New Brunswick, N.J.: Rutgers University Press, 1983), pp. 93–101, 142–144.

33. James H. Smylie, " 'Of Secret and Family Worship': Historical Meditations, 1875–1975," *Journal of Presbyterian History* 58 (Summer 1980): 95–115.

34. See Roland H. Bainton, *Here I Stand: A Life of Martin Luther* (Nashville: Abingdon-Cokesbury Press, 1950), pp. 202–203; Edmund S. Morgan, *Roger Williams: The Church and the State* (New York: Harcourt, Brace & World, 1967), pp. 57–61; on Charles Hodge et al., Darryl G. Hart, "Divided Between Heart and Mind: The Critical Period for Protestant Thought in America," *Journal of Ecclesiastical History* 38 (1987): 254–270; and Karl Barth, "Introductory Essay," in Ludwig Feuerbach, *The Essence of Christianity* (New York: Harper & Row, 1957), pp. x–xxxii.

35. *Calvin: Institutes of the Christian Religion,* ed. John T. McNeill, trans. Ford Lewis Battles (Philadelphia: Westminster Press, 1960), I.i.l.

8: From Old to New Agendas

1. Although opinions differ on just which denominations should be classified as mainline, it is generally agreed that the core of the Protestant mainline consists of denominations whose historic constituency has been of English, Welsh, Scottish, or Irish descent and which have provided much of the leadership in the transition toward more liberal expressions of Christian theol-

ogy. This core consists of the Episcopal Church, the United Church of Christ, the Presbyterian Church (U.S.A.), the United Methodist Church, the American Baptist Churches, and the Christian Church (Disciples of Christ).

2. Robert Booth Fowler, *Unconventional Partners: Religion and Liberal Culture in the United States* (Grand Rapids: Wm. B. Eerdmans Publishing Co., 1989), p. 87. Many church members evidently agree. See, for example, two letters to the editor in the January–February 1989 issue of *Presbyterian Survey.* One letter complains that the "General Assembly has given politics a priority over evangelism," and the other condemns the "left way of thinking that the Presbyterian hierarchy has taken" (79/1:5).

3. Wade Clark Roof and William McKinney, *American Mainline Religion: Its Changing Shape and Future* (New Brunswick, N.J.: Rutgers University Press, 1987), p. 80.

4. Two excellent histories have been written of shifting positions on certain social issues within mainline Protestantism in the years between the two world wars: William Moats Miller, *American Protestantism and Social Issues, 1919–1939* (Chapel Hill: University of North Carolina Press, 1958), and Donald B. Meyer, *The Protestant Search for Political Realism, 1919–1941* (Berkeley and Los Angeles: University of California Press, 1960).

5. The UPCUSA was formed in 1958 by merger with the much smaller United Presbyterian Church of North America.

6. It is correct to refer to the PCUS as a "southern" church because virtually all its congregations were located in the former slaveholding states and Oklahoma, but it is not strictly correct to refer to the PCUSA and the UPCUSA as "northern" because these denominations had congregations in every state. The great majority of their members, however, resided in the Northeast or Middle West.

7. I am indebted to Thomas Heger, Dean R. Hoge, Donald A. Luidens, Jack P. Maddex, John M. Mulder, Donald R. Purkey, Jon R. Stone, Louis Weeks, and Barbara G. Wheeler for criticisms of previous drafts of this essay and for insights into Presbyterian history and how General Assemblies operate. I am also indebted to John Anderson, executive presbyter of the Presbytery of Santa Barbara, and to Eugene Ensley, pastor of Peace Presbyterian Church, Clearwater, Florida, for allowing me to use the collections of General Assembly *Minutes* in their offices.

8. *The Nation* was selected because it has been published continuously since well before 1926 and has consistently taken a

liberal stand on social issues during this period. Moreover, although it has never been antireligious and has sometimes carried articles by religious leaders (for example, Reinhold Niebuhr and Harvey Cox), its general outlook has been thoroughly secular. I am greatly indebted to Gary G. Hughes for examining the indexes of *The Nation* and for reading and excerpting most of the articles we selected as relevant for this study.

9. See Jeffrey K. Hadden, *The Gathering Storm in the Churches* (Garden City, N.Y.: Doubleday & Co., 1969). See also A. James Reichley, *Religion in American Public Life* (Washington, D.C.: Brookings Institution, 1985).

10. General Assembly *Minutes* do, of course, contain the names of the members of committees, task forces, boards, and other important agencies. A study of how these members are selected and what their views are would provide valuable insight into the processes culminating in Assembly actions.

11. Among the other clues occasionally contained in General Assembly *Minutes* are the decision to reject or merely "receive" a committee report, the amendment of a report before its approval, the time consumed in debate, and information included in overtures or committee reports about the unminuted actions of past Assemblies.

12. *Minutes of the General Assembly of the Presbyterian Church U.S.A.* (hereafter cited as GA, PCUSA), 1927, pp. 201–202.

13. GA, PCUSA, 1931, p. 59.

14. See, for example, GA, PCUSA, 1927, p. 247.

15. See, for example, GA, PCUSA, 1930, p. 26.

16. GA, PCUSA, 1929, pp. 73–74. The Kellogg-Briand Pact, formally known as the Paris Peace Pact, was signed in the summer of 1928 by the United States and fifteen European nations. The pact, which outlawed war as a method of settling international disputes, contained many provisions justifying war under various circumstances.

17. GA, PCUSA, 1930, p. 62.

18. GA, PCUSA, 1932, p. 81.

19. GA, PCUSA, 1931, p. 76.

20. Ibid., p. 73.

21. See, for example, GA, PCUSA, 1928, p. 152; GA, PCUSA, 1930, p. 114.

22. GA, PCUSA, 1930, pp. 50–52.

23. On temperance, see *Minutes of the General Assembly of the*

Presbyterian Church U.S. (hereafter cited as GA, PCUS), 1926, pp. 27, 54. On Sabbath observance, see GA, PCUS, 1931, p. 158. On world peace, see GA, PCUS, 1928, p. 44. On marriage and divorce, see GA, PCUS, 1929, pp. 143–144.

24. See, for example, GA, PCUS, 1926, pp. 29, 73, 84; GA, PCUS, 1928, p. 75; GA, PCUS, 1931, p. 157.

25. See, for example, GA, PCUS, 1927, p. 39. On the spirituality doctrine, see Ernest Trice Thompson, *Presbyterians in the South* (Richmond: John Knox Press, 1973), 2:30–31. The doctrine had a few supporters in the northern church, but it was rarely mentioned in General Assembly *Minutes.* In 1932 the PCUSA General Council compared the "theoretical position of our Church" as expressed in the Confession of Faith with "actual practice" and reported that from the earliest years of Presbyterianism in America Synods and General Assemblies had "again and again . . . dealt with 'civil affairs which concern the commonwealth.' " A long list of examples was provided, which included pronouncements on the French and Indian War, the Stamp Act, the Revolutionary War, and the 1805 request of the General Assembly for public funding for its Indian schools (GA, PCUSA, 1932, pp. 267–268). An overture asking for an interpretation of the "intermeddling" section of the Confession was received in 1965, but the Assembly took no action on it (*Minutes of the General Assembly of The United Presbyterian Church U.S.A.* [hereafter cited as GA, UPCUSA], 1965, pp. 29–31, 162).

26. *The Nation* 137 (Dec. 13, 1933): 137.

27. *The Nation* 127 (Sept. 5, 1928): 234–235.

28. *The Nation* 129 (Aug. 28, 1929): 213.

29. *The Nation* 128 (April 10, 1929): 420.

30. For example, in 1934 *The Nation* asserted that "honest sex is not indecent" and complained that the movies were full of "fake sin, fake sex, and fake social and moral values" (139 [Aug. 1, 1934]: 124–126).

31. *Minutes of the General Assembly of the Presbyterian Church (U.S.A.)* (hereafter cited as GA, PC(USA)), 1988, p. 652.

32. Ibid., p. 650.

33. Ibid., p. 84.

34. Ibid., p. 1017.

35. Ibid., p. 1076.

36. Ibid., p. 558.

37. Ibid., pp. 1068–1069.

38. Ibid., p. 1069.

39. Ibid., p. 972.

40. Ibid., p. 1066.

41. Ibid., pp. 1026–1027.

42. Ibid., p. 1073.

43. Ibid., p. 1068. Among the many other issues on which the 1988 Assembly pronounced were disarmament, peacemaking, Korean reunification, Chile, prison reform, gun control, health care, women and work, the income gap, and tax vouchers and credits for education. The positions expressed on all these issues were decidedly liberal.

44. GA, PCUSA, 1914, p. 174.

45. The single pejorative phrase "Jazz with its primeval jungle tom-tom" is the only reference to popular music and dance that I have been able to locate in any document adopted by a northern General Assembly after the mid-1920s. See GA, PCUSA, 1930, p. 77.

46. In 1930 the southern Assembly, in response to an overture on the propriety of worldly amusements, abandoned "enforced obedience to positive prohibitions" and allowed individuals to make their own decisions on the basis of a "Scripturally enlightened conscience" (GA, PCUS, 1930, p. 83). That was the end of the matter in the PCUS.

47. On the loss of interest in the Sabbath, see my essay "On Dropping the Subject: Presbyterians and Sabbath Observance in the Twentieth Century," in *The Presbyterian Predicament,* ed. Milton J Coalter, John M. Mulder, and Louis B. Weeks (Louisville, Ky.: Westminster/John Knox Press, 1990), pp. 90–108.

48. GA, PCUS, 1922, p. 71.

49. GA, PCUS, 1923, pp. 80, 84.

50. GA, PCUSA, 1930, pp. 48–50; GA, PCUSA, 1956, p. 105.

51. The sentiment on the floor of the Assembly was strong enough to override by a vote of more than two to one the majority recommendation of the Standing Committee on Foreign Relations that favored remaining in the Council (GA, PCUS, 1931, p. 47). The PCUS did not rejoin the Federal Council until 1941.

52. GA, PCUSA, 1931, p. 104. The whole matter received national publicity. See *The Nation* 132 (May 6, 1931): 493.

53. GA, PCUS, 1960, pp. 43–45, 75. In a separate action, the UPCUSA approved birth control the year before (GA, UPCUSA, 1959, p. 385).

54. GA, UPCUSA, 1961, p. 444; GA, UPCUSA, 1962, pp. 368–373.

55. On the origin of the social gospel in the mainline denominations, see Charles Howard Hopkins, *The Rise of the Social Gospel in American Protestantism, 1865–1915,* Yale Studies in Religious Education, vol. 14 (New Haven, Conn.: Yale University Press, 1940); and Robert T. Handy, ed., *The Social Gospel in America, 1870–1920* (New York: Oxford University Press, 1966).

56. In this connection it is worth noting that in the first decade of the twentieth century *The Nation* itself was not notably liberal or progressive in political outlook. Its liberal turn came later, though well before 1926.

57. The PCUS, despite its adherence to the spirituality doctrine, led the way in 1890 with a deliverance on world peace (GA, PCUS, 1890, p. 19). The next year the PCUS persuaded the PCUSA to follow suit (GA, PCUSA, 1891, p. 80). Peacemaking is probably also the most popular new agenda item in the church at large. In 1981, for example, thirty-one overtures on the subject were presented to the General Assembly of the UPCUSA (GA, UPCUSA, 1981, p. 57).

58. GA, PCUSA, 1943, pp. 200–201; GA, PCUS, 1943, pp. 32–33, 74. The document was produced by the Commission on a Just and Durable Peace, which held its first conference only a few months after Pearl Harbor. Among the "six pillars of peace" it enumerated were autonomy for the "subject peoples" of the world, the control of military establishments, a world organization of nations, international agreements on the economic and financial acts of national governments, and intellectual and religious liberty for everyone. The commission's work achieved nationwide publicity and may have helped establish a climate of opinion favorable to U.S. participation in the United Nations. See, for example, PCUSA, 1951, pp. 250–251.

59. GA, PCUSA, 1910, pp. 229–233. The 1910 pronouncement was reaffirmed in 1914 and an updated statement was adopted in 1920 (PCUSA, 1932, p. 272). The 1910 pronouncement neither advocated socialism nor defended capitalism in any way. So far as I have been able to determine, these important omissions characterize every subsequent declaration on economic issues adopted by Presbyterian General Assemblies.

60. GA, PCUSA, 1931, p. 102.

61. See GA, PCUSA, 1932, pp. 124–132; GA, 1933, PCUSA, pp. 165–168.

62. GA, PCUS, 1933, p. 38.

63. GA, PCUS, 1934, pp. 33–34. In 1914 the PCUS had

adopted a statement on social service drawn up by a joint committee representing four Presbyterian denominations. See GA, PCUS, 1914, pp. 28, 162–163.

64. GA, PCUSA, 1909, p. 47.

65. GA, PCUSA, 1931, pp. 35, 98.

66. GA, PCUSA, 1910, p. 229.

67. I am indebted to Langdon Gilkey for this observation.

68. *The Nation* 128 (Feb. 27, 1929): 341, 344.

69. *The Nation* 134 (June 22, 1932): 693.

70. Reinhold Niebuhr's personal life was a model of traditional Protestant virtue. Moreover, his views on sexuality, family relations, and personal morality were in keeping with old agenda positions. His biting criticisms of church life were directed to other aspects of mainline Protestant culture, in particular its triumphalism, its complacency, and its neglect of the sinful and tragic dimensions of existence. On the influence Niebuhr may have had in shaping the general outlook of today's mainline Protestant leaders, see my "Taking Stock: Reflections on the End of Another Era," *Journal for the Scientific Study of Religion* 21 (September 1982): 189–200; and "Liberal Protestantism: End of the Road?" *Annals of the American Academy of Political and Social Science* 480 (July 1985): 39–52.

71. In 1965 *The Nation* published an article by Harvey Cox on this subject in which he described "the coming theological mode of the era" as "Christians plunging into the social order to struggle for justice and peace" (201 [Oct. 11, 1965]: 216).

72. See my "Liberal Protestantism: End of the Road?" for a fuller discussion of these attacks. *The Nation* joined in. See its sarcastic 1957 treatment of the new Methodist family magazine *Together,* whose message it perceived to be: "Blessed are the stable-in-heart, kids, for they shall see good weekly pay checks" (184 [Jan. 19, 1957]: 58). A year later *The Nation* published an article by C. Wright Mills complaining that "religion has become a psychiatric aide of the nation-state." With the great powers making plans for World War III, he asked, "Do not the times demand a little Puritan defiance?" (186 [March 8, 1958]: 200–201).

73. GA, PCUS, 1966, p. 126.

74. GA, PCUS, 1967, pp. 150–151.

75. GA, PCUS, 1969, p. 152.

76. Anne Motley Hallum, "Presbyterians as Political Amateurs," in *Religion in American Politics,* ed. Charles W. Dunn (Washington, D.C.: Congressional Quarterly, 1989), pp. 66, 67,

70. Hallum also observes that Presbyterian leaders are not notably effective in influencing Congress or the Administration, in part because of their staunch refusal to compromise and in part because they cannot command the support of a large and enthusiastic constituency.

77. GA, PCUSA, 1931, p. 100.

78. GA, PCUSA, 1932, p. 273.

79. As late as 1948, just prior to the Berlin blockade, the General Assembly adopted a report on social questions that urged Presbyterians to "understand the Russian point of view" (GA, PCUSA, 1948, p. 202), but the next year a report that was otherwise similar in tone contained numerous anti-Communist remarks (GA, PCUSA, 1949, pp. 245–246).

80. During the early 1950s both denominations roundly denounced McCarthyism and urged the U.S. government not to befriend foreign regimes simply because they were anti-Communist, but they often prefaced these statements with condemnations of communism. See, for example, GA, PCUSA, 1951, pp. 253–255.

81. For example, in 1921 the General Assembly had invoked the spirituality doctrine in turning down an invitation from a General Conference Committee of the Methodist Episcopal Church, South, to join it in a campaign to combat efforts to liberalize Sabbath laws (GA, PCUS, 1921, p. 61).

82. After the liberals had persuaded the 1933 General Assembly to create a committee to investigate the economic crisis, a commissioner rose to request reconsideration. By a very slim margin the Assembly then rescinded its action and expunged all evidence of the incident from the *Minutes* (GA, PCUS, 1934, p. 21). Although the next General Assembly did create a permanent committee on moral and social welfare, in framing its first report the committee felt obliged to give the spirituality doctrine its "unqualified assent." It went on to declare, however, that the "Church, in fulfillment of its spiritual function must interpret and present Christ's ideal for the individual and for society . . . [in] every area of human life" (GA, PCUS, 1935, p. 93). This statement was politically astute and probably helped build support for the committee's work, but it did not convince all the traditionalists. For a well-crafted counterargument, see GA, PCUS, 1937, pp. 58–60.

83. Much of the conservatives' hostility to the new agenda was directed against the Federal, and later the National, Council of

Churches. Year after year an abundance of overtures reached the General Assembly asking the church to withdraw from the Council or proposing some other action against it. No sustained opposition to the Council emerged in the northern church.

84. The *Presbyterian Outlook* was the organ of the progressives and the *Presbyterian Journal* was the organ of the traditionalists. Conflict intensified in the PCUS when committee reports began advocating positions on racial issues that opposed the traditional views of most white Southerners.

85. In the long run the conservatives were undoubtedly hindered by the very absence of previous General Assembly pronouncements on many of these issues, including race, on which they might have relied for counterarguments. The *Minutes* include no overtures or other documents containing a theologically grounded defense of either capitalism or racial segregation. On the issue of race, the liberals were also aided by the executive orders, court decisions, and the changing climate of national opinion of the postwar era. A committee report of 1949, for example, asked this pointed question: "Are southern Protestants to allow secular, non-Protestant, and non-southern Christian forces to be the chief instruments of justice in this realm today?" (GA, PCUS, 1949, p. 191).

86. GA, PCUS, 1960, pp. 36–37. See also, GA, PCUS, 1968, pp. 102–103.

87. GA, UPCUSA, 1965, p. 264.

88. The General Assembly "received" but did not adopt the report containing new positions on sexuality and, by a narrow margin, added a reaffirmation of traditional sexual norms (GA, UPCUSA, 1970, pp. 469–471, 548, 680–681, 925–926).

89. GA, UPCUSA, 1972, p. 200. Seventeen overtures on the subject were received.

90. Robert Wuthnow, *The Restructuring of American Religion* (Princeton, N.J.: Princeton University Press, 1988), pp. 215–240. The confrontational style of interaction between liberals and conservatives, which characterizes much of contemporary church life, probably explains Wuthnow's additional finding that hostility between religious liberals and conservatives is greatest among those who actually know someone in the opposite camp. In church circles today, talking things over with one's opponents can make matters worse, not better.

91. *Presbyterian Panel,* The February 1979 Questionnaire: 33–38. The only exception among the many issues investigated was

the right of women to decide whether to have an abortion, a right supported by 65 percent of members but only 56 percent of pastors.

92. Ibid. Among the subjects on which the majority of lay members of the UPCUSA held conservative views in 1980 were those pertaining to capital punishment, policy toward southern Africa, and the direct use of federal funds to provide jobs for the unemployed. The survey did not include issues of sexuality or civil disobedience.

93. In 1978 the UPCUSA General Assembly turned down a task force proposal to permit the ordination of avowed homosexuals. An unusually large number of overtures were received on the subject, virtually all of them urging rejection of the proposals (GA, UPCUSA, 1978, p. 48). In 1988 conservatives persuaded the General Assembly to enlarge the membership of a new task force on sexuality in order to include more advocates of traditional standards and to modify the content of statements on employment discrimination and AIDS so as to remove any implication that the statements might legitimate the employment of homosexual ministers (GA, PC(USA), 1988, pp. 1074–1075, 84–85). The General Assembly also toned down a highly controversial document commending active resistance to the government's military policy. A very large number of overtures and commissioners' resolutions were presented urging rejection or modification of this document (ibid., p. 446).

94. *Presbyterian Panel,* The February 1979 Questionnaire: 28–31. See also the *Presbyterian Panel,* The August 1980 Questionnaire: 6-8. Owing to the lack of good survey data on this subject from the past there is no way of knowing how well informed Presbyterian lay people were earlier in the twentieth century concerning General Assembly endorsements of new agenda positions. It is entirely possible that the laity were even less informed than they are today, which may be another reason for the lack of polarization on social issues in the northern church prior to the 1960s.

95. GA, PCUS, 1974, pp. 218, 306. Seven of the charges dealt explicitly with social issues and several more dealt with them indirectly (ibid., p. 306).

96. A study of congregations that withdrew from the UPCUSA in the 1970s and early 1980s showed the laity to be more alienated by General Assembly pronouncements on social issues than were the clergy, who emphasized instead their disagreements

with denominational statements on theological matters (GA, PC(USA), 1985, pp. 418–419).

97. GA, UPCUSA, 1970, p. 62.

98. GA, PCUS, 1976, p. 117.

99. GA, PC(USA), 1988, p. 1071. There has been no corresponding drop in per capita giving to causes sponsored by local churches. In overall giving, Presbyterians are not less generous now than they were thirty years ago.

100. The General Assembly took no action on the overture (GA, PC(USA), 1988, pp. 1008–1009).

101. *General Assembly News,* Series of 1989, no. 5 (June 14): 2.

102. Other demographic factors contributing to the membership decline are the low birth rates of current church members of child-bearing age and a drop-off in the reception of new members transferring from more conservative denominations. Moreover, as the average age of mainline churchgoers increases, denominational death rates also increase, which makes further membership declines inevitable unless new members can be recruited to replace them. See Roof and McKinney, *American Mainline Religion,* pp. 148–185; Dean R. Hoge and David A. Roozen, eds., *Understanding Church Growth and Decline: 1950–1978* (New York: Pilgrim Press, 1979), pp. 21–41, 42–68, 94–122, 123–143, 179–197, 315–333; Louis B. Weeks, "Why We've Lost Members," *Presbyterian Survey* 79 (May 1989): 20–21.

103. Hoge and Roozen, *Understanding Church Growth and Decline,* p. 328.

104. See Robin D. Perrin, "American Religion in the Post-Aquarian Age: Values and Demographic Factors in Church Growth and Decline," *Journal for the Scientific Study of Religion* 28 (March 1989): 75–89. Hoge and Roozen's *Understanding Church Growth and Decline* reported similar findings. In this regard it is instructive to recall that the statements and actions of the youth delegates to General Assemblies during the turbulent years of the late 1960s and early 1970s invariably expressed displeasure that the church was not moving *more* rapidly to the left. A statement presented by youth delegates to the 1970 southern General Assembly contained this sentence: "We demand the church change or it will be buried in future decades by all youth who will completely give up on the church" (GA, PCUS, 1970, p. 26). In the same year one youth delegate told the UPCUSA Assembly that "the mainstream of this country's young people have already left the Church. They

do not really believe in it anymore" (GA, UPCUSA, 1970, pp. 879, 882).

105. Benton Johnson, "Liberal Protestantism: End of the Road?"; "Taking Stock: Reflections on the End of Another Era"; and "Winning Lost Sheep: A Recovery Course for Liberal Protestantism," in *Liberal Protestantism: Realities and Possibilities,* ed. Robert S. Michaelsen and Wade Clark Roof (New York: Pilgrim Press, 1986), pp. 220–234.

106. GA, PCUS, 1939, p. 117.

107. The General Assembly responded negatively to the overture but did not state its reasons for doing so (GA, PCUS, 1970, pp. 57, 101–102).

108. See my essay "Is There Hope for Liberal Protestantism?" in *Mainstream Protestantism in the Twentieth Century: Its Problems and Prospects* (Louisville, Ky.: [PC(USA)] Committee on Theological Education, 1987), pp. 13–26. This essay reviews the strategies Protestant leaders have adopted in responding effectively to past crises and makes some suggestions about how they might respond to the present crisis.

9: The Tie That No Longer Binds

1. The new denomination originally took the name National Presbyterian Church; the name was changed because a local church in Washington, D.C., already bore it. It is a distinct irony that the Orthodox Presbyterian Church formed by J. Gresham Machen first took the name Presbyterian Church in America.

2. For a fuller account of social and theological change in the PCUS see Ernest Trice Thompson, *Presbyterians in the South,* vol. 3: *1890–1972* (Richmond: John Knox Press, 1973). From the PCA point of view see Morton H. Smith, *How Is the Gold Become Dim: The Decline of the Presbyterian Church, U.S., as Reflected in Its Assembly Actions* 2nd ed. (Jackson, Miss.: The Steering Committee for a Continuing Presbyterian Church, Faithful to the Scripture and Reformed Faith, 1973).

3. Frank Joseph Smith, *The History of the Presbyterian Church in America: The Continuing Church Movement* (Manassas, Va.: Reformation Educational Foundation, 1985), p. 2.

4. Ibid., p. 21.

5. Henry B. Dendy, "Hath God Spoken? If So, Who Should Interpret His Word, Himself or Satan?" *Southern Presbyterian Journal* 1 (May 1942): 4 (hereafter cited as *SPJ* or *PJ*). Frank

Smith, *History of the PCA,* p. 95, says there were instances in which the material was blasphemous and advocated immorality, but without references.

6. See, for example, "Faith and Purpose of the Steering Committee for a Continuing Presbyterian Church," *PJ* 31 (May 24, 1972): 20, and "How It Started," *PJ* 28 (Jan. 7, 1970): 10–11. See also "Council Pounds Wedge a Bit Deeper," *PJ* 28 (Jan. 28, 1970): 12–13; W. Donald Munson, "Should Presbyterianism Survive?" *PJ* 30 (June 16, 1971): 11, 18–19; L. Nelson Bell, "Why," *PJ* 1 (May 1942): 2–3; G. Aiken Taylor, "How We Got Where We Are," *PJ* 30 (Oct. 13, 1971): 7–11; "The 110th General Assembly," *Presbyterian Churchmen United Contact* (July 1970): 1–2; "Why We Are 'Concerned,'" *Concerned Presbyterian* 1 (March 1965): 1; Richard G. Watson, "Concerned Without Comfort," *PJ* 31 (May 3, 1972): 11–12; and, again, Morton Smith, *Gold Become Dim.*

7. Frank Smith, *History of the PCA,* pp. 51–53.

8. The declaration is reprinted in Frank Smith, *History of the PCA,* pp. 43–44.

9. On this issue refer to W. Jack Williamson, "A Plea for a Continuing Church," *PJ* 31 (Aug. 2, 1972): 9–10; "Good News for Bible-Believing Presbyterians!" *The Concerned Presbyterian* (April 1973): 1–2; and Frank Smith, *History of the PCA,* pp. 82–86. The history chronicled here is, of course, much too brief to do justice to the many events and people involved in the formation of the PCA. For a detailed, and often pedantic, recounting, the reader is referred to Smith, *History of the PCA.* By reading that work and selectively in *PJ* one will get a sense of the vitriolic nature of this debate in the PCUS. The formation of the PCA led to anger and dissolution of friendships, particularly at the presbytery and congregational level—but then, family disputes are the most painful of all. See, for one example, "Plans for a Continuing Church Announced," *PJ* 30 (Aug. 25, 1971): 4–5, in which W. Jack Williamson said the PCUS was "both *de facto* and *de jure* apostate."

10. *Minutes of the General Assembly of the Presbyterian Church in America* (hereafter cited as GA, PCA), 1973, p. 41.

11. Ibid., p. 40.

12. Ibid., pp. 41–42.

13. George M. Marsden's thesis in *Fundamentalism and American Culture: The Shaping of Twentieth-Century Evangelicalism, 1870–1925* (New York: Oxford University Press, 1980) contrasts

with Ernest Sandeen's argument, in *The Origins of Fundamentalism* (Philadelphia: Fortress Press, 1968) and "The Princeton Theology: One Source of Biblical Literalism in American Protestantism," *Church History* 31 (September 1962): 307–321, that fundamentalism was discontinuous with nineteenth-century evangelicalism. Also important background for the analysis that follows is Marsden's *Reforming Fundamentalism: Fuller Seminary and the New Evangelicalism* (Grand Rapids: Wm. B. Eerdmans Publishing Co., 1987) and William McLoughlin's *Revivals, Awakenings, and Reform* (Chicago: University of Chicago Press, 1978). Those familiar with Paul Tillich's analysis of culture in terms of heteronomy, autonomy, and theonomy may find those categories informative for understanding the trends delineated here.

14. Marsden, *Fundamentalism and American Culture,* p. 103.

15. Samuel S. Hill, Jr., *The South and the North in American Religion* (Athens, Ga.: University of Georgia Press, 1980), p. 106.

16. Samuel S. Hill, Jr., *Southern Churches in Crisis* (New York: Holt, Rinehart & Winston, 1967), p. 5.

17. "Statistics," GA, PCA, 1973, pp. 205–236.

18. See, for example, an overture from the Presbytery of Southern Mississippi against the National Council of Churches in GA, PCUS, 1971, p. 45; an overture from the Presbytery of Congaree (South Carolina) against amnesty for draft resisters in GA, PCUS, 1974, p. 73; and an overture from the Presbytery of Southern Mississippi regarding draft registration in GA, PCUS, 1981, p. 58. It should be noted that this essay deals primarily with the leadership and clergy of the PCUS and PCA. I do not perceive that, generally speaking, the lay members in congregations remaining in the PCUS and those who went into the PCA were radically different from one another. I believe the difference was in the leadership of churches and the ability of the PCA leaders to convince lay members that the PCUS had fallen into error and forsaken Americanism and social order.

19. L. Nelson Bell, "Why," *SPJ* 1 (May 1942): 2.

20. "A Brief History of PCU," *Presbyterian Churchmen United Contact* (April 1972): 1. It would be interesting to explore what relationship exists between complaints of centralized church power and the argument in the South that the federal government usurped state prerogatives in dismantling desegregation laws.

21. Morton Smith, *Gold Become Dim,* p. 153.

22. "Letter to a Minister," *The Concerned Presbyterian* (April 1973): 10.

23. "What Are You Up To?" *Presbyterian Churchmen United Contact* (June 1972): 3.

24. Robert Wuthnow, *The Restructuring of American Religion: Society and Faith Since World War II* (Princeton, N.J.: Princeton University Press, 1988).

25. Ibid., pp. 146–148.

26. See ibid., ch. 6, "The Growth of Special Purpose Groups" and ch. 9, "Civil Religion: Two Cheers for America." This analysis is reminiscent of the thesis of Martin Marty, *A Nation of Behavers* (Chicago: University of Chicago Press, 1976).

27. Wuthnow, *Restructuring,* p. 98.

28. Morton Howison Smith, *Studies in Southern Presbyterian Theology* (Jackson, Miss.: Presbyterian Reformation Society, and Amsterdam: Jacob Van Campen, 1962), pp. 22–27. He is more certain of subscriptionism here than others; see Walter L. Lingle and John W. Kuykendall, *Presbyterians, Their History and Beliefs,* 4th rev. ed. (Atlanta: John Knox Press, 1978), p. 67, and Sydney E. Ahlstrom, *A Religious History of the American People* (New Haven, Conn.: Yale University Press, 1972), pp. 270–272. Smith makes the same argument in *Gold Become Dim,* pp. 37–39.

29. Morton Smith, *Studies,* ch. 1, "A Survey of Southern Presbyterian History."

30. This point is made repeatedly. For one example see "How It Started," *PJ* 28 (Jan. 7, 1970): 10–11.

31. E.T.S., "Subscription," *SPJ* 12 (June 3, 1953): 6. Similar arguments are found in R. McFerran Crowe, "Consider the Cause," *PJ* 31 (May 3, 1972): 12–13, and Robert F. Gribble, "Speaking of Creeds," *SPJ* 8 (July 1, 1949): 5.

32. This line of inquiry was suggested by Presbyterian historian John Kuykendall. In a conversation he casually wondered how one could explain the presence of a number of northern Presbyterian ministers out of the fundamentalist denominations serving congregations that moved into the PCA.

33. Sandeen, "The Princeton Theology," p. 307.

34. Sandeen, *Origins,* pp. 13–14. Marsden, *Fundamentalism and American Culture,* deals at length with Scottish Common Sense Philosophy, especially among the Princetonians. See pp. 15–21 and ch. 13, "Presbyterians and the Truth." Charles Hodge, in the introduction to his three-volume *Systematic Theology,* defined theology as a science.

35. Marsden, *Fundamentalism and American Culture,* p. 174; pp. 110–120 are also helpful.

36. Charles Hodge, *Systematic Theology* (New York: Charles Scribner's Sons, 1899) 1:177.

37. Morton Smith, *Studies,* p. 81.

38. John Holt Rice quoted in ibid., p. 95.

39. Morton Smith, *Studies,* p. 239. That the Continuing Church adherents relied on the Princetonians for their argument is confirmed by an examination of their work to determine their defense of the inerrantist view of scripture. There is no such defense, only affirmations of the infallibility or inerrancy of the Bible. For instance, William Childs Robinson of Columbia Theological Seminary, an important person in the movement who contributed to the *PJ,* offers no explanation of inerrancy in *The Certainties of the Gospel* (Grand Rapids: Zondervan Publishing House, 1935) or *What Is Christian Faith?* (Grand Rapids: Zondervan Publishing House, 1937). R. C. Sproul, now a professor at Reformed Theological Seminary, delineates the one argument I have found in "The Case for Inerrancy: A Methodological Analysis" in *God's Inerrant Word: An International Symposium on the Trustworthiness of Scripture,* ed. John Warwick Montgomery (Minneapolis: Bethany Fellowship, 1973); it is basically a restatement of the Princeton line (and Sproul himself is a Northerner).

40. Mark A. Noll, ed., *The Princeton Theology, 1812–1921* (Grand Rapids: Baker Book House, 1983), p. 18. Marsden, *Reforming Fundamentalism,* helps us place the PCA in the broader context of resurgent evangelicalism and identifies some connections between Fuller, *Christianity Today,* and southern Presbyterian fundamentalists.

41. Joe Morecraft III, "The Theological Crisis," *Presbyterian Churchmen United Contact* (July 1970): 3.

42. G. Aiken Taylor, "This Has Been Going On a Long Time," *PJ* 31 (May 31, 1972): 12.

43. Morecraft, "Theological Crisis," p. 3.

44. "It's Always Godless," *PJ* 31 (May 24, 1972): 12–13.

45. Wuthnow, *Restructuring,* ch. 7, "The Great Divide: Toward Religious Realignment."

46. Ibid., ch. 12, "A Broader Context: Politics and Faith."

47. Ibid., p. 130.

48. See especially Wade Clark Roof and William McKinney, *American Mainline Religion: Its Changing Shape and Future* (New Brunswick, N.J.: Rutgers University Press, 1987).

Index